WITHDRAWN

Themes in Social Anthropology
edited by David Turton

Buddhism in life

To 'B. Silaratana Thero'

Martin Southwold

Buddhism in life
The anthropological study of religion and the Sinhalese practice of Buddhism

Manchester University Press

Published by
Manchester University Press
Oxford Road, Manchester M13 9PL, U.K.
51 Washington Street, Dover, N.H. 03820, U.S.A.

British Library cataloguing in publication data
Southwold, Martin
  Buddhism in life. – (Themes in social anthropology)
  1. Hinayana Buddhism – History
  2. Buddhism – Sri Lanka
  I. Title   II. Series
  294.3′91′095493   BQ356

  ISBN 0–7190–0971–5

Library of Congress cataloging in publication data
Southwold, Martin
  Buddhism in life.
  (Themes in social anthropology)
  Bibliography: p.
  Includes index.
  1. Buddhism—Sri Lanka. 2. Sri Lanka—Religious life
and customs. I. Title. II. Series.
BQ359.S68 1983   294.3′09549′3   83-9890
ISBN 0–7190–0971–5

Photoset in Century Schoolbook by
Northern Phototypesetting Co., Bolton
Printed in Great Britain by
Biddles Ltd, Guildford, Surrey

Contents

88-7082

Preface

This book is both an account of Buddhism in the lives of the people of some Sinhalese villages where my wife and I did anthropological fieldwork in 1974–75, and a discussion of some basic issues concerning the study and understanding of religions. I explain in the Introduction why I have written on both themes together. Here in the Preface I must indicate to the potential reader what he may and may not expect to find. Inevitably I have not been able to do full justice to either theme. I have not given the comprehensive and detailed account of my observations that one expects to find in an ethnographic monograph, but have rather selected the facts that seem more relevant for interpretation. I have not discussed all the anthropological literature relevant to the study of religion, nor even all that is relevant to the topic on which I have focused discussion, that of belief and its nature and place in religion: I have confined myself to those works which I, for better or for worse, have found most significant. I may be judged to have fallen between two stools; if so, I hope it will be found that the ground between these stools was worth exploring.

While I have addressed myself to my colleagues in the anthropological profession, I have also tried to write for a wider readership. I do think that anthropology is of more than technical, academic importance and I know that Buddhism is of interest, and indeed concern, to many people who are not anthropologists. Inevitably, I have sometimes been too simplistic for one readership and too technical for the other, for which I must ask forbearance.

Much of what I have written is controversial, and more or less contrary to widely accepted opinions and judgements, beliefs and even knowledge. I have sought to provoke debate, and at times I may have overstated my views, as much to overcome my own reluctance to accept them as to combat the positions of others. I have tried to be candid about my own biases and other limitations to encourage proper scepticism about what I argue; and I hope this may mitigate any hurt I may cause by having dealt too bruisingly with views that are cherished by others.

I have criticised, sometimes severely, some of the work of others who have written on the topics I discuss. Though I have tried to be fair, in reviewing their words and mine I can see they have grounds to feel that I have not treated them justly. While I have criticised what I think is wrong in their work, I have largely passed over what I think is right in it: and this is the more unjust as I have evidently learnt a great deal from them. I have not the space to write a balanced appreciation of every book I comment upon: the best I can do is to state plainly that I do not think, and did not mean to imply, that because a book has faults it does not have other merits, which indeed may be much more characteristic of it. I must confess to two bad habits. When I agree with what I read I tend to absorb it so thoroughly that I am unaware that I learnt it from someone else, and hence fail to give him credit for it. And when I first absorb what someone else has said and afterwards come to think it is wrong, my struggles to rid my own mind of error tend to get vented in animus against those I blame for having misled me. If for these reasons I have expressed my criticisms too strongly, and have failed to acknowledge that many of the points I make were already made in books I criticise, or others I do not refer to at all, I must apologise – and, more importantly, ask the reader to assume that books I criticise have more merit than appears from what I say about them.

I am especially concerned not to cause hurt to any readers I may have among the Sinhalese, to whom I am so indebted, not only for having taught me about Buddhism, but for innumerable other kindnesses. As Buddhists they are of course accustomed to searching and unconventional argument in the pursuit of truth. But some of them may feel I have gone too far in describing some of the more worldly and earthy aspects of Buddhism as I observed it. These are matters which most Sinhalese know about, and are quite ready to talk about among friends: it may appear a breach of confidence and hospitality that I, their guest, have chosen to publish them more widely. Taken out of context, some of the things I tell are not flattering, and might have been told to disparage the Sinhalese and their religion. I hope it will be plain that nothing is further from my intention. It is just because I have and express so much esteem for the Sinhalese and their Buddhism that I have sought to avoid easy flattery. It is my central and sincere contention that the real Buddhism of real people in real life is more to be valued and admired than the idealised image of Buddhism that is more often presented.

The fieldwork from which this book derives was carried out in Sri Lanka from August 1974 to September 1975. I take this opportunity to express my gratitude to the many people without whose help I could not have written it. First and foremost to the Sinhalese villagers who taught me the better part of what I know about Buddhism, and whose unfailing friendship and kindness made the year we spent with them as happy as it was instructive, and the latter not least because of the former. I think I have made my appreciation and esteem for them clear enough in what I have written to be able to forgo further words here. What I have said of the villagers goes also for the many Sri Lankans whom we met in many places and for whom no kindness was too much to help strangers in their land. I thank also the Sri Lankan Government, which is remarkably tolerant of and helpful to foreigners who seek to do research in their country; and to its many officers who generously went out of their way to help us.

I thank next my more immediate colleagues in the research. Above all, my wife Sarah, herself an anthropologist, who not merely assisted in the fieldwork but in fact did the greater part of it. I am as indebted to her also for her constant encouragement, help, and forbearance during the travails of writing (and for forbearance, at least, I must thank our young sons, Hugh and Andrew). Second only to her, I owe thanks to our four Sinhalese research assistants (of whom at any one time we employed two), without whom we could have achieved little: Messrs Tilakasiri Gamage, Bandula de Silva, Gamini Wickremasinghe, and Chandra Vitarana. Their hard work, loyalty, intelligence, and perception of what was needed could not have been bettered; and they were good friends too. We are especially grateful to Mr Gamage, the only one of the four who was able to work with us throughout the year we spent in Sri Lanka, and who did further research for us after we left. I hope he knows how much our insight into Sinhalese life is indebted to his sensitivity and integrity.

We have recently been reminded that the anthropologist should tell his readers how much he relied on interpreters, and about their social backgrounds (Obeyesekere, 1981, pp. 10–11). Neither my wife nor I acquired sufficient skill in the Sinhala language to be able to conduct more than a simple conversation: nearly all our interviews and informative conversations were conducted through one of our research assistants as interpreter. This procedure certainly has drawbacks, but I am confident we did not lose more information by it than would have been lost through reliance on the linguistic competence we could have acquired for ourselves in the time available. After a time we could follow Sinhala well enough to check on our interpreters; and they understood our work well enough often to ask the appropriate questions before we had spoken them. It became a surprisingly effective working relationship.

Mr. Gamage comes from a middle-class family of modest status, living in a village on the outskirts of Kandy; he is a graduate in Sociology, and had worked as an assistant to other anthropologists. Mr. Wickremasinghe comes from a family of similar status in a Low Country village, and he too is a Sociology graduate. Mr. de Silva's parents are of similar standing, and live in a suburb of Colombo; though well educated and very able, he did not go to university. What he lacked in sociological training he more than made up for in alacrity of apprehension and linguistic sensitivity – he used, for example, without even trying, to speak to me in British English and to my wife, who is American, in American English. Mr. Vitarana comes from a small town in the Kandyan Highlands, but has lived in several other parts. He is of somewhat humbler background and formal education than the others, but he has worked as research assistant to a number of anthropologists, including Professor Bruce Kapferer, who seconded him to us to help us get started: his experience, and considerable knowledge of the Buddhist clergy, proved invaluable.

Two of our four assistants are of Goyigama caste, and two of high castes not indigenous in our area – the villagers soon decided that this was of no consequence, as they had come from outside to do a job. All are Buddhists by adherence, though only one by much more – the others were somewhat laid back in the matter. In age they ranged between twenty and thirty. All of them found it easy to relate to the villagers, and became well liked for the most part; Mr. Gamage in particular became so much a part of the community that when we had to depart the villagers begged us to let him stay.

I thank also the British Social Science Research Council for a Research Grant (No. HR 2969/1) which generously supported our fieldwork in Sri Lanka and met various ancillary costs. I am also grateful to the University of Manchester for a grant from its Hayter Travel Fund, which enabled me to make a preliminary visit to Sri Lanka in the Long Vacation of 1973. And for much else, not least the grant of a sabbatical year in 1979–80 without which I could never have made what progress I have in solving the problems my research threw up.

I am indebted also to many academic colleagues both in Manchester and elsewhere. I am especially grateful to a former Manchester colleague, Professor Bruce Kapferer, who was largely responsible for persuading me to work in Sri Lanka, and more narrowly in Kurunegala District. Moreover, he was most generous of his time in introducing me to the country and people when I visited in 1973, and in lending us his own research assistant, Mr. Vitarana, for three months to get us started in 1974.

Among so many to whom I am indebted, I have chosen to dedicate this book to the Buddhist priest I call Silaratana. In writing it I have become conscious of how much of what I understand I owe to him: in a very real sense he has been my principal teacher. I hope I have managed to convey not unfaithfully what I learnt from him, as from many others. The many faults of this account are mine entirely; whatever merits it may have I transfer to my many helpers as an inadequate token of gratitude.

April 1982   Martin Southwold
Department of Social Anthropology
University of Manchester

A note on terminology and orthography

I have tried to use only English words for descriptive purposes; I discuss the more controversial ones, and the problems of translation they raise, in the Appendix. For key Buddhist concepts I have had to use indigenous terms, since English words would distort the meaning. Some Buddhist terms, such as Nirvana, Dharma, Sangha, are sufficiently familiar that I have used them as if they were English words, with capitals; for all of them, except Nirvana, I do explain their meaning. Less familiar words, in Sinhala or in Pali, the language of the scriptures, are printed in italics, and I define each of them that I use. Other Sinhala or Pali words are merely cited to show what lies behind my English translations.

I have followed the orthography of Gombrich (1971), which is a romanisation of the Sinhala orthography – except that I sometimes write *-ē* for *-aya*, to represent the sound more closely. Vowels are as in Italian, except that *ä* represents the vowel in English 'cat'; long vowels are shown by a dash over, so that, for example, *ē* is the vowel sound in our 'fête' – but long *ä* is written as *ää*; unmarked *a*, especially terminally, is often a neutral vowel. Consonants are mainly as in English, with some exceptions. *t* and *d* are dental sounds, part-way to our two sounds spelled as 'th', whereas *ṭ* and *ḍ* are retroflex; *h* written after a consonant aspirates it. *c* is approximately as in English 'ch'. Some of the sounds I have written as *s* are often or always sounded more like English 'sh'. *ñ* is as in Spanish *mañana*, i.e. like 'ny'. Syllables are not stressed, but to our ear those with long vowels or dipthongs, or with doubled or compound consonants, sound more prominent. On the other hand short vowels and soft consonants are often hardly sounded at all, so that, for example, *hāmuduruvō* usually sounds like '*hāmdrū*', or 'hondrewe' as Knox (1681) rendered it in his English spelling.

For their privacy, I have given pseudonyms to the villagers I write about, and their villages. For verisimilitude, I have mostly lifted the pseudonyms from the real names of other people and places. I am not, of course, writing about the people and places that bear those names in real life: e.g. though there is a village called Gonnawa, it is not the one I refer to by that name. The places, and some of the people, I do write about are easily identifiable by anyone with local knowledge: should anyone feel that he has been slandered, through my error or indiscretion, I can but sincerely apologise.

A note on notes

Notes to the text appear at the end of each chapter. Those which add to what is said in the text are indicated by an asterisk as well as a number – e.g. 'Buddhism[1*]'. Notes indicated by a number without an asterisk are mostly citations of works quoted or referred to, and probably not relevant to the non-specialist reader.

1

Introduction

This book is about Buddhism as an anthropologist sees it: Buddhism as it is thought and practised by Buddhist people in a Buddhist society. It is also about religion generally: it is a discussion of some of our ideas about religion and about how to study and understand it. In particular, I discuss belief and its place in religion, and how misunderstandings about this lead us astray. I had better explain how these various themes are linked together, and why I have tackled them all in one book.

An anthropologist tries to observe and describe what a particular people do and think, and not to confuse this with what they, or others, say they ought to do and think. Thus I have already hinted that the Buddhism an anthropologist observes may be different from Buddhism in some other, more ideal sense: and in fact it is so. Let me call the Buddhism of observable reality – Buddhism as thought and practised by ordinary Buddhists – 'empirical' or 'actual' Buddhism.

Most anthropologists, myself included, who have studied actual Buddhism have done so among villagers, that is, the ordinary people of the countryside. This is sensible, since most people in the present homelands of (Theravāda) Buddhism[1]* – Sri Lanka (Ceylon), Burma, and Thailand, mainly – are in fact villagers; and also because anthropologists are most at home and competent at working with ordinary people in villages. But it has had the consequence that we have fallen into the habit of identifying actual Buddhism with the Buddhism of villagers. This is an oversimplification: there are people in Buddhist nations who are not villagers, and it is possible that their actual Buddhism is different from that of villagers.

Through overlooking this we have confounded, and confused, two different distinctions. One is the distinction between religion in actuality, as practised in the lives of real people, and a religious ideal or myth; the other is a distinction between the actual religions of different categories, or classes, of people. By identifying actual Buddhism with the religion[2]* of villagers, or peasants, we have made an opening for the depreciatory prejudices that urban intellectuals tend to have about such people. Leach, for example, pointed to the distinction between ideal and actual, terming these 'philosophical' and 'practical' religion respectively. He remarked, 'In studies of comparative religion a failure to take into account this distinction between philosophical religion and practical religion has often led to grave misunderstanding,'[3] and he went on to summarise, most aptly, the distortions it has produced in the study of Buddhism. But he proceeded to identify 'practical Buddhism' as the Buddhism of 'ordinary village people'; and he had already defined 'practical' as referring to 'the ordering of categories in all unsophisticated forms of human thinking'.[4]

It is quite true that the actual Buddhism that I, like most other anthropologists, learnt about and have to describe is the Buddhism of villagers; but in saying this we must be careful not to assume too hastily that it is theirs peculiarly and distinctively, so that its peculiar features are to be explained by the peculiar character of villagers. Still more, we should avoid speaking of villagers and their thought as 'unsophisticated'. This is a word of many senses, some of which are applicable to villagers; but its principal function, or effect, is to convey a connotation of depreciation.

This connotation is especially unfortunate since in any case it is very difficult to consider actual Buddhism, more particularly that of villagers, without depreciatory bias. As I have indicated, and shall show, the actual Buddhism of villagers is unmistakably, and notably, different from Buddhism as we understand it – 'we' being mainly educated people in Western countries. Actual Buddhism plainly appears to be more human and worldly, more ritualistic and superstitious, than what we take to be 'Buddhism'; it is therefore very natural to take it to be a deviant, not to say degraded, development from 'true' or 'pure' Buddhism, which we also assume to have been the original form of the religion. As Spiro put it, in his study of the Buddhism of Burmese villagers, '. . . early Buddhism . . . could hardly have perdured as the religion of an unsophisticated peasantry without undergoing important changes'.[5]

Nearly everything that has been written about the actual Buddhism of villagers – let us call it 'village Buddhism' for short – is pervaded by the assumption that it is a deviation from, and evidently inferior to, an earlier and truer form of Buddhism which alone is wholly authentic. Many writers have stated it plainly – most notably, among more recent and professional scholars, Spiro, in the book I have just quoted. In others it is implicit: it seems the inevitable conclusion from the facts they present, and they do little to contest it. I do not share it; yet I see very well that if I were simply to describe the facts I observed most readers would be led to the same conclusion, which I think is false. This is the basic reason why I cannot simply report my observations, and why, in order to convey a true picture, I have to go a long way about to refute the mistakes which lead us to misapprehend and misjudge the reality.

The mistaken assessment of village Buddhism, which I shall call the 'conventional judgement', is not confined to books. Gombrich, who also studied village Buddhism in Sri Lanka, remarks on 'the frequency with which I had been told, by books and by people, that Sinhalese village Buddhism was corrupt';[6] and he goes on to explain why he thinks that judgement mistaken. I had a similar experience: quite a few Sinhalese, mainly but not entirely English-speaking, told me very positively that village Buddhism 'is corrupt', or 'is not true Buddhism', or 'is not really Buddhism at all'. This might have confirmed the prejudice I had acquired from the literature, and perhaps initially it did. But I could not help noticing that the people who spoke like this – mostly English-speaking Sinhalese, who would categorise themselves as of the 'middle class', and thus not 'villagers' – in various other respects spoke disparagingly of villagers and their ways. I did not find what they said either accurate or engaging; on the contrary it provoked me enough to challenge, privately, their claim that village Buddhism was not true Buddhism.

When I returned to England in 1975, after fourteen months' fieldwork in Sinhalese villages, I wanted to write an account of my observations. Since what I had observed was little different from what others who have studied village Buddhism, whether in Sri Lanka, or Burma, or Thailand, had observed, my account would not be very different from theirs.[7]* I found I just could not write it; and when I tried to diagnose what prevented me, I discovered it was a rooted refusal to state, or even imply, that village Buddhism is not true Buddhism. I felt, and felt strongly, just the opposite. I felt it because I greatly liked and admired the village Buddhists I had known, more than I did most people who assured me that they knew something else to be the true Buddhism. I felt that if we had to rank different varieties of Buddhism, the Buddhism of the better people should be accounted the better Buddhism. And besides, Buddhism as the villagers explained it made good sense to me, whereas I had long since formed an unfavourable judgement of 'true Buddhism'.

There was no sense in trying to overturn the conventional judgement on grounds so subjective and flimsy. Like other scholars, I had formed my opinion on the basis of prejudice, feeling, and intuition, and then set to work to find more solid arguments to support it. In the first place I realised that 'true Buddhism' had no valid claim to the title. As Gombrich had pointed out, but I had forgotten, this 'true Buddhism' was largely the product of mainly Western scholars, in the late nineteenth and early twentieth centuries; from them it had passed, directly and through various channels of popularisation, to form the standard view of

Buddhism of most Western people, and heavily to influence the view of
Western-educated people in Buddhist societies.[8] If it seems too sardonic
to go on referring to this as 'true Buddhism', perhaps we may call it
'Western Buddhism'; and with Gombrich, following Bechert, its product
among Sinhalese Buddhists may be termed 'Buddhist Modernism'.[9]

I suppose that many people who speak slightingly of village Buddhism
because it differs from 'true Buddhism' are not aware how far the latter is
a Western concoction. If they were, they might have misgivings about the
arrogance of our conventional judgement, which takes it so easily for
granted that we in the West know what Buddhism truly is, while actual
Buddhists do not.[10*] But the judgement itself would still seem sound.

The scholars who formed our Western view studied the Pali
scriptures[11*] in order to recover from them the life-story and teaching of
the Buddha. If they succeeded in doing so, as they claimed to have done,
then what they produced would have a unique claim to be authentic
Buddhism: for the word itself means the -ism, or doctrine, of the Buddha.
But they did not succeed, and could not have succeeded, for the
scriptures cannot yield us such information. No doubt the scriptures
contain the teaching of the Buddha, or some of it; but they contain much
else besides, and there is no objective basis on which to separate the one
from the other. There is no scientifically or historically valid way in which
we can determine what the Buddha taught, except perhaps in terms far
too general and hazy to decide that one interpretation of Buddhism is
more or less authentic than another.

I shall argue the case for this conclusion later (Chapter 10). It is
evidently unorthodox, against the consensual Western interpretation of
Buddhism, and unwelcome to those who have found a more than
academic interest in Buddhism. If we cannot say what the Buddha
taught, how can we know what Buddhism is, and by what criterion can we
know what is more and what less authentic? These questions are indeed
unanswerable within our conventional framework, and need to be recast.
We should not be asking about Buddhism as we ordinarily understand
the term, for if there is any such thing it is certainly of secondary
importance. Sinhalese Buddhists did not speak of 'Buddhism', and had
no term which could properly be so translated until one was introduced
with Christian concepts. The word they now use, '*Buddhāgama*', which
does seem to translate as 'Buddhism', is compounded from the word
āgama: this was introduced from Sanskrit by Christian missionaries to
signify their notion of 'religion', for which they could find no term in the
Sinhala language.[12] The more indigenous terms, which Gombrich[13]
(though not I) found still to be used more frequently, are *Buddha Dharma*
(or *Dhamma*), and *Buddha Sāsana*. The term *Dharma*,[14*] which is
normally translated as 'doctrine', does not really mean that; as its proper

meaning is crucial for understanding, I shall discuss it more fully later (Chapter 12). For the present, let us say it means Reality. *Buddha Sāsana* means 'Buddhism as a spatio-temporal phenomenon':[15] I shall render it as 'Buddhendom', by analogy with 'Christendom'.

Buddhism as the teaching of the Buddha is unknowable except in outline, and therefore of little use to us; but Buddhism as Buddhendom is thoroughly knowable, if we care to look. Buddhendom is more than religion, as we ordinarily understand that term: it is Buddhist civilisation[16] and life. In its more specifically religious aspect it is what I have called 'actual Buddhism', of which village Buddhism is now, and always has been, by far the largest component. If we seek a criterion of what authentic Buddhism is, it can only be Buddhendom, actual Buddhism. I do not say that village Buddhism is the only authentic variety of Buddhism, but I do say that it is wholly authentic, for there seems to be no valid criterion by which it could be judged otherwise. Not 'true Buddhism', which is a Western deviation; not the teaching of the Buddha, which is insufficiently knowable; not the scriptures, which are what they are, the ingenious but ambiguous compositions of peculiar people, worthy of respect as another component of authentic Buddhism, but not of unique authority nor indeed import.[17*]

To me, this conclusion is congenial, both because I strongly approve of village Buddhism, and because it implies that as an anthropologist I am peculiarly privileged to know what Buddhism is. To readers who do not share my predispositions, it is likely to seem rebarbative. They may well, for a start, react by pointing out how arrogant it is of me to claim to understand Buddhism better than most of the scholars who have preceded me[18*]. It would indeed be so if I claimed it on my own authority, but I do not. Basically, I am reporting as Buddhism what the Buddhists I knew taught me; my own contribution is only to clear away the tangle of confusions which have prevented us from perceiving this as what it is.

Why is it that these conclusions are likely to seem so hard to accept? Why is it that I, predisposed as I was in their favour, had such a long and hard struggle fully to grasp and accept them as true? Why is it that Gombrich, who seems to have been led to a similar conclusion, expressed it so hesitantly, even evasively, when he wrote, as the last sentence in his book: 'If this is popular Buddhism, could it be that *Vox populi vox Buddhae?*'[19] And why is it that, having thus expressed himself, he allowed to stand on an earlier page a passage which directly contradicts it (see below, Chapter 6)?

Quite clearly, it is because of the powerful hold which the Western view of Buddhism has on our minds. But why that powerful hold? In part it is a legacy of the conceit of colonialism, and of the disdain which intellectuals of the middle class have for rustics. But it goes much deeper. The Western view of Buddhism seems self-evidently true because it is rooted in our usual notions of religion. We think that Buddhism must be essentially and criterially the teaching of its alleged founder because that is how we think of Christianity; and we think that the Buddhist scriptures must be the key to Buddhism because that is how we think, under the influence of Protestantism, of the place of the Christian scriptures in our own religion. Both errors are sustained by errors of historical method. It may well be true that both religions began with the teachings of their eponymous founders, which to that extent are their origins: but it does not follow that those teachings are the key to the religions when they are, in point of fact, unknowable. It may well be, indeed is, true that the scriptures are the best sources we have for knowing what those teachings were: but it does not follow that those sources are good enough, or even much good at all, for that purpose. These errors would have been recognised long ago if they had not been sustained by, as they sustain, a more fundamental mistake. 'Our modern habit,' the great Scottish theologian William Robertson Smith wrote nearly a century ago, 'is to look at religion from the side of belief rather than of practice,' and he went on to explain what a serious error this is in the study of religions.[20] The fundamental error in the study of Buddhism has been to approach it from the side of belief, doctrine, rather than of practice.[21]*

I should have known better, since Robertson Smith's alternative approach is standard in the theory, and much of the practice, of social anthropology. To a small extent I did: I did not often ask my informants what they believed, except as a joke. But I was not very successful in following through the real implications of Robertson Smith's analysis of religion. My view of Buddhism was shaped by the tradition of Buddhist studies, which has been little affected by anthropology and less by Robertson Smith; on the contrary it is rooted, however implicitly, in the contrary assumption that belief, doctrine, is fundamental in religion. This has indeed determined how Buddhism is perceived, and its terms translated, in ways which make Robertson Smith's approach seem inapplicable. I was not much concerned with what the village Buddhists I knew believed, and indeed doubted whether there was much that they did believe, in any clear and relevant sense; but I never did, while I was doing my research in Sri Lanka, get free from the delusion that since their practice was at variance with Buddhist doctrine, it was the former, and not the latter, which was defective.

In this way I see misapprehension about the place of belief in religion, and hence about its nature, as basic to the misunderstanding of Buddhism that I have shared but now seek to rebut. I focus on it the more because my own analysis of Buddhism has been whetted on those of Gombrich and Spiro, in both of which notions of belief have explicit and central prominence. I criticise at some length later Gombrich's use of these notions, and their harmful effects on his analysis (Chapter 13). I shall also make my dissent from Spiro's analysis plain enough (e.g. Chapter 6), though I do not directly tackle its roots in an undue concern with belief. Let me therefore blandly remark that I know no other anthropological study of religion so lavishly peppered with belief-terms (the words 'belief' and 'believe'), and that Spiro himself acknowledges the bias: 'If I seem unduly to stress beliefs and ideas . . .'.[22] He declares his stance when he writes, implicitly against Robertson Smith, 'Although religious sociology has typically argued for the priority of ritual over myth, of behaviour over thought, of action over ideas, this argument is based more on dogma than on evidence,' and goes on to express his scorn for 'an intellectual zeitgeist in which ideas are only responsive to, but are never the guides of, behaviour . . .'.[23]*

There is little merit in describing facts as an end in itself; there is positive demerit in doing so when one knows that thereby, because of the preconceptions with which they will be received, they will convey a false picture and understanding of reality. It is for this reason that I have considered it more necessary to rebut the preconceptions than to elaborate the facts. Having found that my account of village Buddhism had to be largely an argument on the theory of religion, I decided to present it as such. Thus this book, though it can be seen as a view of village Buddhism developed through theoretical revision, amounts as much, if not more, to an essay on the study and understanding of religion, illustrated from my experience of Buddhism.[24]* I think that this is a good way to discuss matters of theory. To some people – and I am one of them – theoretical discussions can be fascinating in themselves. In the end, however, I find them, rather like American bread, more gaseous than satisfying, unless they are tied to genuine empirical or practical problems. I think mine are, for they grow out of a need to understand what I observed of Buddhism, and to make both academic and personal sense of it.

Thus this book, though it mixes empirical description with theoretical discussions in a proportion unusual in anthropological writing, does seem to me a fitting response to the problem I have had to tackle. I do regret that my concern with theoretical issues has left me all too little space to describe the village Buddhism I observed. By far the larger part of my observations goes unreported here, and I have hardly attempted to give a systematic description of village Buddhism. There is some advantage in this, since the culture and society of Sinhalese Buddhists is rich and complex, and it is only too easy to miss the wood for the trees. When, with Robertson Smith's advice in mind, I asked village Buddhists what as Buddhists they were required to do, some of them replied 'not to kill animals'. As I relate below (Chapter 6), this struck me at the time as amazingly naive and simplistic; but when I had learnt the context by which it is to be expanded, I came to see it as an admirable summary of what Buddhism is about. In all seriousness I do think that Buddhism is essentially as simple as that, and undue elaboration of its outworks and ornaments can confuse as much as illuminate. If, nevertheless, I have presented village Buddhism too sketchily for the reader to see what we are talking about, I can but apologise, and suggest that much of the detail I have omitted may be found in Gombrich's admirable study, *Precept and Practice: Traditional Buddhism in the Rural Highlands of Ceylon* (1971).[25]*

I have, before now, been chided for too much use of the pronoun 'I' in my writing, and have been advised to write rather in the impersonal style more conventional in anthropological and other scientific literature. I have plainly neglected that advice. In part I have done so from distaste for the antics of 'we' and 'one' and 'the present author' where English style demands one should write 'I'; but there are more than stylistic considerations at issue. Anthropology is very much more than autobiography, but if it is less it is the worse for it. We do think of ourselves as scientists, objectively observing and analysing the data, and we are right to do so, lest we lapse from standards of honesty and objectivity, rigour and open-mindedness. But the ideal of Science, like that of Nirvana, is not to be embraced too literally and exclusively. We seek to be scientists, but we are also men among men, both in conducting research and in what we make of it. We study by participant observation, meaning by that that we seek to understand a society and culture by becoming, as far as we can, a member of it; and our principal instrument of enquiry is ourselves, as human persons relating to others. In consequence, what we produce is bounded by our personal limitations; it had better be enriched by our personal assets, which extend far beyond what gifts we may have as scientists in the ordinary sense.

This is why I have freely resorted to value judgements of people and their conduct, have attached weight to my subjective impressions and feelings, and have drawn upon my own religious experiences, in analysing Buddhism: all of which social scientists as a rule sedulously avoid. So long as I tried to exclude my personal feelings and assessments from my intellectual analysis I was divided against myself and unable to proceed: this book emerged as an integration of what I had striven to keep apart. An anthropologist is a man – and a woman – and if he strives to be less than a man he defeats his anthropology. This, at least, is surely true when the topic is religion: was it not always absurd to expect to understand religion by excluding value judgements, emotions, and personal experience, which are of its essence? I am indeed a flawed instrument; but so long as I strove to be a narrow social scientist I was maimed as well.

Even natural scientists have described the standard style of presenting the results of research as misleading, and have called for greater candour in reporting what one actually did (e.g. Medawar, 'Is the scientific paper a fraud?', 1964).[26] This seems to me especially relevant for social anthropology, where research is in fact so much a matter of personal encounter and experience. For this reason, basically, it has seemed to me appropriate to present my research largely in an autobiographical framework, telling it as it was. Since I am not the first anthropologist to have done this,[27]* I think the method requires no further general defence.

But there is further a special reason why I have written in this style, and indeed found it impossible to write otherwise. The interest of most anthropologists in what they research on is, I suppose, largely academic, and this makes it possible for them to adopt a largely impersonal and detached attitude. I had thought that my interest in Sinhalese Buddhism was academic too; it was only in writing this book that I learnt how much I had deceived myself, how much Buddhism and its understanding were matters of deep personal concern to me. That alone has prevented me from pretending to be impersonal. Moreover, the principal keys to my understanding of village Buddhism were in fact personal, highly subjective experiences, and it would be duplicitous in me to try to conceal this fact.

It would also be foolish of me to imagine that the subjective experiences that carried so much weight with me could be a foundation for public knowledge, which is science.[28] They belong to the process of discovery rather than of proof; and this of course is why I have sought to prove, or support, by other means, the conclusions to which they led.

Since my encounter with Buddhism has been a very personal matter, its fruits may well be more than usually prejudiced and idiosyncratic. If this is so, the fact that I have been candid about my prejudices and feelings, as well as I know them, may help the reader to allow for my biases. I have also made further efforts to keep within hailing distance of objectivity and balance. Where I have been aware of facts that conflicted with my own preferred interpretation, I have felt it my duty to report them, even where this has led me into further problems it would have been more expedient to evade. In particular, I have felt obliged to write plainly about the sexual morals of Buddhist clergy, and especially of the two who most influenced my understanding of Buddhism, although I know that this will offend the sense of propriety of many Sinhalese. Worse, since I judge these two good and authoritative Buddhists, while I know that they do not conform in spirit to the sexual morality of the Vinaya Rule,[29]* I have suggested the heresy that the Vinaya Rule, in this respect at least, is not authentically Buddhist.

Because I have had, in the cause of candour, to report of these men and others matters it were better not said in print, I have had to protect them by hiding the persons and villages I mention behind pseudonyms – even though some of them specifically asked, and I promised, they they should appear under their own names.[30]

I have also made an effort to discover and report prejudices which may have biased my interpretation. In particular, in reading over my field-notes, I have noticed that the clergy, and some of the laymen, who have most influenced my understanding of Buddhism have been disproportionately adherents of political parties of the left. This makes me suspicious, since my own sympathies incline in that direction. Inevitably, in selecting people with whom to work and to talk, I tended to prefer those whom I found congenial, and I cannot doubt that, unconsciously, this led me to be more open to clerics of the left. How far different interpretations of Buddhism correlate with different political allegiances I cannot say: my data are sufficient only to suggest that the correlation may be real, though it is very far from perfect. I must add that, however strong it may be, one should be very cautious in giving it a causal interpretation: my guess is that political allegiances do not determine views of Buddhism, nor vice versa, but rather that both result from a basic cast of sympathy and disposition. The reader should bear in mind that an anthropologist who inclined to the right might very well, and sincerely, see Buddhism in a way quite different from mine.[31*]

Notes to Chapter 1

1 There are two major varieties or schools of Buddhism. They are sometimes called Mahāyāna and Hīnayāna; but as the latter term is pejorative (it means literally 'Lesser Vehicle') it is better to use the term preferred by its adherents, 'Theravāda'. Unless otherwise specified, by 'Buddhism' I refer to its Theravāda variety. Mahāyāna Buddhism appears to be similar in many respects, but it would take me too far afield to attempt to discuss it.

2 I am assuming that Buddhism can be regarded as a religion, although this has sometimes been denied. I discussed the issue in an article (Southwold, 1978), and make some further remarks in Chapter 13. I state my position summarily at the end of the Appendix.

3 Leach (1968a), p. 1.

4 Ibid.

5 Spiro (1971), p. 45.

6 Gombrich (1971), p. 45.

7 Spiro writes, '. . . I believe it is fair to say that wherever it is found, Theravāda Buddhism is remarkably similar to the Buddhism I observed in Burma'. Its Burmese form differs from its Thai or Sinhalese form 'in only minor ways'. 'The differences are variations on a common set of themes' (1971, p. 16). So far as I can judge, knowing Burmese and Thai Buddhism only from the literature, I agree. I assume that what is true of one of the local forms of Theravāda Buddhism should be true also of the others, except in matters where the relatively minor factual differences are plainly relevant.

8   Gombrich (1971), pp. 50–6.

9   Gombrich (1971), p. 56 n.; Bechert (1966).

10 Gombrich suggests such misgivings when he writes sarcastically, 'The reader may be wondering what "the true Buddhist dogma" is which Dr. Wirz comprehends "in its real profoundness" while it eludes so many Buddhist monks' (1971, p. 50).

11 These are the scriptures of the Theravāda Buddhists, so called because they are written in Pali, a dead language of northern India. The scriptures of Mahāyāna and other schools were mostly written in Sanskrit, though some survive only in translations into other languages. For the most part, the Sanskrit scriptures were composed later than those of the Pali canon, and are therefore taken to be less reliable as historical sources for the Buddha's life and teaching.

12 Malalgoda (1972), p. 164.

13 1971, p. 60.

14 'Dharma' is the Sinhala and Sanskrit form, and 'Dhamma' the Pali form, of the same word. Sinhalese Buddhists use the two forms interchangeably, and so do I.

15 Gombrich (1971), p. 60; see also my Appendix.

16 Cf. Ling (1973), especially Chapter 2.

17 Tambiah writes, '... the canonical texts of Buddhism (just as the Bible of Christianity or the core texts of any other religion) are complex and rich in meaning, full of redundancies and variations, and by the same token paradoxical, ambiguous, and capable of different levels of interpretation at various points ... the texts themselves portray dialectical tensions, polarities and complementarities, in the treatment of basic issues' (1976, p. 402). He illustrates the point by reviewing some of the very different interpretations of Nirvana that Western scholars have derived from the scriptures (1976, pp. 402–5).

18 As I shall show, my understanding is similar to that of several more eminent scholars. I am original mainly in my readiness to suppose that villagers may well understand Buddhism better than most learned intellectuals.

19 Gombrich (1971), p. 327.

20 Smith [1889] (1927), p. 16.

21 I deal with this at length in Chapters 11 and 12.

22 1971, p. 5.

23 1971, p. 92. I must point out that Spiro distorts the position he rejects. Neither Robertson Smith, nor I, nor any serious sociologist of religion I know of, maintains that ideas are *never* the guides of behaviour: we argue that in the main ideas are more shaped by practice than practice by ideas. And evidence is produced, notably by Robertson Smith, as we shall see in Chapter 11.

24 The General Editor of this series, Dr. David Turton, suggested to me that I might contribute a book of this latter kind, and I found it more appropriate to what I have to say than the more usual format of an anthropological monograph would have been.

25 This is by far the fullest and most reliable account of Sinhalese village Buddhism. The basic facts can also be found in shorter accounts of Sinhalese Buddhism, notably the articles by Ames and Obeyesekere, and for the most

part resemble those reported from Burma and Thailand, notably by Spiro and Tambiah (see Bibliography).

26   See also work cited in Ornstein (1973, 1975) – notably the passage from Bruner (1962), pp. 2–5, quoted in Ornstein (1975), pp. 86–8.

27   See particularly Read (1966) and Robertson (1978). Bowen (1954) is an earlier and distinguished example. It is significant that, at the time she wrote, Bowen felt that an autobiographical account could not be regarded as social anthropology: in a prefatory note she remarks, 'When I write as a social anthropologist and within the canons of that discipline, I write under another name. Here I have written simply as a human being . . .' (1954, p. 5). Today, however, anthropologists regard the book as one of the most valuable of the works on the Tiv by Laura Bohannan and her husband. Recently, Obeyesekere, referring to his own research, has written forcibly on the relevance of personal features of the anthropologist, and the value of his utilising and acknowledging them (1981, pp. 8–11). Compare with Bowen's remark above his statement, 'What is sad is the pretense anthropologists must keep up that they are objective *tools* (a sorry admission for a human being)' (p. 8).

28   Ziman defines science as public knowledge (1968, p. 8 and *passim*).

29   The Vinaya Rule is the code of discipline, closely detailed in scripture, which should regulate the conduct of members of the Sangha, the Buddhist clergy.

30   Obeyesekere remarks that most of his informants wanted to be referred to by their own names, but that he has refrained from doing so (1981, p. xii).

31   Since these are matters in which passion and prejudice may subvert judgement, I must emphasise that I am *not* presenting a Marxist view of Buddhism, and that personally I am neither a Marxist nor even a Socialist. It should occasion no surprise that egalitarian views in both religion and politics may be associated, and similarly élitist views in both areas, since this is observable in our own society. I suspect that it has not been suggested before because we tend to think of Buddhism as a somewhat idealised abstraction, rather than as set in the full complexity of human life. A proper apprehension of that complexity should also enjoin caution in attributing causal connections without adequate evidence.

2

The village: Polgama

As a young man I had been fascinated by Buddhism, as I supposed it to be, and had read extensively on it. I chose to do fieldwork on Buddhism in Sri Lanka largely in order to realise this otherwise idle asset; and, like other anthropologists, decided to focus my research on villagers. In the early 1970s three distinguished studies of village Buddhism had appeared, one each for Sri Lanka, Burma, and Thailand.[1] Each of them struck me as weak on sociological analysis, and indeed data, and I hoped to be able to advance understanding by laying greater stress on this: by relating Buddhism to the structure of social relations in the communities which sustained it, I thought that each might illuminate the other.

In choosing an area in which to work I wanted one which had not already been much studied by other anthropologists, and where I might hope to find reasonably typical villages. In both respects Kurunegala District looked promising. It lies on the west of Sri Lanka, on the coastal plain and foothills of the central uplands; Kurunegala, its principal town and administrative centre, is some fifty-five miles (88 km) north-east of Colombo, the modern capital of Sri Lanka, and twenty-five miles (40 km) north-west of Kandy, the traditional capital of the Sinhalese.

The Sinhalese country, which is the greater part of Sri Lanka, is divided into two major ecological zones: the Wet Zone, which is the south-western quadrant of the island, in which two crops of paddy (rice) can be grown in a year by reliance on rainfall alone, and the Dry Zone in which two annual paddy crops can be obtained only by use of irrigation reservoirs or 'tanks'.[2] These different agricultural systems have sociological correlates. The southern part of Kurunegala District is in the Wet Zone, the northern in the Dry; I thought this might make it possible for me to compare villages of both types within a quite small distance. The Sinhalese country is also divided into two sub-cultural divisions: the Low Country on the southern and western coastal plains, which came under colonial rule in the sixteenth century, and the Up-Country, or

Kandyan region, which remained independent of the colonial powers until 1815.

Kurunegala District (then known as *Hat Korale*) was part of the Kandyan kingdom; I thought that, since it was on the plains, it might also have elements of Low Country culture. This proved not to be so, except to the extent that Low Country people and culture have diffused into the District, as they have into other Kandyan areas. It is true that the lower-lying parts of the western Kandyan kingdom, from Kurunegala District northwards to Anuradhapura and beyond, were not closely controlled from Kandy, and had and have some sub-cultural peculiarities of their own. So far as I know these are not of great significance – though, as I shall note, Robert Knox, the best observer of the Sinhalese, in the seventeenth century, remarked notable differences in character between the people of the lowlands and those of the uplands (below, Chapter 5).

I had hoped I might be able to study two or three villages comparatively, but this proved to be quite unrealistic: although I was greatly helped by my wife Sarah, and each of us worked with a Sinhalese research assistant/interpreter, it took us a full year to unravel the complexities of the first village we chose to study, and then perhaps not altogether adequately. Only in that one village, which I call Polgama, did we make an intensive study, with a village census.[3]* We were able to learn, less systematically, about several neighbouring villages, and made some enquiries in others within cycling range; essentially ours was a study of Polgama and its vicinity. Since the factors which led us to choose Polgama for study, and other features of the village which we were to discover later, raise questions about its typicality, and about the possible bias which led us there, I shall consider these at some length later. Here I outline some of its basic characteristics.

Polgama is eight miles (13 km) north of Kurunegala town, on a minor metalled road which leads to nowhere of much importance. It is linked to the town by two bus services, which were infrequent and unreliable. Kurunegala is not a large town – in 1972 its population was about 28,000[4] – but proximity to it was of some social significance to Polgama: some of the villagers had settled there because of it, and some 7% of household heads were employed in the town.

Polgama is about 300 ft (90 m) above sea level, and is technically in the narrow transitional, or Intermediate Zone, between the Wet and Dry Zones, where paddy cultivation without tanks is possible but unreliable. Because of features of local terrain, Polgama actually receives less rainfall than other villages near-by, and because the soil is sandy benefits less from it: it is really a Dry Zone village without a tank. In both the growing seasons of 1974–75, when we were there, practically no paddy was harvested, and little sown, in Polgama; and in the previous eight growing seasons most people recalled only one or two good harvests.[5*] This was a period of relative drought in Sri Lanka, as in much of the Tropics; nevertheless we observed that paddy was harvested in other villages just a few miles away, which had tanks or higher rainfall. I suspect that in Polgama paddy cultivation is normally unsuccessful, and only in wetter years do many farmers harvest enough to supply even their own households. One villager told us as much. Many said that paddy farming was their principal occupation, which it certainly was not when we were there, nor I suspect in most years; these statements reflect the high prestige of paddy farming among Sinhalese villagers. In reality, the principal crop was the coconut, some of which was consumed domestically, but most sold to copra merchants; and a variety of other crops were grown on a small scale, mostly for domestic consumption. Most households had, and needed to have, several sources of income, and there was a wide variety of occupations, including employment in the village, in other villages or on coconut estates near-by, in Kurunegala and even in Colombo. This was a village with a very mixed economy in reality, though not in the perception of most of the villagers, who saw themselves as farmers, indeed paddy farmers.

The people, or most of them, also spoke of themselves as poor. They certainly were by Western standards, though this was not the comparison that they were making. They said they were poorer than they had been in the recent past, and this was surely true: because of the drought, the rise in oil prices, and other factors, Sri Lanka as a whole was suffering severe economic stringency in the mid-1970s. They also spoke of themselves as poorer than other Sinhalese, including those in near-by villages. This is more questionable, though in the absence of sufficiently detailed statistics it is difficult to be certain.[6*] By the measure of visible signs of wealth, I think it likely that many Sinhalese in areas of better rainfall or irrigation, or other economic resources, were more prosperous than those of Polgama, and the same could be said of at least one village in the vicinity of Polgama. But other near-by villages, lacking the employment opportunities that the accessibility of Polgama provided, or with a greater pressure of population on the land, were probably or certainly poorer. Polgama people saw themselves as poorer partly because, unrealistically, they tended to estimate prosperity in terms of paddy yields, and partly because this expressed a more diffuse dissatisfaction with their lot. The majority of villagers were poor, in the sense that they had less food and other resources than they had come to expect, and saw other people, including some in the village, enjoy; and some families certainly went hungry. But no one actually starved, and the village was not characterised by grinding poverty; on the contrary, it was modestly prosperous for the area, and most households had some surplus beyond the basic needs of subsistence.

In 1974–75 the village had a population of some 730 persons, divided between 144 households, occupying less than one square mile (2 km²). Like most Sinhalese villages outside the Dry Zone, the settlement was not nucleated, for houses stood among their coconut trees and other dry-land (*goda idam*) crops, on the slightly higher land which surrounded and separated the paddy fields: most of them were strung along the two metalled roads, and lesser tracks, with other houses, linked by footpaths, behind them. The settlement had no evident centre, and its boundaries were somewhat arbitrary, especially on the south, where it was contiguous with the village of Gonnawa, which, with its several permanent shops, its police station, sub-post office and secondary school, and its railway station, was a place of more importance.

Polgama was a mixed-caste village,[7] in which the largest single community (41% of household heads) claimed to be Radala. Among the Sinhalese, the highest and largest caste is that of the Goyigama, which probably comprises more than half the total population;[8*] the Radala are those of the highest-ranking of the three sections into which the caste is divided. In the days of the Kandyan kingdom the Radala were the aristocracy: administrative officers and their families, who held considerable estates of land and resided upon them in their *valavva*, roughly 'manor houses'. Today the term has a less definite meaning, but is considered appropriate for descendants of the aristocrats who still have high social standing and maintain their *valavva*. By the latter two criteria those of Polgama have lost their status, and are now ordinary Goyigama, as one of them told us; but in fact most of them insist that they are Radala, and I shall not quibble.

According to 'Radala' informants, the village of Polgama, with several square miles of surrounding land, was granted by the king, apparently in the eighteenth century, to their ancestor.[9*] As he, and some of his descendants, held minor administrative offices under the king or the British, the family were perhaps Radala, very minor gentry, at that time. Around 1900 they sold, or as they say were cheated out of, most of their land to people opening up coconut estates in the area; and falling to litigation among themselves, they lost more to pay the fees of lawyers. Today none of the Radala people owns more than a few acres of land, and many of them are quite poor; the richer members of the village are not of their community.

One part of the village, known as the Old Village (*mul gama*) has a concentration of Radala families; it was the site of the original *valavva*, though there is no building there now to which anyone would give the title. In the last century the senior man of the family built two new *valavvas* a little higher up the hill, between which he distributed his three wives. Though neither of these stands today, two of the three largest houses in the village happen to occupy their approximate sites. One was built by a man I call Joseph Salgado, of Karāva caste, who migrated to the area and bought land there around 1930. He was evidently a man of energy and ability, and hence of some wealth, and was considerably respected by his fellow villagers. When we asked people who they considered to be leaders of the village, most people said they could think of no one; but among those who could, Salgado was one of the two men most often named. Both of them had died shortly before we came to Polgama. His widow and children, some of them adult, lived on in the two-storey house, and were respected by, and friendly with, their Radala and Goyigama neighbours. One of the sons was thought to be seeking to marry a daughter of one of these Radala families, and to be using sorcery (*huniyam*) to that end; the family took this seriously enough to use magic to counteract the sorcery.

The Karāva caste, whose traditional occupation is that of fishermen, is not indigenous to the Kandyan region. In the Low Country its members have been so successful economically that they are generally regarded as more or less equal in status with the Goyigama. In the Up-Country too, similar status equality with the Goyigama is commonly accorded to Karāva immigrants. In Polgama this extended, sometimes, to eating together in the home. But not to intermarriage, the ban on which is the most emphasised symbol of caste exclusiveness. The Radala of Polgama exert themselves strenuously to prevent intermarriage even with ordinary Goyigama – but have not entirely prevented their sons and daughters from marrying even into low castes. I doubt if Salgado's son did wish to marry the girl. The suspicion that he did, elaborated in the idiom of sorcery, was symbolic. The Radala felt, in traditional idiom, that Polgama was their village, but presumably sensed that in reality it was not. Many villagers were 'outsiders', i.e. immigrants, mostly non-Radala, who had come to live there, for the most part during the course of the previous thirty years;[10]* most of the villagers who had wealth or other attributes of high status other than caste were outsiders. The Salgados had been typical; in his lifetime Joseph Salgado had been among the more prosperous and influential men in the village, and in a way he had the *valavva* – though no one said as much to me.[11]* The last tenuous claim of the Radala to be the real, exclusive, aristocracy of the village would have dissolved had they been compelled to admit his family to connubium.

The identity, boundaries, and social structure of Sinhalese villages are commonly tenuous matters[12] – especially when the village is neither an economic unit centred on a tank, or a common estate of land, nor a social unit based on unity of caste and kinship. Polgama is regarded as one village because it was defined as such under the Kandyan kingdom;[13]* but in terms of present-day social realities it is little more than an arbitrary division of the countryside. While neighbourhood, and close kinship, count for something, most kinds of social relationship spread across the boundaries of the village, and there is little of important common interest to unite the villagers as such. There are no distinctive leaders because there is no common cause or interest in which people could be led, nor does anyone control sufficient resources to be able to dominate many of his fellows. For the Radala the village is still an arena in which to play out their largely imaginary game of traditional status; for most other people, outsiders especially, it is little more than a *pied à terre*.

The most evident respect in which a village is a distinct community is in relation to its Buddhist 'temple' (*pansala*). It is in a sense the parish of the temple, though Sinhalese do not speak in such an idiom. It seems to be normal for one village to have one temple, though smaller or poorer villages may have none, and larger villages more than one. The lay people of the village are expected to provide material support for the temple and its resident clergy, who in return provide ritual and other services to the villagers. Buddhist lay people are free to attend or worship at any temple, or at none, though in fact only a few people at Polgama regularly attend at any temple but that in the village. They have less freedom to invite Buddhist clergy to participate in rites held at their homes, which, especially funeral and other mortuary ceremonies, are regarded as of greater religious importance. Here the convention is that one must invite the incumbent[14] of one's own village temple, and only through him other Buddhist clergy; clergy should not respond to such invitations directly from laymen of other villages, and usually do not. In this sense the incumbent of the village temple has a ritual monopoly over his village, which corresponds to and sanctions his claim to support from it.[15*]

The material and financial affairs of the temple should be run by a committee of Buddhist laymen, usually called the *Dāyake Sabhāva*, the 'committee of donors'. In my area at least these were often inert or ineffective. In Polgama the village priest – or 'monk' in the more usual but inappropriate terminology (see Appendix) – largely managed the affairs of the temple himself, sometimes with the aid of a body known as the Temple Association. Its members were mainly 'insiders', especially of the Radala families. The village priest, whom I call Sīlaratana, though he was born in another village a few miles away, was himself of a junior line of these Radala, by descent from a woman. Control of temple affairs was one of the ways in which the Radala sought to assert their traditional status: in principle appropriately, since the Buddhist clergy and temples are symbols for the traditional identity and values of Sinhalese society; but in practice with difficulty, since Sīlaratana did not share their conservative values and liked to associate with poor and low-caste people. He was also a man of strong and dominant character.

The principal function of the Temple Association was to raise funds, and the major need for funds had for thirty years been to build a more fitting *āvasa*, or presbytery, for the village temple. This project had signally and repeatedly failed, and we were offered a variety of excuses for this: fund-raising attempts had been thwarted by the jealousies of leading Radala; Sīlaratana had embezzled what funds had been raised; an astrologer had read in the stars that the *āvasa* would be built in the incumbency of the seventh Polgama priest (Sīlaratana was the sixth). One man, however, told us he reckoned the real reason was this: if the funds ever were raised, most of them would have to come from outsiders, as the insiders were too indigent: in that case the prestige, and indeed religious Merit, of building the *āvasa* would be accounted to the outsiders, and this the insiders were too jealous to allow.

I said there were two fine houses on the sites of the two former *valavvas*. One was that of Joseph Salgado; the other was that of David Pieris, another Karāva immigrant to the village. David's father had come to the vicinity as a trader and had settled there, but had later left. David had returned, settled in Polgama, and gone into business as a copra merchant, at which he was moderately successful: he was probably the second richest man in the village when we were there, and was generally liked and respected, as he was reckoned a fair dealer who readily extended credit (at a price) to those who sold him coconuts. He was more of an outsider than Salgado, since he was not only Karāva but Roman Catholic – one of only fourteen non-Buddhist households heads in Polgama; and he told us he made a point of keeping out of village politics, lest his trade suffer. His wife, however, was a Buddhist and active supporter of the temple. David, of course, did not himself participate in public Buddhist practices, though each year he lent his tractors and trailers to support the nominally religious *perahāra*, or procession, which Sīlaratana organised with much energy and ostentation.

Their marriage was not only across religious categories but also across castes: Mrs Pieris, another outsider, was of Batgama caste, which is generally said, out of earshot to its members, to be of very low rank.[16*] Caste is very much a matter of kindreds and their relations within the local community, and such a marriage between established families of the village would have been strongly resisted and resented. It is a measure of how much the Pierises were regarded as outsiders that we heard no one criticise them, and saw no one ostracise them,[17*] on account of their irregular marriage – Sīlaratana, in fact, boasted to me that it was he who had urged them to marry.

In 1981 we learnt by correspondence that funds had at last been raised to build the new presbytery (*āvasa*), and building work had commenced: and a principal benefactor was David Pieris. This was so neat a solution to the villagers' dilemma that I kicked myself for not having predicted it:

David was so much of an outsider that insiders did not have to feel unduly jealous of him. I cannot, of course, say how far everyone finds this a satisfactory solution; not do I know whether any Radala people feel unease that a man who, in a loose sense, has a *valavva* has also made himself a major benefactor of the village temple.

All this throws some light on the sociology of the village – though I must point out that the affairs of the temple are not of very large concern to anyone, except Sīlaratana and his pupil-novices who may expect to succeed to his incumbency. It throws less on the significance of village Buddhism. Buddhist activities are part of village life, and provide one of many resources for status emulation; the priest, the temple, and activities centred on them, are to some extent symbols of village identity and pride, and Buddhism to a notable extent symbolises traditional Sinhalese values. But I cannot delude myself that these and similar observations tell us much about the significance of Buddhism to the villagers: they are indeed quite explicit that the affairs of the temple, and indeed the activities of the priest, are at best accessory to the practice of Buddhism.

My hope to throw light on village Buddhism through sociological analysis was in large measure disappointed. I can see why. Buddhism is not a product of village life, and while it is of course adapted to meet the needs and conditions of the lives of villagers, its social significance to them is not primarily to reflect or endorse the social structure of the village, which is in any case pretty tenuous. On the contrary, its symbolic social significance is rather to express the fact that its practitioners are not villagers merely, but members of a grander society and civilisation. Moreover Buddhism, especially among religions, is not of this world: I was constantly told that it is not concerned with *laukika*, worldly affairs, but with the *lōkōttara*, the supra-mundane, which is defined as the opposite of the *laukika*. This is an exaggeration, for Buddhism in practice is concerned with worldly affairs, and *lōkōttara* also means 'pre-eminent in the world'.[18] I shall have to discuss these terms more fully later (below, Chapter 7). For the present I remark that their implication is that Buddhism is not, or should not be, concerned to reflect and endorse social life as it is, but rather to transform it. The sociology of Buddhism tells us more about the failure of people to be the Buddhists they seek to be than it does about what they seek and why. To make sense of these latter became increasingly the aim of my research.

Notes to Chapter 2

1   Gombrich (1971), Spiro (1971), Tambiah (1970).
2   Wickremeratne (1977), p. 237.

3   Several aspects of Sinhalese life, especially the economic, are extremely complex. Suspecting that we might not succeed in getting full data from each of the 144 households in Polgama, we concentrated our efforts on a 50% sample – every second household. We gave lower priority to getting less extensive data on the remaining households, and in fact did not get data from all of them. The statistics I report are therefore based on the completed main sample.

4   Department of Census and Statistics (1973), p. 16.

5   People's experiences varied, since whether or not one got a harvest sometimes depended on the location of one's plot in the paddy field. People's recollections also varied, partly in relation to political attitudes. Harvests are largely dependent on rainfall; and many Sinhalese believe that failure of the rains is a judgement on, or supernatural result of, bad government. Hence those who were politically hostile to the left-wing Government that had been in power since 1970 were more inclined to report bad harvests.

6   It commonly took us several hours to determine the land-holding and income of a single household in Polgama; hence I have reservations about the accuracy of more extensive statistics.

7   Ryan (1953) is still the best authority on Sinhalese caste.

8   The Census of Sri Lanka does not record caste, so accurate figures are not available. Obeyesekere quotes Ryan's estimate that the Goyigama make up more than 50% of the population, but thinks the true figure is close to 60% (Obeyesekere, 1974, p. 371).

9   The village is said to have existed long before this, and probably belonged to another caste.

10 Thirty-nine per cent of household heads were non-Radala and were not born in Polgama; 77% of household heads were not born in Polgama.

11 Though Salgado's house may not have been on the exact site of the old *valavva*, it looked more like a *valavva* than any of its neighbours.

12 Cf. Pieris (1956), pp. 39–40.

13 This is what villagers said; in fact Polgama seems to have been regarded as a section or satellite of Gonnawa, and was not recognised as a quite distinct village until about 1920.

14 *Vihāradhipāti.*

15 Both laymen and clergy told me that the final sanction a priest would exercise over a villager who adamantly refused to give any material support was refusal to attend, and invite other clergy to attend, mortuary ceremonies. It was clearly regarded as a dire sanction.

16 This is the caste usually termed Padu in the literature. Its members reject that term, which seems to be a term of opprobrium for low-caste people generally rather than a specific caste name.

17 In fact they employed a Radala lady of the village as a domestic servant.

18 Carter (1924), p. 555.

3

Silaratana and the clerical norm

From my voracious, if unprofessional, reading of earlier years, I knew more about Buddhism than most anthropologists would; and this was indeed the asset I had hoped it would be. Buddhist concepts and idiom, which often appear abstruse on first acquaintance, were to me familiar, so I was rarely puzzled by what people were saying, and could easily hold my own even in quite recondite debates with Buddhist clergy. It was evident to everyone that I was a serious scholar and worth taking seriously. But I also paid a price. Puzzles are what science is about, and in not being puzzled I was often at a loss to see what I should be finding out. I understood too easily what people were talking about: when I heard an allusion to a concept already familiar to me, I often assumed too hastily that the speaker had just the concept that I had, rather than letting him explain his own thought in his own terms. Above all, my perception was distorted by what I have called 'the conventional judgement', that village Buddhism is not true Buddhism. Unwittingly, the real progress of my research was the outgrowing of that prejudice.

I did not, so far as I knew, go to Sri Lanka as a Buddhist. In my youth I had felt strongly attracted to what I took to be Buddhism, but had later come to find it repugnant; later still, I had become indifferent, and thought I had left all this far behind me. If I had not, I should not have gone to study any kind of Buddhism, for I thought then that strong feelings, one way or another, would be incompatible with the objectivity and impartiality necessary to a scientist. But I felt confident that I had become neutral and detached; and took it for granted that if 'authentic' Buddhism had no personal appeal for me, village Buddhism, which I 'knew' to be inauthentic and corrupt besides, could have none.

In the summer vacation of 1973, the year before I planned to begin my fieldwork in Sri Lanka, I made a preparatory visit to get to know what I might find, and to plan the fieldwork as far as possible. I found Sri Lanka quite as attractive as I had been told I should. Unexpectedly, I noticed how moved I was to find myself surrounded by the conventional marks of Buddhist devotion, temples, images, and monks in saffron robes. The Sinhalese I met assured me – and I did not doubt it – that all this was outward sham, the temples nests of superstition, the images tawdry, the clergy mostly rogues. But for all that, spontaneously I felt the sense of rest, of warmth and welcome, that one feels on coming home after travelling long in foreign parts. I felt this was my home. If I had ever confessed this to my Sinhalese friends, they would have told me it showed I must have been a Buddhist in a previous birth; and in a certain, figurative, way I suppose they would have been right. But I simply relaxed in the comfort of it, not thinking how much it called in question my supposed detachment.

When I came back to Sri Lanka with my wife in 1974, our first task, after having engaged two Sinhalese research assistants, was to find a suitable village in which to begin fieldwork within Kurunegala District. Since, in the event, we were to do nearly all our work in that village, the selection I made, and the way I made it, introduced potential bias which I must frankly acknowledge.

I suspected that if I went to senior Buddhist 'ecclesiastics' for advice, they would steer me not to a typical village, but to one where I might be impressed by the atypical state of Buddhist piety. (When, much later, I did meet such an ecclesiastic, that was just the advice I was offered.) Bypassing that pitfall, I went instead to the local administration for advice, and was extraordinarily fortunate. The Government Agent, the administrative officer in charge of Kurunegala District, then Mr. Chandrananda de Silva, was a man of unusual ability. He understood at once what I was after – better than I did myself – and after giving me a brilliant summary of the characteristics of the District, suggested three areas in it which might be most suitable for my research. One of these was near Kurunegala town, and he graciously offered to ask one of his senior clerks, Mr. Siri Ratnayake, who lived in the area, to show me around if I wished.

Naturally I did, and the next day Mr. Ratnayake, my research assistant and I set out on bicycles to explore. I was looking for a village which was predominantly high-caste, not so large or dispersed that fieldwork would be difficult, and where the Buddhist temple owned significant estates (which I took to be the traditional and usual pattern). After visiting and rejecting several possible villages which turned out not to satisfy these criteria, we came to Polgama. Our guide told us that the village priest here was an unusual character: among other things, he had devoted the greater part of his efforts to the economic and social development of the village, through the Rural Development Society (*Grama Sangwardhana Samitiya*) he had founded and led. This tickled me, in view of the solemn words I had read of the incompatibility of Buddhism and economic development,[1] and my appetite was whetted.

I was later to learn that Mr. Ratnayake was very friendly with Sīlaratana; and I see in my notes that when I first spoke to him he had suggested Polgama as one of two villages I was most likely to find suitable for my research. Subtly, and probably unconsciously, I suppose he steered me towards the choice of Polgama. This is remarkable, since Sīlaratana is not the kind of priest of whom most English-educated Sinhalese, of whom Mr. Ratnayake was one, would approve; on the contrary, most other English-speakers whom I met considered him more or less disgraceful.

When we met Sīlaratana he welcomed us warmly – as indeed most priests do – and I took an immediate liking to him. In the notes I wrote that evening I remarked, 'He appeared a very shrewd and kindly man'; and I was impressed too by his robust common sense and forthright manner of speaking. I told him that I was planning to write a book on village Buddhism, and wanted to examine particularly social relationships in the village, especially those between lay people and clergy. He applauded and said that was just the right way to go about things. I was flattered, and encouraged that my social anthropological approach was so readily grasped and approved. I had misgivings that Polgama was a good deal larger than the kind of village I would have preferred; and when Sīlaratana also told me that his temple had no estates,[2*] I said regretfully that Polgama would not be suitable. Not a bit abashed, he replied that I was all mixed up (and I daresay, from my knowledge of him, that his actual expression was a good deal more picturesque):[3*] 'You say you want to study relations between priests and villagers: well, go to a village where the temple has estates and you'll find there aren't any. It's only priests like me, who have to depend on the villagers for their meals, who trouble to cultivate good relations with them. But don't take my word for it: go and see for yourself. Why not go to Dikväva, a few miles down the road, where the priest has estates, and ask him what his relations with his people are like?'

I was much impressed with this, both by the robust good sense and by the frankness and lack of deference to the foreign scholar. I felt this was the kind of man I could really work with, and I think I decided there and then to do so. I was doubtless influenced, too, by his evident keenness that I should work in his village. But, to show him that I would not too readily take his word for anything, we did go to Dikväva. The priest there was most welcoming, and told us unprompted that his relations with the villagers were deplorable: most of them would have nothing to do with him or the temple, mainly because they resented the fact that it owned most of the best paddy land in the village.

We returned to Polgama, when I met the headman (*grama sēvaka*), who was administratively responsible for six villages, including Polgama where he lived. As with Sīlaratana, I took an immediate liking to him, and found that he understood at once the kind of research that I wanted to do, and was most co-operative. Somewhat appalled at my own temerity, I at once committed ourselves to begin our research in Polgama.

I see now, what I did not suspect at the time, that my decision was probably influenced by the kind of sympathies which, as I pointed out in Chapter 1, tend to find expression in political attitudes. Sīlaratana was somewhat left-wing in his politics: he had been a strong supporter of the moderately socialist Sri Lanka Freedom Party (SLFP). The headman was a member of the Communist Party, more I am sure from indignation at social injustice than from commitment to Marxism, of which he seemed to know little. As I tend to find such people most congenial in my own country, I suspect that my own sympathies affected the liking I took to both these men, which clearly influenced my choice of Polgama as a village in which to work. I note also that Dhammatilaka, the priest whom I came to know best after Sīlaratana, and who also did much to shape my own ideas, had a similar view of Buddhism and politics, and was also an active supporter of the Sri Lanka Freedom Party. I came to know him better than others primarily because all of us, my wife, our research assistants and I, liked him a great deal, and often called in at his temple for the pleasure of his company.

I suppose that by preferring to work with people I warmed to I made it more likely that I would encounter an interpretation of Buddhism which would fall in with my own predilections, and hence seem to me 'true'. Presumably all anthropological research is to some extent steered by such personal bias: the best corrective is to inform the reader of it, if one can. On the other hand, I must point out that the Buddhism I saw and report is not merely self-projection. Sīlaratana and Dhammatilaka do exist, and there are many priests like them; and as I shall argue, it would seem that most Buddhist clergy are more like than unlike them. If this should prove to be an exaggeration, it is a healthy one: for the view of Buddhism that I shall present is at least a large part of reality, and one that has hitherto received too little attention, having been too easily dismissed because of attachment to the more usual stereotypes of the Buddhist 'monk' or '*bhikkhu*' (see Appendix).

Had I foreseen that in choosing a village in which to begin fieldwork I was choosing the only one we should study, I might have agonised more than I did over the choice – and probably done no better. I thought Sīlaratana an interesting and attractive person, and I was intrigued by his unfamiliar idea of Buddhism. I assumed that he must be untypical of Buddhist clergy, but was not unduly concerned, since we planned to work in two or three different villages anyway, and reckoned it not too crucial where we began. However, after four months in Polgama our information about the village was plainly incomplete and superficial: as was evident from the fact that the data we were then getting was much better than we had got earlier. It made little sense to get inadequate data on several villages, so we decided we should stay longer in Polgama until we could feel confident that we knew the village well. I suspected then that this was going to entail our spending the whole year there, in a village I would not have chosen as the only one in which I would study village Buddhism at all thoroughly. I had realised that Sīlaratana was less untypical than I had initially supposed, and I still liked him and his approach to Buddhism. But I had come largely to share the opinion of most people who knew him, that he was a bad priest with little real interest in religion. Because of the importance of the priest as the religious focus and leader of a village, it seemed to me that Polgama could not easily be defended as a place in which to spend so long studying village Buddhism. The arguments for not leaving yet were sound, but I felt they were rationalisations. When I was honest with myself, I saw that in large part the basis of my reluctance to move on was the fact that I had come to like the people of Polgama so much I could not bear to leave. I thought this was unprofessional, and I had a bad conscience about it.

I found it very difficult to make up my mind about Sīlaratana. Few people in the village had a good word to say for him, and many of them, and other people round about who knew him, forthrightly criticised him. Uncomfortably, I saw that there was at least something in what they said. 'Nothing but a businessman (*mudalāli*)' – and it was true he did engage a little in commerce, mostly with laughable incompetence. 'He's just a politician, not a priest' – and he certainly had been very active in politics, though even then I doubted the validity of the distinction.[4] 'All he is interested in is boasting and self-advertisement' – and there was certainly a lot of truth in that. 'He never meditates' – even his friends conceded that, and Sīlaratana himself could not have been more unconvincing in denying it. There were nastier and more specific charges. 'That whore who lives next to the temple, she has been his mistress for years. And he has had other women [several of them named]. And that boy, the one who sells peanuts at the temple at festivals, that's his son.' Several people told us, what it was obvious others were darkly hinting, that most of the money the villagers had ever collected for improving the temple buildings had been embezzled by Sīlaratana and passed to his sister's son.

It was easy to suspect that much of this was slander, especially as it mainly came from his political opponents. I was to learn that Sinhalese rarely have a good word to say for anyone active in a political party opposed to the one they support themselves; and Sīlaratana had campaigned very actively for the party repudiated by the great majority of the villagers.[5*] Eventually I was to realise that in each of the four villages near-by which I knew well enough to form any judgement there was considerable disgruntlement with the village priest, sometimes expressed in scathing criticism. To be sure, I did not hear any of them accused of unchastity, though I probably would have done if I had been more in the villagers' confidence: for it is a common saying that every temple has a well worn footpath at the back leading to the house of the priest's mistress. On the most jaundiced view this must be an exaggeration. Again it is quite common to be told that most priests are bad priests, and many of them arrant rogues: that I am sure there must be good priests somewhere in Sri Lanka but I don't know where they are. Emboldened by this, I included on the survey questionnaire which we used with a 50% sample of householders (or their wives) a question 'Are Buddhist priests mostly good people?' No fewer than 37% of the Buddhist respondents replied that they were mostly bad,[6*] some of them offering us greater statistical precision – as do some people in more informal contexts – with statements that 75%, 90%, 99% of them were bad. This considerably restored my confidence, since I knew that such statements were absurd, not only because those who made them could not have had such extensive knowledge, but also because most of the priests I knew, and they knew, plainly did not merit such disparagement – and the only one who did had in fact been virtually expelled from the Sangha, the order of clergy, by his colleagues (see below, on Gunajoti). Why Sinhalese should so often and so wildly disparage their clergy, even to a foreigner, and even though they know it is a specific sin to do so, is a question I shall return to briefly later (Chapter 9); but even quite early on it taught me to be sceptical of what they said about particular priests such as Silaratana.

On the two more specific charges I mentioned I was eventually to realise also that the critics had overreached themselves and thus undermined their own credibility. Obviously there is no way I can know for certain whether Silaratana had or had not maintained his clerical vow of celibacy; and since he had plainly not been a blatant sinner like Gunajoti, I am not sure that it matters much. But, for what it is worth, a number of considerations give me some confidence that at least one of the charges against him was blatant fabrication, and that on balance he is more likely to have maintained his vow than not.[7*]

On the other charge, of peculation, I feel even more confident. In the first place, there were other reasons why the villagers could never raise the funds to improve the temple, which they were anxious not to acknowledge; I have discussed these already. In the second place, we asked Silaratana's sister's son about the matter, and I felt sure he was not lying when he replied. With an easy laugh, he gestured at his house – he was one of the richest men in the village – and said, 'Well, look at me, and

remember how poor Sīlaratana is. What do you think? Yes, it is true that I
go rather secretively to visit him in the temple most evenings, and it is
true that money changes hands. But in which direction, would you
think?' In the third place, we asked the local headman (*grama sēvaka*),
who was a good friend of Sīlaratana's, and of ours, if he thought there was
any truth in the story. He considered it for a moment, and then with
disarming frankness replied: 'I would not think so. It is quite true that he
is hopelessly incompetent at managing money, it slips through his hands
like water. If he has been stealing it, what has he got to show for it? The
thing is, he has always been a soft touch for any poor priest who comes by
begging for money and calls him *Nāyaka Thero*:[8]* Sīlaratana will just
give him whatever he has got, without thinking.'

That is not untypical: where I have been able to investigate charges
that were made against Sīlaratana, what looked to be the truth turned
out to be rather innocent, if not indeed to his credit. One of the blacker
marks against him I ought perhaps to have taken rather seriously, rather
than laughing about it as I did. We had decided to move into Polgama,
but were waiting as requested for the next auspicious day, when I thought
I heard my research assistant refer to Sīlaratana's 'cinema'. Incredulous,
I asked if I could possibly have heard aright, and my assistant said oh yes,
the 'monk' owns this cinema, just across the road from the temple:
performances every Monday and Wednesday, 7 and 9.30 p.m. Even I,
relatively ignorant as I then was, recognised this as outrageous: for I knew
that one of the Ten Precepts, which form the basis of proper conduct for a
cleric, forbids the handling of gold and silver, commonly understood as
handling money; and another forbids a cleric to watch theatrical shows
and dancing, which would surely extend to cinema performances. I was to
find that my reaction of astonishment to this revelation was common also
to educated Sinhalese with whom I shared it: those who took a somewhat
idealistic view of Buddhism were quite appalled, while those whose
outlook was more realistic laughed as much as I did. Eccentric this
enterprise undoubtedly was, but probably quite innocent: when I asked
Sīlaratana himself about it, he said that he had started the cinema to
show religious films to the people, and these he had watched; but the
somewhat scanty stock of religious films was soon worked through, so he
took to hiring, but not watching, more secular films in the hope of raising
funds for the temple. He could have added that it was really no different
from the amateur dramas and entertainments that many temples
organise to raise funds.

At Polgama the presbytery (*āvasa*), that is, the building on the temple
compound in which the priest and novices reside, was indeed
extraordinary. An educated middle-class lady whom we knew, who had
visited Polgama a number of times, once exclaimed to us indignantly that
it was nothing better than a pigsty. A similar judgement, in less extreme

terms, was expressed to us by several of the villagers, and it was evident that many, perhaps most, of them were ashamed of the condition of the presbytery. We have observed that they tried for many years to raise the funds to build a new one. It was easy to see why. The actual presbytery at Polgama was a somewhat dilapidated mud-walled building with a rusty corrugated iron roof; Silaratana's sporadic efforts to improve the overall appearance of the place included an array of flowers in pots, one of which proved, on closer inspection, to be a superannuated piss-pot. The contrast with every other presbytery I saw, save in the very poorest villages, was striking. Every normal presbytery is a well built house with brick walls and a tiled roof – objectively among the finer residences in the village. Villagers definitely take invidious pride in the condition of the buildings at their village temple – it is this as much as anything that motivates them to raise, or try to raise, funds to improve them. I heard only one man ever express satisfaction with the condition of the Polgama presbytery, and that was Silaratana himself. On a number of occasions he boasted to me that he was not like most village priests whose chief ambition was to get themselves a fine presbytery in which to reside: he didn't care about things like that, he had always been more concerned to help poor people. This may have been exaggerated, but it was basically true.[9]*

Silaratana told me that when he came to Polgama, in 1940, simply taking over the temple, which had been without an incumbent for a dozen years, the village was a poor and primitive place, little more than jungle. From what I was able to piece together from other sources, I am clear that that account was exaggerated. On the other hand, from the evidence I have, it seems likely that, relative to its condition in 1974, the Polgama of 1940 would have been small, poor, and backward, and the lives of the villagers somewhat harsh.[10]* Silaratana told me that he saw that his first task must be to work to improve the economic and social conditions of the villagers, since there is little to be gained by preaching Dhamma (doctrine) to people too wretched to be able to pay much attention. It was to this end that he had founded the Polgama Rural Development Society and worked energetically for many years as its President. He spoke with pride of numerous improvements and benefits which the Society had been instrumental in bringing to the village. (Objectively, it would appear that Silaratana exaggerated, no doubt sincerely, the actual role of the Society and himself in the development of the village: nevertheless it was real and seems to have impressed a number of visitors to the village.)[11]* It was with the same end in view that around 1952 he became very active, and locally prominent, in supporting the moderately left-wing political party, the Sri Lanka Freedom Party (SLFP), which was being formed at that time under a national political leader, S. W. R. D. Bandaranaike. The local Member of Parliament (M.P.) at that time was from the more conservative United Independence Party (UNP). Silaratana presented to him a list of five demands,[12]* all for needed social or economic improvements of Polgama and its vicinity, and asked him if he supported them. When the M.P. demurred, Silaratana told him that he would actively oppose him – it seems to have been a somewhat heated quarrel[13]* – and vigorously set to work to do so. From that time Silaratana was an active, and locally notorious, supporter of the SLFP, which earned him the detestation, no doubt variable over time in depth and in extent, of many of the villagers, who were inveterate stalwarts of the UNP.[14]* Silaratana also boasted to me that he had always made especial efforts to help the poorest people, and those of low caste. Perhaps that was exaggerated too, but I saw a good deal of evidence that it was substantially true. I suspected, too, that it might not be wholly unconnected with the spiteful judgements often expressed of him by the less unfortunate.[15]*

Though all this seemed to me rather admirable, I was at a loss to understand what it had to do with the calling of a Buddhist cleric – the more so as many villagers and others insisted that it had nothing to do with it, but was on the contrary clear evidence of Silaratana's failure in and indifference to his calling. On a number of occasions I asked Silaratana what was his authority for interpreting his vocation in the Sangha in this way, and his answers left me little the wiser. Usually he replied by saying that Lord Buddha had charged his followers, the first *bhikkhus* of the Sangha, to go out and teach the multitudes the Dhamma (doctrine), and that was why he, Silaratana, devoted himself to social service. I knew that, according to the scriptures, the Buddha had indeed delivered this charge,[16] and also that it was the fundamental legitimation of the teaching activity of the Sangha throughout history. But Silaratana's application of it seemed to me a *non sequitur*, and if he understood its logic, he never made it clear to me.

On another occasion he told me an anecdote about Ānanda, Lord Buddha's favourite disciple, with the sly amusement which usually accompanied his telling of such stories. Once, he said, there was a very poor man who heard of the Buddha's Dhamma, and determined to go and hear it from the Master's own lips. After walking many days without food, he came at last before Ānanda and begged him to teach him the Dhamma. Ānanda took one look at him and despatched him to the kitchens to get a good meal first, remarking to the other monks that it is useless to preach to a hungry man, who will be thinking too much of his stomach to pay much heed to the Dhamma.

I asked my colleague Dr. Lance Cousins,[17] who is an authority on Theravāda Buddhism and often visits Sri Lanka, if he had ever heard of this story. He told me he had heard it often, as it is commonly told by clergy who want to warrant their application to social service. It comes from the Commentarial literature, which by scholars, though not by most actual Buddhists, is considered less authoritative than the Canonical scriptures: from the Dhammapada Commentary.[18] But in the Commentary, and as Dr. Cousins has heard it, the story is told of the Buddha himself, not of Ānanda.

The mistake, if mistake there was, was not mine. Silaratana told the tale with his characteristic vigour and vividness, and I could not repeatedly have substituted the name of Ānanda if it had not been spoken. It is quite conceivable that a variant of the story featuring Ānanda exists in oral tradition, if not in that part of it that has been incorporated into the vast bulk of the Commentarial literature. But my guess is that Silaratana was simply inaccurate. If he was, that seems to me thoroughly characteristic of his attitude to scripture, and indeed that of village clergy generally. I sometimes suspected that some of the more amusing anecdotes he threw off about Lord Buddha he had made up himself – a practice to which, it would seem, the authors of scripture themselves were not always averse.[19]

In sermons, village clergy often quote from scripture (translating from Pali into Sinhala), or paraphrase closely; and in rituals they chant the actual Pali words of selected scriptures. In less formal contexts I was struck by the vagueness of their scriptural references. Quite often they will remark on something that Lord Buddha (allegedly) did or said, or will preface a remark by 'It says in scripture';[20] and laymen less frequently do the same. Usually what they said corresponded to a hazy recollection of my own, and I think that, if I had had the books to hand, I could have found a similar passage. But what they said was usually a very free paraphrase, and they never offered chapter and verse, nor even the name of the scripture they may have been referring to. On other occasions when I asked them if they knew of some particular scripture which I named, more often than not they seemed not to know what I was talking about.

I have described the difficulty I had in extracting from Silaratana a clear scriptural warrant for his devotion to social service. Because I normally felt satisfied that they had it, I did not often ask clergy for their scriptural warrant for what they said. I do remember one occasion when I did. We were about to leave after a conversation with Dhammatilaka when he said, 'Lord Buddha told us to enjoy life.' This was so unlike my own impression that I did demand his authority. He referred me to the Dhammapada Commentary, which on another occasion he had said was his favourite scripture. This seems somewhat flimsy authority for such a statement – though on quite other grounds it now seems to me true[21] (see below, Chapter 6).

I do not mean to say that the clergy are ignorant of scripture; on the contrary, they seemed to me to have a good grasp of at least the better part of it. They undoubtedly study scriptures during their education as novices, and probably read parts of them as priests, as some of my informants claimed to do. But the situation regarding scripture is very different from what is familiar to us from our Christian tradition. Our Bible can be carried in the hand – indeed, thus, by an extraordinary chance, Robert Knox bought a copy in Bandara Coswatta[22] – and the chief part of it, the New Testament, can be read in a few days. But the Canonical scriptures of the Buddhists fill shelves, quite apart from the Commentarial literature, which in fact most people regard as just as scriptural. No ordinary priest could read all this literature, nor could he own more than a small part of it. Rationally, in these circumstances, it is considered more important to understand the Dhamma, the meaning of the scriptures, than to have detailed knowledge of the books. 'The monk is expected to carry all his learning in his head,' Malalasekera writes; 'And the person who trusts to books for reference is contemptuously referred to as "he who has a big book at home, but does not know a thing".'[23]

Whether Sīlaratana simply made a mistake, or was using a less familiar version of the story, I find it suggestive that he did prefer to tell it of Ānanda. According to scripture, Ānanda, though the favourite disciple and chosen successor of the Buddha, was the only leading disciple who had not attained Nirvana. The more liberal and humane interpretation of Buddhism, which strongly colours village Buddhism, is empirically and logically connected with the view that there is no hurry about attaining Nirvana (see below, Chapter 6). I wonder – I have as yet no further evidence – whether the figure of Ānanda may not serve, as he aptly might, as a mythical patron of this interpretation of Buddhism (see also below, Chapter 12).

It does seem rather plain that Sīlaratana's scriptural warrant for interpreting his vocation very largely in terms of social service was weak. On the one hand he referred to a passage in Canonical scripture which had no obvious bearing on the point; on the other he quoted – more probably, misquoted – a story from the less authoritative Commentarial literature. He neglected, I was later to discover, a passage from Canonical scripture which does very fully and plainly authorise application to social service, and is apparently used for that purpose in Burma;[24] probably, he was ignorant of it. It seemed to me that on such a liberal interpretation of scripture almost anything could be authorised, and therefore nothing really was. I still think so, but I no longer pass the unfavourable judgement I did then. On the contrary, I see now that the relaxed attitude to scripture characteristic of Sīlaratana and village Buddhists generally is both healthier and more scientific than its opposite, which has been characteristic of Protestant Christians, and many Muslims. I shall enlarge on this later (Chapter 10).

I have one piece of evidence that Silaratana's failure to provide, to me at least, any clear canonical legitimation for his commitment to social service is not peculiar. In 1973 a conference ('Seminar') was held in Sri Lanka on the theme of 'Religion and Development in Asian Societies'. Among the published papers there is just one[25] by a Buddhist cleric – evidently erudite, and presumably a leader among those who interpret their calling as one of social service. The learned author makes an impassioned case, citing many scriptural passages, none of them of any evident relevance. The first he cites is the one that Silaratana did, relating the Buddha's charge to his first disciples, and after a further display of irrelevant erudition he declares, with peccable logic, 'The conclusion is thus quite clear that the motive and aim underlying the Buddha's request to his first sixty disciples is nothing but the idea of social service.'[26]

Though he simultaneously overstates his case and fails to support it, the author, like Silaratana, is basically correct. It puzzled me for a long time how people so committed to a cause could be so inadequate in finding authority for it. I have realised, of late, that, as an anthropologist ought to have guessed, the failure lies with us rather than with them. The trouble lies with our, characteristically Western, misinterpretation of the key term 'Dhamma' as 'doctrine'. I shall have to discuss this term later and at some length (Chapter 12), and there I shall show that while the concept comprehends doctrine, its real meaning is very much deeper and wider, and comprehends social service quite as much.

If I had understood that,[27]* when I was in Sri Lanka, I might have appreciated Silaratana better; as it was, I never felt quite sure whether I should regard him as an amusing rogue, or as something of a rough, original saint. But I did feel almost sure that one thing he was was a bad Buddhist priest, and to that extent untypical. I felt depressed that I had stuck myself with studying a village that was quite unsuitable for making a study of village Buddhism. Had I been more detached, I might have reflected that depression is a normal sympton in an anthropologist learning to adapt himself to another culture, and for that reason have discounted it.

There were four things mainly that occasioned me some hope that perhaps Silaratana was not quite as bad as gloomily I took him to be – and objectively are grounds for more confidence than that.

First, he was President of the local *Sangha Sabhāva*, the chapter of clergy within the same Nikāya,[28]* which meets from time to time to discuss matters of common interest, especially clerical discipline. He was also Secretary of the Kurunegala Branch of the *Sāsana* Protection Society, a body established by the Government's Ministry of Cultural

Affairs to promote the interests of Buddhism in the District. Though the first of these offices might have come to him largely on the basis of seniority, it is unlikely that he would have held either if his clerical colleagues had disapproved of him as many laymen claimed to do.

Second, I noticed – he made sure that I did – that Sīlaratana was not unsuccessful in inviting other clergy to attend festivals at his temple. On one extended occasion there were twenty visiting clergy (including novices), among them the Principal and six of the staff from a well respected *pirivena* (seminary) in Kurunegala town. If they had considered Sīlaratana disreputable, they would not have come: I know that priests find excuses for declining such invitations from others they dislike, and that ostracism is a normal way for Buddhist clergy to show disapproval of a colleague, when his misconduct does not merit more formal and severe reprobation.

Thirdly, I often recalled that Sīlaratana had evidently been keen that I should work in his village – why else should he have contested my statement that it seemed unsuitable for my purposes? It was evident, too, that he continued to be pleased and proud that I was working there, knowing as he had from the outset that I intended to write a book about my observations. I knew he was somewhat vain, but I also knew that he was intelligent and shrewd, and he did not take me for a fool either. Although there were some things he tried to conceal, he was remarkably frank about many others which could easily be seen as discreditable. Quite plainly, he could not have seen himself, as some laymen claimed to see him, as a bad priest who had failed in his vocation: on the contrary, he must have been confident that he was a good Buddhist priest. I, too, often felt that he was, though I found it hard to make sense of this conceptually.

Finally, I was considerably reassured by some of the more hard-headed and well informed Sinhalese whom I spoke to, most of them Government officers. When I told them about Sīlaratana – those who did not know him already – and said I guessed he must be untypical of Buddhist priests, they disagreed. They assured me that he seemed rather typical of the village clergy they had known in their own experience, in the Kandyan areas at least,[29*] and if anything rather better than average. In his devotion to social service, they said, he was not wholly typical, but not remarkably atypical either, since it is a substantial minority[30*] of village clergy who apply themselves to social service.

I heard similar judgements also from other Sinhalese Government officers whom I met later, in England. As the ethnographic literature provides hardly any reliable information on the character of Buddhist priests in other villages, I regard such statements by honest and responsible men as the best comparative evidence available. Clergy, like other human beings, differ among themselves, and Sīlaratana in particular had a strongly marked personality. So far as I can judge, he

does not fall outside the normal and predictable range of variation, and in
that sense is typical enough of village priests.

It is not uncommon for Sinhalese to slander those who differ from them
politically, or whose prominence they envy, and much of the criticism of
Silaratana that I heard can be attributed to this. Some of it, however,
arose from comparing him unfavourably with a role-model which he, like
other priests, does not accept as normative. The reader, too, may be
inclined to criticise him on similar grounds, for he is plainly little like the
standard image we tend to have of the Buddhist monk, and regard as
normative. Spiro, for example, expresses this standard view of ours, when
he writes that, according to 'normative' or 'nibbanic' Buddhism,
'physical retreat from the world is not sufficient . . . Salvation can only be
achieved by a total and radical rejection of the world in all its aspects . . .
those who have the spiritual attainments necessary to renounce the world
. . . alone are sons of the Buddha.'[31]

It is central to my argument that that view of Buddhism is seriously
mistaken, and that for most actual Buddhists it is not normative,
exclusively or even primarily, if at all; what is actually normative is a
role-model to which Silaratana, and most other village clergy I know,
conform rather well. I shall develop that argument at length later, in
Chapters 9 and 12. My concern here has been to exemplify that norm, and
to show the difficulties I had through not having recognised it. While I do
not of course claim that Silaratana's conduct conforms to the norm
perfectly – like the rest of us, he is human – I am, with that qualification,
presenting him as an example of a good Buddhist priest. In this I am
making an ethnographic assertion, which I shall support, as to what the
norm is. I am making a more theoretical claim, which I shall also support,
that this is a wholly authentic Buddhist norm. I am also, quite
deliberately, making a value judgement that this is a good norm and that
those who conform to it, as much as can reasonably be expected of a
human being, are good Buddhists – as Spiro would say, 'sons of the
Buddha'.

These are controversial matters, and my case would be weakened if it
could be shown that Silaratana is in fact a bad cleric, as his critics
claimed, and that he and other village clergy stand condemned by a
binding Buddhist norm. I do have evidence that points in that direction,
and honesty requires me to present it. It is distasteful to me to relate facts
about my friends by which they may seem to stand condemned; I should
be even more reluctant than I am to do so if I did not feel able to argue that
such condemnation is misplaced.

A person enters the Sangha by the ceremony of Robing, usually
between the ages of ten and twelve, and thereby becomes a novice (see

Appendix). He becomes the pupil (*sisyayā*) of the cleric who robes him, and the latter becomes his Teacher (*ācārya*). The relationship between pupil and Teacher is a close one, which clerics compare to that between son and father, and it terminates only[32]* if one of them disrobes, i.e. leaves the Sangha and returns to lay life. The Teacher is responsible for the education and training of his pupil, and also for his maintenance: the pupil normally resides with his Teacher, unless he is boarded out to receive instruction, usually at a *pirivena* (seminary). Even after the pupil receives ordination (*upasampadā*), usually at the age of about twenty, and becomes thereby a mature cleric, a full member of the Sangha, his Teacher remains responsible for his support – though some young priests are able to maintain themselves by obtaining a post as teacher in a *pirivena* or school, or more rarely by being given the incumbency of a vacant temple. A pupil normally expects to succeed to the incumbency of his Teacher's temple when the Teacher dies. Many Teachers take on more pupils than they have incumbencies to pass on, and this commonly leads to quarrels with the pupils, especially those of them who expect that their Teacher means to withhold the succession from them.

Sīlaratana told me, as did a number of laymen, that in his youth he had twice disrobed but had been persuaded to resume his clerical status.[33]* He said he had done so as a result of fierce quarrels with his Teacher, whom I call Gunajoti. He did not say what the cause of the quarrels was; but on another occasion he told me that Gunajoti had told the villagers, in very strong terms, that his pupils were not fit to succeed to his temple,[34]* and they had reported this to Sīlaratana. This was in the village I call Henagala, about two miles (3 km) from Polgama. Later, Gunajoti sold this temple to priests of another fraternity (the Rāmañña Nikāya); this was a scandalous transaction, though not, as most of my informants supposed, strictly illegal.[35]* It seemed a fair inference that the quarrels had been about the succession to the temple, and that Sīlaratana had disrobed because he saw little prospect of succeeding to an incumbency. In 1940 Sīlaratana had had a third quarrel with his Teacher; this time, instead of disrobing, he had walked out and taken over the temple at Polgama, which had been without any incumbent for a dozen years. Sīlaratana had at most a tenuous claim to be considered for the Polgama incumbency, which was in the gift of the priests of the Gonnawa temple; but since they had been unable to fill the incumbency they did not contest his act. As Sīlaratana was a kinsman of the leading families of Polgama, they did not object either. This appeared to confirm that the cause of the quarrels was Sīlaratana's concern to get a temple of his own.

However, in the last month of our fieldwork I interviewed an old man, who was one of the Radala people of Polgama, and had lived in the village for many years, though after family quarrels he had moved to another village near by. He was wilfully indiscreet, and among other things he told me that Sīlaratana had disrobed because he was determined to marry a girl, whose relatives had adamantly refused their consent and compelled him to re-robe. As is common among the Sinhalese, her relatives were also his; and as Sīlaratana had been orphaned since the age of eight, they had probably had more than usual power to compel him to obey. I checked this story with good informants in Polgama; they were evidently shocked that I had heard it, but agreed that it was true.

I do not find this discreditable to Sīlaratana, and I do not think the reader would if I had space to recount all the relevant background. In particular, I should point out that, by common consent, Gunajoti was a most disagreeable man and an exceptionally bad priest: eventually his colleagues in the Sangha tried him on the charge of brazenly keeping a mistress, and withheld the penalty of expulsion from the Sangha only out of deference to Sīlaratana – who now takes care of him in his old age. However, the villagers clearly thought it discreditable: on most matters they were remarkably frank and truthful, but no one in Polgama had as much as hinted what the facts were here. This is the more notable as many of those who knew the facts were not slow to slander Sīlaratana on other charges.

It is not immediately obvious why people were so reticent about this history; it is not uncommon for novices or even priests to leave the Sangha in order to marry, and it has always been permissible, if somewhat shameful, to do so. But Sīlaratana could hardly have reached the point of being determined to marry the girl without having committed numerous offences against the meticulous sexual provisions of the Vinaya Rule of discipline by which clergy are bound; and in this sense the history does raise sensitive issues.

Spiro devotes some space to analysis of the *Pātimokkha*, the most familiar compendium of the Vinaya Rule.[36] He shows that a high proportion of the more strongly sanctioned rules are concerned with sex.[37] One of the four *pārājika* rules, for which the prescribed penalty is expulsion from the Sangha, is that which forbids 'sexual intercourse either with a human being or with an animal';[38] I was told that nearly all expulsions are for breach of this rule. Spiro writes that '. . . the extinction of sexuality is, alone, one of the sure signs of sainthood', and 'If sexual desire is the greatest of all temptations, succumbing to that desire is, for the monk, the greatest of all derelictions.'[39] He concludes, 'The main object of the Rule, then, is to lead to the suppression, and ultimately the extinction, of bodily – and especially sexual – desire.'[40] He quotes also from other sources – notably the *Mahā Parinibbāna Suttanta*, which has the Buddha say that monks should avoid seeing women if possible, and if not, should avoid talking to them.[41] Spiro describes the Rule, particularly on sexual matters, as 'ascetic', and refers to the 'phobic antisexual and

antifeminine ideology of monastic Buddhism'.[42] It is hard to disagree
with these assessments.

Lay villagers do not seem to know about the detailed provisions of the
Vinaya Rule, but they are aware of its spirit; they see that the conduct of
their clergy, notably in sexual matters, is not in accordance with it, and
they disapprove. Rather characteristically, they usually show this
disapproval indirectly, by joking about the matter and/or by
exaggeration, as when they remark that all priests have mistresses. (I
know that some priests have mistresses, but doubt if most do.) On less
heinous matters, village priests constantly and unabashedly breach
minor sexual provisions of the Rule, including some of those mentioned
by Spiro.[43] More significantly, since the Buddhist ethic is primarily one of
intention, though they curb their sexual desires, they seem to make little
effort to suppress them. Rather, they allow, if not indulge them. Quite
plainly they welcome and enjoy the company of women, and find them
attractive, in a way which is not asexual, though it is perfectly seemly by
normal standards.

Spiro claims that 'latent homosexuality' is among the salient features
of the personalities of typical Burmese clergy.[42] I put this statement to a
number of Sinhalese – not villagers – and asked them if they thought it
was true of clergy in Sri Lanka. Each of them found the suggestion
hilarious, since fascination with women, if not concupiscence, is held to
be characteristic of most Sinhalese clergy. We remarked it ourselves, and
not least in Dhammatilaka. It was a joke between our research assistants
and me that any conversation with him was sure, sooner or later, to get on
to the topics of women and sex – I quote a typical example below (Chapter
6).

This is an area of conduct in which village priests plainly do fall short of
standards which they, all other Buddhists, and the scriptures, accept as
normative. By ordinary standards their conduct is innocent, but it is not
by that of the Vinaya Rule. Since I shall argue, as Buddhists do, that a
person's understanding of religion must be judged by an assessment of his
ethical conduct (see below, Chapter 5); and since I hold, as Buddhists do,
that its sexual ethic is of central importance in an ethical system, this
counts against my contention that village priests, and in particular
Silaratana and Dhammatilaka, are good exemplars of authentic
Buddhism.

Spiro suggests that 'the sexual decorum of the Burmese monks and
their fidelity to their sexual vows' contrasts with what is reported of clergy
in Thailand and Sri Lanka; while his citations of such reports exaggerate
by their brevity, they otherwise correspond fairly well with my
observations among the Sinhalese.[44] He also remarks that the fear of
women and 'latent homosexuality', which he found to be salient features

of the personalities of Burmese monks, 'receive cultural support from the phobic antisexual and antifeminine ideology of monastic Buddhism'.[42] By this measure Burmese clergy seem to be better, by accepted Buddhist normative standards, than those of Sri Lanka and, apparently, Thailand. This seems unlikely, and in fact Spiro's evidence does not support it.

The sample of Burmese monks on which, almost entirely, Spiro based his assessment of the character of Burmese monks is not, as he supposed, typical of Burmese clergy generally – on the contrary, it is demonstrably untypical.[45]* He excluded from his discussion those whose vocation he judged not to be genuine;[46] his sample was therefore of those whose Buddhism he considered normative, in terms of his, the usual Western interpretation of Buddhism. As Obeyesekere remarks, 'The analysis of unconscious motivation is appropriate to forest monks or meditating monks rather than to village monks in general.'[47] Thus the comparison, presented as one between Burmese clergy and those of Sri Lanka and Thailand, is actually one between the meditating monks esteemed by the Western interpretation of Buddhism, and those village clergy I am arguing are better Buddhists. The evidence I have presented regarding sexual conduct and the Vinaya Rule therefore counts against my principal thesis. Since it is quite clear that my village priests are better Buddhists than the meditating monks, at least of Spiro's sample (see Chapter 6 below), I am bound to question the authenticity of the Vinaya Rule.

This is indeed an undertaking of some enormity, since I have never heard any Buddhist question the normative status of the Vinaya Rule, which indeed they all regard as fundamental to Buddhism. I cannot honestly shirk the issue; but since it would unbalance this book to develop my arguments in full, I shall simply outline the major points to be made.

While there is no sound historical evidence that the Vinaya Rule does derive from the Buddha, there is clear evidence that parts of it, at least, do not.[48] There is significant evidence that its basis should be regarded with considerable suspicion. According to Frauwallner (1956), the earliest known work of Buddhist literature is a book called the *Skandhaka*, the text of which can be recovered from the scriptures of at least four Buddhist schools.[49] It consisted of an exposition of the Vinaya Rule, together with a biography of the Buddha and some historical information about events after the Buddha's death,[50] and included what later became detached to form the *Mahā Parinibbāna Suttanta* (MPNS).[51] As I shall show later (Chapter 10), Frauwallner argues that the 'biographical' and 'historical' portions of the *Skandhaka* are distinctly unreliable as history, because of its author's evidently wilful working methods;[52] he is notably scathing about the account in the MPNS.[53] Since Frauwallner attributes the same working methods to the exposition of the Vinaya Rule,[54] that part of the work must come under similar suspicion. There is too much reason to attribute parts of it to the invention of the author of the *Skandhaka*, and to traditions which he used without knowing their origin, to allow confidence that the Rule in every – maybe any – particular stems from the Buddha himself. Spiro points out that the asceticism of the Vinaya Rule has much in common with that of the Indian religious tradition.[55] It is quite possible that the Buddha himself was an Indian traditionalist in this respect; it is also possible that he was not, and that the sexual asceticism of the Rule is the product of his more traditionalist followers, such as the author of the *Skandhaka* and the creators of the traditions which he reworked.

Christian history suggests what may be a parallel. We know that a rule of celibacy for the clergy, together with phobic and ascetic attitudes to sex similar to those of the Vinaya Rule, came to be established in the Catholic Church. We also know that it was not original. At least one of the heads of the Early Church, St. Peter, was a married man. So little was celibacy considered important for the religious life that none of the Evangelists thought it worth mentioning that Jesus was unmarried.[56] When St. Paul, in Chapter 7 of the First Epistle to the Corinthians, wrote on celibacy, recommending it very cautiously only to those who had God's gift for it,[57] he made it quite explicit that he had 'no instructions from the Lord' in the matter.[58] I am not arguing that the original sexual ethic of Buddhism must have been identical to that of early Christianity: in view of the large differences between the traditional cultures of India and of the Hebrews, this is improbable. I am merely remarking that, since in one case it is plain that a clergy introduced a rule of compulsory celibacy which had not been original, and which was actually inconsistent with scripture, it is a reasonable surmise that the Buddhist rule of celibacy also may not have been original.

The weightiest, though least demonstrable, consideration, is that the phobic and obsessive attitude to sex of the Vinaya Rule is out of harmony with the reverence for life and concern with equanimity and mindfulness which are basic to Buddhist ethics; and is also unwise in theory and harmful in practice. Except that his estimate of marriage is somewhat grudging – and it later became more generous[59] – St. Paul's view, in I Corinthians 7, can hardly be faulted.[60]* The celibate can serve God more single-mindedly[61] if he has God's gift for it; if a person has not, it is more seemly to marry, and there is nothing wrong in it.[62] 'Better be married than burn with vain desire'[63] – as it seems Buddhist priests tend to do.

There is no proof that the historical Buddha was as wise as St. Paul – though it is not unreasonable to allow him the benefit of the doubt. We cannot say whether, in constituting the Sangha, he foresaw that he was laying the foundation of an order of clergy, rather than establishing a select community of religious virtuosos. For our present purpose it hardly matters. As there is reasonable doubt whether the sexual ethic of the Vinaya Rule stems from the Buddha himself, its claim to authority is weaker than is usually supposed. Since one can argue that it is not a wise ethic to impose on an order of clergy, and does not harmonise with the basic spirit of Buddhist ethics, one should hesitate before condemning those clergy who do not entirely endorse it in their lives. That village priests both strain against the spirit of the Rule and regularly flout its pettier provisions is not unequivocal proof that they are bad Buddhists. It may rather be evidence of their good sense.[64*]

Notes to Chapter 3

1 Primarily Weber (1958), chapter VI, especially pp. 213, 216, 222. Also Pfanner and Ingersoll (1962); Nash (1965), pp. 156–65; Spiro (1971), pp. 427–37, 453–68; and for a more recent review, Ling (1980).

2 It does in fact own about three acres, but the income from these is practically insignificant.

3 My research assistants were impressed by the vivid, colloquial, and sometimes earthy style of Sinhala that Silaratana used even in sermons: they said they had never heard another cleric use this idiom in preaching, and thought it was unusually effective with villagers. His style was striking even in translation – I could appreciate the imagery if not the finer nuances of the language.

4 Cf. Ling (1973), notably pp. 26, 122, 140–5.

5 In our first fortnight in Polgama a middle-class resident of the village told me that Silaratana was not much liked, as he was regarded as a businessman and a politician, very left-wing. He added that he reckoned about 80% of the villagers were supporters of the UNP, the conservative party. Though we though it imprudent to ask people directly about politics, our own observations tend to confirm his assessment. Several other non-villagers who knew Polgama well also told us they thought Silaratana was unpopular largely on account of his politics; and Silaratana told us that twenty years earlier he had been ostracised on this account.

6 Thirty-five per cent said they were mostly good, 19% that there were good and bad, 10% that they did not know.

7 It would be tasteless to review my evidence; and I think I have said more than enough to establish my objectivity.

8 A *Nāyaka* is a cleric of senior rank, and Silaratana did not have this title. The allusion to Silaratana's vanity shows that the headman was not merely flattering him.

9 It may seem inconsistent that Silaratana is now having a new presbytery built. I noticed in 1974–75 that his political views had become more conservative than they had been. But I guess the principal factor is that as he approaches the end of his life he must be increasingly concerned to have a pupil succeed himself in his incumbency, which is more likely if the presbytery is respectable.

10 The area was malarious before the Malaria Eradication Compaign of the

1940s, and I was told that land was cheap primarily for that reason. Economic conditions must have been poor at a time when the world market for copra was depressed.

11 I read through Sīlaratana's Visitors' Book; even with the obligatory handful of salt some of the remarks of visitors are laudatory. In 1974–75 local administrative officers told us that the Society had done good work in the past.

12 He told us that these were (1) that the Rural Development Society be registered, (2) that a Government dispensary be provided, (3) that the local school be developed, (4) that land should be distributed to poor people (he had forgotten the fifth).

13 Other informants told us that this M.P. was in fact active in getting facilities, especially schools, for his constituency. I suspect that Sīlaratana had already decided to oppose him, and the demands were largely a pretext.

14 Sīlaratana told us that leading villagers had plotted to forcibly deprive him of his incumbency; and when he had thwarted that, everyone had refused to feed him, and even shopkeepers refused to sell him food. When I asked laymen about this they became extremely embarrassed and changed the subject. I take this as confirming the story, if not in every detail.

15 Several very poor and mostly low-caste people lived near the temple, and Sīlaratana said he had facilitated their settling there out of compassion. One of these was said by others to have been his principal mistress and mother of his child: that smacks to me more of spite than fact.

16 *Vinaya Pitaka, Mahāvagga I*, 11, 1; quoted in Dutt (1962), p. 17.

17 Of the Department of Comparative Religion, University of Manchester.

18 Burlingame (1921), pp. 75–6.

19 See, for example, Frauwallner (1956), p. 163.

20 Usually they say 'in *bana* books' or 'in Dhamma books'.

21 Cf. Rahula (1967), pp. 27–8.

22 Knox [1681] (1966), pp. 239–41.

23 Malalasekera (1928), pp. 45–6.

24 *Samyutta Nikāya I*, 5, 7; quoted in Sarkisyanz (1965), p. 41.

25 Ratanasara (1974).

26 *Ibid.*, p. 16.

27 I had in fact read a good deal on the concept of Dhamma, but I failed to see its relevance.

28 The Sinhalese Buddhist clergy is divided into three major groupings, the Siam Nikāya, Amarapura Nikāya, and Rāmañña Nikāya. These are largely organisational groupings, based partly on caste, and are hardly distinguishable in terms of doctrine or religious practice. Thus they are not sects, but may reasonably be called fraternities.

29 It is commonly said that clergy in the Low Country are more strict in their observances. Some of the reports I have heard about them induce me to suspend judgement.

30 Between a quarter and a third of them, I was told. I doubt if anyone has actually counted.

31 1971, pp. 65, 64.

32 It is not terminated by death; clerics speak with pride of their deceased

Teachers, and indeed of more remote forebears in the pupillary line.

33 More probably he was a novice when he disrobed rather than an ordained priest, but I failed to clarify this.

34 He had said that giving his pupils a temple would be like giving a dog an unhusked coconot – a proverb for a useless gift (Senaveratna, 1936, p. 38).

35 Wijekulasuriya (1963, pp. 38, 39) shows that a priest is entitled to transfer his incumbency to another, and that his pupils have no claim against him for the loss of their expectation to succeed. His cases do not refer to the element of purchase; both buyer and seller would be in breach of the Vinaya Rule, but I do not think the issue would be justiciable in the civil courts, nor normally provable in any forum.

36 Spiro (1971), pp. 292–304.

37 *Ibid.*, pp. 292–3.

38 Page 292.

39 Page 296.

40 Page 299.

41 Page 297.

42 Page 343.

43 Page 298.

44 Page 368 n. 7.

45 Spiro selected a sample of twenty-one monks for intensive study (1971, p. 24). Careful reading shows that his analysis of the character and motivations of Burmese monks (chapters 14 and 15) is based almost entirely on the members of this sample. A majority of them had become monks not directly from the novitiate but after some experience of adult lay life (p. 333). Spiro claims that this was also true of a majority of the monks in the villages he surveyed, but is not prepared to assert it of the total monastic population (p. 333, text and n. 8). He also reports, '... a large percentage – perhaps the majority – of monks have already found founded families when they decided to join the Order ... for them to enter the monastery is to abandon wife and children. Often families are left not only without husband and father, but also destitute, with no one to care or provide for them' (p. 345).

Now if Spiro's sample were typical, these latter remarks would have to be true of Burmese monks generally. We would thus have a society in which a large and highly esteemed estate was recruited largely through the abandonment and even destitution of families. (Spiro estimates that the total monastic population of Burma proper is around 800,000, or between five and ten per cent of the male population (p. 284).) This is an inherently improbable social formation. If it really existed, the pattern of recruitment to the clergy in Burma would be quite different from that in Thailand and Sri Lanka. In those two countries, otherwise so similar, most ordained clergy are recruited directly from the novitiate; and in Sri Lanka, at least, married men are not ordained unless they have made adequate provision for their dependants. If there really were this difference, it could not have escaped comment; but I have been unable to find discussion or mention of it anywhere, even in Spiro's book. It is far more probable that there is no such difference, and hence that Spiro's sample is not representative.

46 Spiro (1971), pp. 321–3.

47   Obeyesekere (1981), p. 42.
48   See Dutt (1962), pp. 74–7; Frauwallner (1956), p. 65.
49   Page 4.
50   Page 65.
51   Page 46.
52   Pages 163–4.
53   Pages 159, 163.
54   Pages 53, 65.
55   1971, pp. 294–5.
56   Nineham (1963), p. 35.
57   Verses 7, 9, 36.
58   Verse 25, NEB.
59   Col. 5, v. 18 f., Eph. 5, v. 22 f.
60   It should be read in a modern translation, and with the aid of a commentary to place what Paul wrote in its context. Without these precautions it is easily and often misunderstood.
61   Verses 32–5.
62   Verse 36.
63   Verse 9, NEB.
64   The comparable rule of celibacy for Roman Catholic priests has often been contested on theological grounds. I know of no such argument among Buddhist clergy. It is notable, however, that for more than a century the majority of clergy in the Kandyan kingdom were *ganninanses*, a kind of cleric who was not bound by the vow of celibacy, though they were not all married (Malalgoda, 1976, pp. 57–8). Sinhalese today speak of them as disgraceful, and Malalgoda's account of them implies a similar judgement. This may of course derive from the rhetoric of the subsequent reform, and the tendency of Sinhalese to disparage their clergy unreasonably. Knox, who lived in the Kandyan Kingdom from 1660 to 1679, indicates that the majority of clergy at that time were *ganninanses* ([1681] 1966, pp. 139–40); although he was a committed Christian, he does not disparage the morality of the Buddhist clergy. I am not arguing that the *ganninanses* originated from opposition to celibacy: I merely draw attention to the fact that for at least one extended period Sinhalese Buddhism was carried on by a clergy not obligatorily celibate, and was not necessarily the worse for it. The same may have been true of some earlier periods: Carrithers quotes from the *Mahāvamsa* a statement that 'in the villages owned by the Sangha the morality of the monks consisted only in supporting their wives and children' (*Mahāvamsa* LXXVII, 3–4, quoted in Carrithers, 1979, p. 198).

4

Rebirth and belief

When I was not worrying too much about what to make of Sīlaratana, I found myself happy with the village Buddhism of which I was an increasingly participant observer. It overtook me unawares, and I found myself half converted before I had even thought such a thing possible. I have remarked that I began with the firm if naive conviction that village Buddhism was a corruption of a Buddhism I had thoroughly rejected anyway. There was also another bar. I remember from my visit in 1973 one of the first conversations I ever had about Buddhism with a Sinhalese; and being told, not dogmatically but as a matter of simple fact, that one could not be a Buddhist if one did not believe in Rebirth. I was to hear this asserted many times later, during the year we spent in Polgama, and only by a few denied. But this first time that I heard it I remember feeling notably reassured: I took it as a guarantee that I was not in the slightest peril of converting to Buddhism, for I knew that I never would, or could, believe in Rebirth. It was therefore with a mixture of surprise and wry amusement that I observed one day, after we had been living in Polgama some nine months, that I was in fact believing, or half believing it. And by then it was too late.

What I have just said raises some large issues, two of them at least quite central to what I have to say. As my informants said, the doctrine, tenet, notion – whatever it may be – of Rebirth is indeed basic in actual Buddhism: if there is one thing at least we can confidently assert that actual Buddhists believe, this is it. Its saliency has been noted in all the accounts I know of actual Buddhism. I must therefore explain exactly what it is, and what is its place in the system of actual Buddhism: and I shall have to show that these are a good deal more subtle than they have usually been taken to be. Similarly, as the reader may have noticed, puzzles and misgivings about just what we mean, or should mean, if we should, by 'believing' or 'believing in', as well as 'half believing', and about how these concepts, if that is what they are, are to be understood in relation to religious practice – these have arisen already, and will do more. It will, I hope, become clear that misconceptions on these matters are basic to the misunderstanding of Buddhism, and of religion generally. We shall have to take time to clear the matter up.

I shall say more about Rebirth, and much more about belief, later. I begin to discuss them here since my own experience with them was an important basis for my thoughts on both topics.

All of us take it for granted that whatever normal being is born and lives will inevitably die. Buddhists seem to take it equally for granted that whatever normal being dies will inevitably be reborn and live again – on and on and on to the end of time. This is the notion of rebirth in the less specific sense. Buddhists invariably associate it with what is logically a separable doctrine, that of Karma, which asserts that whatever good deed a being does will inexorably bring him a happy consequence, and whatever evil deed an unhappy consequence: it is the notion of just deserts made into an inexorable law of nature. Since very few Buddhists seem to think of these two notions as separable, it is their combination that I refer to as the doctrine of Rebirth in the larger, more specifically Buddhist, sense.[1*] In this combination, it is maintained that the condition of life into which a being is reborn is determined by the causal efficacy of the good and evil deeds that he has done in his previous lives, particularly the last. With us, while normal beings are subject to the law of mortality, God (at least) is exempt. With Buddhists, while the chain of unending rebirths is the doom of normal beings, the attainment of Nirvana brings release: and this is often spoken of as its greatest boon. This implies, what formal doctrine plainly states, and what actual Buddhists at least pay lip service to, that the certainty of Rebirth, the fact that life is unending, is the most terrible of the ills that flesh is heir to. For people like us, who fear to end in death and crave a promise of immortality, such an evaluation seems weird or incredible or both. This is, for those who write books forgetting that Buddhists are people like us, a major reason for claiming that Buddhism is life-denying. For authors who have studied actual Buddhists and therefore know better, two alternative conclusions are possible. For Spiro, and for Gombrich when he agrees with him, as for many other authors, Buddhists, more particularly village Buddhists, believe that rebirth is real, but also really believe that it is a good thing: they desire more and better lives in the future, and shun what they claim to seek, the Nirvana that would terminate it all (see below, Chapter 6). Since this is precisely what I seek to rebut, I must, and shall, argue that it is too simple to suppose that Buddhists believe Rebirth in just and only that sense. What their believing Rebirth amounts to is thus a crux.

What my non-believing, believing and half-believing Rebirth amounts to, and how these relate to those of Sinhalese, must also be clarified. How was it that when I first heard Rebirth made indirectly relevant to me I knew, or thought I knew, I never should believe that? I was well aware that I had no kind of proof that such a process did not occur, just as I assumed – not quite accurately – that Sinhalese had no kind of proof that it did. I could see that either was a perfectly reasonable view to hold, that Sinhalese were no more irrational or superstitious to believe it than I was to disbelieve it. Indeed, I could see that if one grew up believing it, as Sinhalese did, its truth would appear quite obvious, a matter of basic fact: I already sensed, what later experience seemed fully to confirm, that that was indeed how Sinhalese saw it. But I saw that, by the same measure, if one grew up as I had disbelieving – or rather, unbelieving – it, its untruth would appear equally obvious and matter-of-fact, and did. I could entertain the idea, and be entertained by it, discuss it, explore it, concede it as a hypothesis, willingly suspend disbelief. But believe it, never.

What is it to believe? It is to hold a proposition, a statement, true – in the most usual sense, at least, it is to attribute or concede factuality to that which is thought of or imagined. And similarly, to believe in is, in part, to find factuality, or at least an aura of factuality,[2] in that to which it is directed. And whence the conviction, more or less, of factuality? Not, in this case – nor I think in the case of any other genuinely religious axiom – from reasoned proof, for there is none. It seemed to me very plain that I must find with Rebirth as I already had with God: that, having been brought up an atheist, however much I wanted to believe in God (as I have), however easily and indeed meaningfully I used theological concepts (as I have, and do), when I face myself I know that for me He simply does not exist. He is not within my panoply of factuality, and I knew no way He could be: similarly it would and must be with Rebirth.

And yet it wasn't. I realised that I had come in large part to believe Rebirth one day when I was daydreaming, playing with various speculative analyses and scenarios. Still playing, I noticed with sardonic glee, but also a frisson of alarm, that in every one of them it had come naturally to me to assume the reality of Rebirth. Was this not factuality, of the premise that sprang with ease, without rebuff, into the mind? I was puzzled, for I was clear that the logic of the case was the same as it had ever been: yet factuality was there, not yet solid and immovable, but plainly quite substantial. And it remained although I reproved myself for believing what I did not believe.

I should have understood this experience better if I had read Evans-Pritchard's account of a similar experience he had had in the course of his fieldwork. In his paper 'Some Reminiscences and Reflections on Fieldwork', he remarks that he has often been asked whether, when he lived among the Azande, he accepted their ideas about witchcraft. In the course of a most insightful discussion of the point he tells us: 'In their culture, in the set of ideas I then lived in, I accepted them; in a kind of way I believed them.' And he concludes with the pregnant sentence, 'If one must act as though one believed, one ends in believing, or half-believing as one acts.'[3]

I suggest that Evans-Pritchard has run together two points it is necessary to distinguish. It is true that if one acts as though one believed one ends in believing,[4*] and it is a point that village and other Buddhists often emphasise. Indeed, as I shall analyse their system it seems to be a fundamental principle. I shall even argue that there is no other way in which one can wholly believe a religious tenet, and that this is why Robertson Smith's principle of the primacy of practice over belief, which he derived from empirical observation, is necessarily true, though not the whole truth. But it does not exactly apply to my own experience that I have related. I cannot think of any act, other than of thought and speech, that I did which distinctively implied belief in Rebirth, as Evans-Pritchard's acts of oracle consultation implied belief in witchcraft: indeed, I think there are no such acts available.

I mean by this that I can think of no significant act which is entailed by the reality of Rebirth which is not as strongly entailed without it. In this sense the doctrine is practically meaningless. If this is plain to me, then it must be that many Sinhalese are more or less aware of it too. Indeed, it is plain in the familiar passages of scripture[5] in which the Buddha is represented as saying that the way of life he recommends is wholly warranted by its fruits in this life, even if rebirth is unreal. This in itself suggests that the Rebirth doctrine is important to Sinhalese not only in its literal sense.

The aura of factuality that Rebirth came to have for me was generated less by my action than by my interaction, with people, within a culture, and that culture within me. Most obviously, I was talking with people who assumed the reality of Rebirth, so that it would have been tedious and discourteous of me constantly to dissent: much easier to assent, at least to the extent of suspending disbelief, and in my own part of the conversation to speak on the basis of their assumption. Real too, though harder to pin down, was the fact that I was talking, acting, and living in and by a culture which is subtly pervaded by the assumption of Rebirth. But this, though it might account for a superficial veneer, does not account for the fact that the concept entered into me. I spent not one but three years among the Baganda, and became far more fluent in their language than I ever did in Sinhala: but their concepts hardly penetrated me.[6*] What did make the difference was that I found the Sinhalese people and their culture most attractive, so that I welcomed and opened out to them. Moreover, I found the concept of Rebirth itself, as the Sinhalese use it, most attractive.

As might be expected from the fact that it is practically meaningless, the concept of Rebirth can be used to explain or warrant almost anything, albeit vacuously. (Religion, unlike nature, craves a vacuum: it is vacuity which gives religious concepts much of their value.) These uses divide into two categories. There is the retrospective application, where a person's present condition is explained as the result of hypothetical deeds he did in a previous birth. And there is the prospective application where doing good deeds, and eschewing evil, in the present is warranted in terms of the hypothetical fruits in the next birth.

Retrospectively, the concept is sometimes used in some cultures (e.g. Burma)[7] to argue that since the condition of the poor is the result of the evil deeds they did in a past birth, and cannot change until the karmic consequences have been fully worked out, there is no need, or possibility, of doing anything to help them. I find this repugnant. But I heard this argument used only once in Sri Lanka – though my wife tells me she encountered it more often. It is more common to hear people who are themselves poor or otherwise unfortunate attribute their own condition to their misdeeds in a previous life. This is rather healthy, when it does not lead to fatalism: and I found it often led to unusual efforts to improve matters by generating good karma now. Another application I often encountered was to explain present happy circumstances in terms of past good deeds. Thus people sometimes told me I deserved my present good fortune as an academic because I must have studied hard in my previous life as well as this one. Often, when it was evident that a Sinhalese and I greatly liked each other, he would tell me we must have been brothers in a previous birth. I found this a charming fancy.

More often, and more seriously, it is the prospective application that is employed. People very frequently say, and seem to mean it, that they are trying to do good and avoid evil for the sake of their prospects in their next life. Logically, of course, this is nonsense: what possible difference can it make to me whether a future person who bears the results of my present deeds is or is not *me*, when I can never know the difference? But if a logical nonsense can make the sense of moral responsibility more tangible, and if thereby it motivates more effectively, as it seems to do, one's moral endeavour, then I find it welcome. In these ways I liked the notion of Rebirth.

If this account is correct, I should have ceased to believe Rebirth once I ceased to interact with Sinhalese in Sinhalese culture. And so I did. Back in England, Rebirth ceased to have any factuality for me, so much so that it took effort to recall what it had been like to half believe it in Sri Lanka. But then, some years later, it acquired another kind of factuality. I read,

in Jeffrey Iverson's *More Lives than One?* (1977), accounts of how some
people, under hypnosis, had recalled and even relived what appeared to
be stretches of their previous lives. I was aware that such data can be
accounted for by more than one hypothesis;[8] nevertheless it seemed to me
that there was at least a strong *prima facie* case for the reality of rebirth.
(It was because Sinhalese often cite reports of apparent recollections of
past lives that I wrote earlier that it is not quite accurate to say they have
no kind of proof of the truth of their doctrine.) Thus I found myself once
again half believing in rebirth, but this time on a different sort of basis,
namely reasoned inference from evidence. Subjectively I found this felt
quite different from the kind of half-belief, on a different kind of basis,
that I had experienced in Sri Lanka. I reasoned that if even one person
actually did remember her past lives, then the Sinhalese were probably
right in their belief that rebirth is part of the human condition: and to the
extent that I had accepted that, I knew that I had had other lives in the
past and would have others in the future. I had barely got used to thinking
this when I realised that the truth of rebirth made hardly any practical
difference, for the reason I have outlined above. Certainly, if it is possible
to recall one's past lives under hypnosis, there should be some slight
interest in doing so: but I found it too slight to motivate me to look for a
hypnotist. Thus, within a few days of supposing that rebirth might be
real, I found it uninteresting. I did from time to time read other accounts
of hypnotic 'regressions', but almost wholly for amusement. I must
concede, however, that my surreptitious part-belief that perhaps rebirth
was factual had some emotional value for me: it made me feel more
indifferent to my death than I normally do. I think this was also so when I
half believed it in Sri Lanka.

I have related this story, of my own beliefs about Rebirth, in part
because they throw some light on the Sinhalese concept, and have
implications for what their own belief may be. More, however, because
they throw light on different kinds of belief which are related to different
sources of the aura of factuality. Factuality may come by reasoned
inference from evidence; this, I think, can never strictly be the case for
religious, mystical, concepts for which there cannot be decisive evidence.
It may come from acting as though one believes: this is appropriate in
matters of religion, and I think no one has ever wholly believed without it.
It may come from interacting within a culture which is pervaded by the
tenet as axiomatic: this too is normal in matters of religion. Finally, the
feeling one has towards a supposed entity, whether it be of hope, or trust,
or love, or of fear or hatred, generates about it an aura of factuality: this
too is basic in religion, as in witchcraft, sorcery, and much else.[9]* For me,
this analysis clarifies distinctions that are necessary if we are to grasp
what is meant by saying that people believe, or believe in, something. It
explains, too, why religion is so stable in traditional society, for belief

stands firm on each of the latter three bases, and is further propped up by inability to infer correctly from empirical evidence. It suggests, too, that those Christians who are so anxious to prove from evidence that God exists may be suffering from deficiency in the appropriate foundations of their faith.

The story has a final twist, which throws light on yet another aspect of these matters. I have recently read the definitive work on the hypnotic evidence for memories of past lives, Ian Wilson's *Mind out of Time?* (1981). Wilson shows, conclusively I think, that these 'regressions' provide no evidence for the reality of rebirth, for in too many cases clearly, and in most or all presumably, the personality the subject experiences under hypnosis is not a recollection of a life he lived long ago, but a construction of his unconscious mind, woven around buried memories of history once read. Brilliantly he suggests that the 'past lives' produced by a good subject under hypnosis have much in common with the multiple personalities occasionally generated by persons who have suffered unbearable traumas in childhood; and he reminds us that the cure for this terrifying psychic disorder lies through the reintegration of the separated personalities into a whole person, whether this is achieved largely through the patient's own endeavour, as in the case of Chris Sizemore ('Eve'), or through the guidance of an insightful therapist, as with 'Sybil Dorsett'.[10*] Paradoxically, this, which should have demolished what lingering belief I still had in the doctrine of Rebirth, has instead augmented it, but in a different direction. The imaging of mental disorders as possession by devils, as in the New Testament and many other cultures, is a valuable way of thinking figuratively about the phenomena, so long as it is not taken literally. Similarly, and with the same precaution, I find the notions of Rebirth a valuable figurative way of taking hold upon the mysteries of the unconscious. When I wrote earlier (Chapter 3) of feeling myself in my real home when I found about me in Sri Lanka the outward forms of Buddhism, I said the Sinhalese would doubtless have explained this by my having been a Buddhist in my previous birth: 'and in a certain figurative, way I suppose they would have been right'. What I had in mind was that that experience should have shown me that, for all my conscious confidence that I had put Buddhism far behind me, deeper down and in truth I had never ceased to be a Buddhist, however little I understood what this meant. It was necessary that I tell the reader this, lest he suppose, as I did at the time, that my fieldwork was an exercise in looking at village Buddhism from the outside, objectively. I tried to make it this, and I try in this account to make clear what is more and what is less objective. But the larger truth, of which at the time I was at most dimly and fleetingly conscious, was that in Polgama I was looking for what lay buried in myself, and in seeking an order in village Buddhism I was seeking most to put myself in order. Hence the emotionality of my experience.

I have not had the opportunity to put to any Sinhalese this hypothesis that in talking of Rebirth they are talking figuratively of elements or aspects of the inner man, the mind or psyche. But I am confident that many of them at least would find nothing strange about it – might even ask me how I could ever have supposed otherwise. For it is common among Buddhists, even some village Buddhists, to recognise and indeed to state that mystical entities, spirits, such as gods and demons, are in reality projections of one's own mind.[11] It is most characteristic of Buddhist thought, even as one encounters it among apparently unsophisticated villagers, to think of mind as the creator of the most significant aspects of reality as it is experienced. Because of their culture they may well take Rebirth to have independent factuality, but I think the meaning it has for them has to be explored along the figurative or symbolic dimension. Indeed, I suggest that this may be true of all religions: that however much or little belief is assent to factuality, it is also recognition of symbolic worth or 'truth'.[12]

Rebirth theory may also function as a kind of intellectual catalyst. I once talked with a priest of the modernist persuasion, who had been invited to Polgama, at some trouble and expense, from a town about seventy miles away, by two of the villagers, one of them Banda (see below, pp. 65, 202–3). Banda told me that they had brought him primarily to explain to me what true Buddhism is. The priest told me that Buddhism is scientific. I remarked that Rebirth theory did not seem scientific to me, and there was no evidence to support it. He replied by observing that I, an Englishman, was speaking to him in a Sinhalese village: could I tell him how this had come about? I told him how I had flown in an aircraft to Sri Lanka, travelled by train to Kurunegala, and then by car to Polgama. Yes, he said, he had no doubt these events had occurred: but what made me so sure that they had happened to one and the same person, namely me? I had to think about this; then I replied that I knew each had occurred to me because I remembered my participation in each. All right, he said: you are sure that you are one person in what you consider different stages of your present life because you remember. Then you must agree that if a person remembers events of a previous life, that shows it is the same person in the present life as in the previous one.

It did not seem to me that he was trying to prove to me the truth of Rebirth theory; indeed, shortly afterwards he remarked that when people had asked Lord Buddha about Rebirth he had told them not to worry about it. I think the object of his remarks was the effect they actually had on me, to make me see how flimsy and ill-considered was the basis for my confidence in the continuity and identity of myself in this life. That is, of course, the central thrust of Buddhist philosphical analysis: the central and most distinctive Buddhist concept is that of *anatta*, that our sense of the reality and continuity of self is in large part illusory. Thus Rebirth theory, though superficially it seems to contradict *anatta*, can in fact serve to focus attention on it.

Notes to Chapter 4

1 I do not mean that it is uniquely Buddhist: it is found also in Jainism and in much of Hindu religion.
2 The phrase is that of Geertz (1966, p. 24).
3 Evans-Pritchard 1976, p. 244.
4 Provided that one 'entertains' the notion to be believed, that is, has it in mind (cf. Braithwaite 1967, pp. 29–30).
5 E.g. *Kālāma Sutta* (*Anguttara Nikāya, Tika Nipāta, Mahāvagga, Sutta* 65).
6 Since the Baganda were mostly Christian, I would not have perceived their major religious concepts as distinctively theirs. But there are other matters on which my experience of the two cultures is more closely comparable, and on these too I found myself more receptive to Sinhalese than to Ganda ideas.
7 Cf. Spiro 1971, pp. 439–40, 446–7.
8 E.g. in Stevenson 1960.
9 As when we perceive real persons or groups as threatening because of our own feelings of fear or hostility towards them.
10 On 'Eve' the best source is Sizemore and Pittillo 1978; on 'Sybil', Schreiber 1975. Though the widespread fascination with such cases may owe something to their bizarre and dramatic nature, I think it owes as much to their relevance to common experience: as Wilson suggests, 'Do we all have a little of the multiple personality about us?' (1981, p. 173).
11 Cf. Ortner 1978, p. 99.
12 Cf. Southwold 1979, pp. 635–41; Sperber 1975, pp. 102–6.

5

The Buddhists of Polgama

When I found myself in Polgama half believing in Rebirth, it was a measure of the extent to which I had become absorbed in Sinhalese culture, but I do not think it had any causative effect on my attitude to Buddhism. My supposition that the impossibility of my believing Rebirth was a bar to my becoming a Buddhist was the bluster of my conscious mind, and its dissolution altered nothing. It was other things that were drawing me to village Buddhism. One was the augmentation of the sense of being in my real home which I had felt in 1973. For all the outward nonsense of it, I felt a deep sense of peace and rightness in participating in Buddhist forms of life. Another, and very important, was the withering contempt that Sīlaratana and some other people expressed for the meditating monks (the cynosures of Western Buddhism, and its Sinhalese followers) who go off solitary, or in sets, to the jungles away from ordinary men, seeking by ascetic meditation to grab for themselves a Nirvana, selfish and soon; and their contrary insistence that a good Buddhist cleric must seek his salvation in teaching and serving others – as, Sīlaratana once said in a sermon, Lord Buddha himself could have attained Nirvana thousands of births before he did, but chose rather to wait until he could bring others with him. Here, for the first time clearly, I encountered an interpretation of Buddhism which made good sense to me, as I had found, by experience, the Western interpretation did not. I had learnt already – from, for example, Rahula (1967), pp. 76–7, and Ling (1973), pp. 122–8 – that there was an inherent absurdity in the notion of a selfish, or even solitary Nirvana: for Nirvana is defined as the complete realisation of *anatta*, the doctrine that the sense of separate self is the root of all that is wrong. It was only later that I was to learn, through study, that through much if not all of the history of Buddhendom, something like Sīlaratana's view has been the standard view of most Buddhist clergy – and, by a reasonable surmise, of most laymen too (see below, Chapter 9). In very large part, it is Buddhism.

Buddhism has often been described as a life-denying religion. On a narrow and blinkered interpretation of texts and dogmas, it is; but I did not find it so in Sinhalese villages. My most enduring memory, on the contrary, is one of happiness. Villagers suffer numerous privations and woes from which my wife and I were exempt: but I could not mistake in their lives an impressive and infectious tenor of laughter and serenity, which was closely connected with their Buddhism. It was not the least of the things which led me to feel that our conventional judgement of village Buddhism must be wrong.

Their laughter especially, and the fact that there was so much that they, and I, found to laugh about in village Buddhism as it actually is. Perhaps I react unduly against the kind of po-faced piety that I find truly life-denying, but I have never, since I grew up, been able to take seriously a religion that was not enveloped in laughter. In Uganda, twenty years earlier, I had been deeply impressed by the Catholic missionaries of the White Fathers Order: they were men of breath-taking practical piety, who seemed always to have a smile about their lips, frequently dissolving into earthy, indeed bawdy, laughter. They might easily have won me to become a Catholic, had I not been too immature to stomach the superstition – instead of seeing in it the richest part of the joke. This is why I have related some of Sīlaratana's more risible eccentricities, without which he would have been diminished in my eyes. Although for long I puzzled whether to place Sīlaratana as an amusing rogue or as something of a rough, original saint, he was in fact both, and I esteemed him the more for it: just as, in extension, it was the combination of similar qualities in village Buddhists generally that so much attracted me.

Much as these things drew me, it was not they that made it impossible for me to agree that village Buddhism is not true Buddhism. It was the quality, the goodness of the village Buddhists. This may not, I suppose, appear a datum that has any place in scientific analysis; I shall argue below that it is relevant, even uniquely relevant. The fact, of course, is not securely established, and I see myself that my conviction that the villagers of Polgama were among the best people I have ever known is thoroughly subjective and emotional. It is easier to cite evidence against it than for it. Very properly, my wife reminds me that they were a good deal less kind and innocent in their dealings with one another than they were to us, their guests. Among themselves they were often envious, malicious, and given to slander; suspicions of sorcery (*huniyam*) seemed to be rife, and I have strong evidence that it was at least sometimes practised. They sometimes cheated one another, took life, drank, if not to excess, and were certainly less chaste than they pretended. All this I know, and some of it I tell. It is less easy to evidence their goodness, for my conviction of it derives much less from this or that piece of evidence than from my overall sense of the tenor of their lives, and the admiration it evoked in me.

I am confident that this is more than a matter of mere subjective sentiment, because it was not only I who admired the people of Polgama. My wife, more critical than I, yet loved them more warmly. My wife and I each employed a Sinhalese research assistant, and since two of them left during the course of the year, we employed four altogether. They came from different parts of Sri Lanka, and one of them knew at first hand the Sinhalese of several regions. Each of them told us, with some astonishment, that the people of Polgama were the best, the kindest, the most 'innocent' people they had ever met. I heard the same judgement from several residents of the village who had migrated there from other parts.

I did not record the Sinhala terms that lay behind these epithets; and one of them, 'innocent', does not bear the sense in the somewhat archaic Sri Lankan dialect of English that it does in modern English. Thus it does not mean 'simple-minded', though it does connote simplicity. It does not mean 'naive', though it certainly connotes lack of sophistication in the basic pejorative sense of that word. It does not mean 'without guilt', though it does suggest guilelessness and goodness. One sees the sense from another usage of the word: what we would call a 'harmless' snake, i.e. non-venomous, Sinhalese speaking English always term an 'innocent' snake. But 'innocent' applied to people does not mean what we understand by 'harmless', i.e. 'insignificant, negligible'. Rather the word carries its original, etymological sense, of doing harm or injury to none. The Buddhist value of *ahimsa*, non-violence, has been absorbed; indeed, I guess that the Sinhala word behind 'innocent' was *'ahimsaka'*. Perhaps 'gentle' is as near to a synonym as can be provided.

So we found them – as other visitors to Buddhist countries have, sometimes, found the people.[1] Silaratana used to boast to me that the virtues of the Polgama people – notably the rarity of crime or drunkenness among them – were attributable to his own teaching and admonishment, and I think there may be some truth in that. But I cannot say that I noticed any difference between the people of Polgama and those of other villages round about; and, unlike our research assistants, I cannot compare the people of this area to Sinhalese of other parts. But I think it possible that there may be an objective regional difference.

Many Sinhalese, together with foreign anthropologists, consider Robert Knox to be still the most reliable and insightful author who has ever described the Sinhalese.[2] The son of an English sea captain, he was, together with his father and other shipmates, captured by the Sinhalese in 1660 and held captive for nineteen years. Their lives were not made hard, except that all escape from the Kandyan kingdom was effectively forbidden; they were settled in various villages, where the villagers were commanded to provide them with their food, and they were allowed to do much as they pleased, and to travel in the kingdom if not too near its borders. Robert Knox spent the first four years of his captivity in the village of Bandara Coswatta, which is about fifteen miles (25 km) from Polgama; the rest of his time in villages in the higher part of the kingdom, nearer to its capital Kandy, though he travelled widely.[3] He wrote of the Sinhalese:

The natures of the inhabitants of the mountains and lowlands are very different. They of the low lands are kind, pitiful, helpful, honest and plain, compassionating strangers, which we found by our own experience among them. They of the Uplands are ill-natured, false, unkind, though outwardly fair and seemingly courteous, and of more complaisant carriage, speech, and better behaviour, than the low-landers.[4]

Knox was acquainted with lowlanders of various parts, and was much moved by the kindness of those in the area of modern Trincomalee, among whom he spent the first weeks of his captivity.[5] But, scrupulously accurate as he always was, he would not have written these words if he had not found them true of the people of Bandara Coswatta, the lowlanders he knew best. That I also found them true of the people of Polgama, fifteen miles away, though three hundred years later, leads me to surmise that, for whatever reason, the people of the area in which we worked simply are remarkably kind, pitiful, helpful, honest and plain, compassionating strangers, which we found by our own experience among them.

The reader has every right to be sceptical. The author must, with whatever misgivings, report these impressions rather than suppress them: for, fallible as they are, I know that they were crucial to my experience and judgement, and shall show them to be logically decisive also.

In order to do so, I must make two further claims. The first of them seems reasonable enough, though not undeniably true; the second may be found contentious, as it flatly contradicts the positivist assumptions that have had so much influence on the study of religion, not least in anthropology. The first is this: that if of Buddhism, or any other major historical religion, there are two distinct interpretations each claiming to be the more authentic version, then that interpretation which can be shown to be more true should be reckoned the more authentic: for it is more probable that a religious civilisation that has endured and flourished for two and a half millennia is based on truth than that it is based on error. The second is that it is meaningful to speak of a religion, or interpretation of a religion, as true, and as more true than another, and that there is a satisfactory empirical test for such truth. This claim will not be so readily conceded that it can stand without being argued.

There is a delightful Buddhist scripture, much admired by educated Buddhists of the modernist persuasion, though not, so far as I could tell, familiar to village Buddhists,[6] which deals with this very point. The *Kālāma Sutta*[7] purports to relate a discourse of the Buddha. There is no more reason in this case than in any other to suppose that it actually does; but this one has the delightful feature of cutting the ground from under anyone who supposes that that matters. For it represents the Buddha as saying that to determine truth one should not rely upon the authority of a teacher or of a scripture. So, if he did say it, he says it doesn't matter that he did; if he did not, then this scripture is an imposture, hence we recognise that at least some scriptures can be impostures, and since there is no way of knowing which are and which are not, there is no way of knowing what the Buddha did say. And hence we need some other criterion of truth – which this somewhat Cretan[8]* scripture does provide.

According to this ingenious yarn, then, some people called the Kālāmas came to the Buddha and complained that they were visited by so many various religious teachers, each expounding his own doctrine and pulling those of the others to pieces, that they were thoroughly confused as to how to decide what was true and what was false. Lord Buddha said they had reason to be confused, and told them truth cannot be determined by relying upon tradition, or upon what is in a scripture, or upon specious reasoning, or upon reliance on the word of a teacher (and so forth). He told them instead to adhere to whatever they found by observation led to good conduct in a man, to the absence of greed, hate and delusion, and to avoid whatever led to the opposite.

There is a remarkable parallel in the Christian scriptures (though the Cretan structure is much less obvious). According to *this* yarn Christ said, 'Beware of false prophets. . . . By their fruits ye shall know them. Do men gather grapes of thorns, or figs of thistles? Even so every good tree bringeth forth good fruit; but the corrupt tree bringeth forth evil fruit. A good tree cannot bring forth evil fruit, neither can a corrupt tree bring forth good fruit.'[9] What amounts to the same argument, highly compressed and not attributed to Christ, is used in I John 3, v. 17 (R.V.): 'But whoso hath the world's goods, and beholdeth his brother in need, and shutteth up his compassion from him, how doth the love of God abide in him?'

It is plainly unimportant who said these words: even if we *knew* that Christ said them we should still need to determine whether he was a false prophet . . . his authority depends on the validity of the words, not vice versa. Reflection will show that any religion which makes universal claims – is not content to rely only on the aura of factuality attaching to a religion already established in a culture – must rely upon the criterion proposed in these passages as the ultimate basis of its claims to be true, for none other will stand up. Useless to claim that its doctrines are true, since, as both scriptures acknowledge, such claims can be and are made falsely: and, since the axiomatic doctrines – concerning, say, God or Nirvana – are always unverifiable before they have been assented to, nothing else can provide adequate reason for such assent. This shows, from another angle, the necessity of the primacy of practice over belief.

Although the argument is very holy, in the sense of full of holes, for the purpose of proving to anyone whatever that a particular religion is true, it is strong for the purpose for which we require it, that of showing village Buddhism to be truer than Buddhist Modernism. No modernist (and no Western Buddhist) would deny that absence of hate, greed and delusion are Buddhist virtues. Few would deny, since it is one of their favourite scriptures, the authenticity of the *Kālāma Sutta*; and if they did they would be forked by it, as we saw, and could produce no sounder criterion. The only question could be, in whom are the virtues more manifest? I cannot claim that hate, greed and delusion are absent among village Buddhists, for their traces are all too evident. They seemed to me rather more evident in the kind of people most ready to disparage village Buddhism. By less exacting, but still consensual, Buddhist standards of good conduct I am clear that it is village Buddhists who excel. The truth of this factual premise cannot be placed beyond reasonable doubt, as I have already conceded; but my present purpose is to show that the logic of the inference is sound, and that the criterion applied is the proper one. The argument suggests a conclusion, but to establish it we shall need arguments of other kinds.

Is the argument in principle sound for showing the truth of a religion to an unbeliever? The criterion for truth proposed is very different from the criteria accepted in science; for this reason, I think, most social scientists would dismiss the question as meaningless or irrelevant. I am less confident that the kind of truth recognised in science, and the criteria appropriate to it, are all that should concern the anthropologist. If religion is part of human life it is part of our concern; and if religion is, as I judge it to be, a valid mode of human cognition, we should not disqualify ourselves from assessing its forms through exclusive insistence upon a mode of thought with which we feel more comfortable. Whether a particular religion, or even religion generally, is true, in the sense which fits its own peculiar kind of rationality, is a question not compulsory but permissible for the anthropologist to raise, though not of course to claim to settle.

Notes to Chapter 5

1 E.g. Ling (1973), p. 137.
2 Saparamadu (1966), pp. vii, xxxii, xxxv.
3 *Ibid.*, pp. xvii, xxxiii.
4 Knox [1681] (1966), p. 121.
5 *Ibid.*, pp. 228–9.
6 As Gombrich also reports (1971, p. 263).
7 *Anguttara Nikāya, Tika Nipāta, Mahāvagga, Sutta* 65; it is summarised in Rahula (1967), pp. 2–3.
8 By this term I draw attention to the fact that the logical structure of this discourse has something in common with that of a family of logical antinomies or paradoxes which are similarly self-referential. 'The oldest contradiction of the kind in question is the *Epimenides*. Epimenides the Cretan said that all Cretans were liars, and all other statements made by Cretans were certainly lies. Was this a lie? The simplest form of this contradiction is afforded by the man who says "I am lying"; if he is lying, he is speaking the truth, and vice-versa.' (Whitehead and Russell 1927, p. 60.) These paradoxes have had a significant role in the development of logic, and their occurrence sometimes indicates that a basic question is at issue. I suggest that such a basic question is raised whenever a religious teacher acknowledges that the word of a religious teacher is not *ipso facto* authoritative.
9 Matthew, 7, vv. 15–18 (R.V.).

6

Problem and dissolvement

It will have been noticed that I have so far written little, except obliquely, of the content of village Buddhism, which one would expect of an anthropologist, and much of my personal experience, which one would not. I, too, have found this puzzling.

In the Preface to his *Nuer Religion* (1956), Evans-Pritchard stated cautiously – but not cautiously enough for many of his readers: 'It may be said that in describing and interpreting a primitive religion it should make no difference whether the writer is an agnostic or a Christian, Jew, Muslim, Hindu, or whatever he may be, but in fact it makes a great deal of difference, for even in a descriptive study judgement can in no way be avoided.'[1] Some years later he expressed his view more boldly:

On this point I find myself in agreement with Schmidt in his confutation of Renan: 'If religion is essentially of the inner life, it follows that it can be truly grasped only from within. But beyond a doubt, this can be better done by one in whose inward consciousness an expression of religion plays a part. There is but too much danger that the other [the non-believer] will talk of religion as a blind man might of colours, or one totally devoid of ear, of a beautiful musical composition.'[2]

If Fr. Schmidt could say, with implicit reference to his own Catholic Christianity, that religion is essentially of the inner life, the same can be said with at least equal emphasis of Buddhism. It very frequently is said by village, and other, Buddhists, for whom it is a commonplace that Buddhism is really in the mind. Not only in the mind, for Buddhists are no less emphatic that practice and states of mind are inseparable, each determining the other. But the practice that village Buddhists are chiefly referring to is not of the kind that the anthropologist of religion sets his sights upon: it is not ritual but rather ethical conduct. For much of the time I was looking past what I should have been recording, and no longer know how to describe it specifically.[3]*

Village Buddhists, unlike many Buddhist modernists, do not despise ritual. But, as I shall recount more fully later (Chapter 12), they do consider it unimportant and optional, in religious if not always in social terms. If I were to offer as an account of village Buddhism the fullest description that I can of ritual acts, I should, I fear, be rather like the observer 'totally devoid of ear' who described a symphony concert in terms of the hammerings and frottings of the performers, and the gymnastics of the conductor. Still less am I willing to offer an extended account of the beliefs of village Buddhists, most of which I doubt if they believe, but themselves are apt to describe as embroidery on what Buddhism really is. The reality of village Buddhism is mostly shared between inward experience, to which I have access mainly through participating in it, and a tenor of life which, since I cannot separate it out from the totality of what I saw, I have to illustrate by anecdote.

The best I can do to bring matters to a focus is to take up more fully the principal problem which, for better or for worse, did absorb, or distract me. It is the problem of the conventional judgement on village Buddhism, and why it will not do.

The content of the conventional judgement, its basis, and its apparent inevitability, are admirably illustrated in a paragraph from Gombrich's book, part of which I quote:

It was the aim of Buddha to attain *nirvāna*, a mystical release from normal states of consciousness; it is attained in life, and someone who has attained it is not reborn: he escapes from the wheel of rebirth, to which all creatures are tied. Rebirth the Buddha considered misery; the peace of *nirvāna* was the only good worth having. But most Sinhalese villagers do not want *nirvāna* – yet. They are like St. Augustine who prayed "Make me chaste and continent, O Lord – but not yet". They say they want to be born in heaven; some of them would even like to be reborn in a favourable station on earth . . . This shifting of an aim, from *nirvāna* to heaven or even to earth . . .[4]

This reads like an elegant summary of the central conclusion of Spiro's book (1971), which he develops at length in his chapter III. What Gombrich (like most other commentators) identifies as the doctrine of the Buddha, Spiro does not: terming it 'nibbanic Buddhism',[5] he identifies it as the doctrine of the canonical scriptures, while remaining agnostic as to whether it was indeed the Buddha's teaching. Since he calls it 'early', 'canonical', and 'normative', and says that Buddhists themselves identify it as the Buddha's teaching,[6] the practical effect is much the same. Apart from this, the parallelism is striking. Spiro too sees the Buddhism of villagers as showing a 'shift in the goal',[7] and it is from nirvana to a happy rebirth on earth or in heaven.[8] The Burmese, he writes, 'have not rejected nirvana, they merely – like St. Augustine in the matter of celibacy – wish to defer it'.[9]

In fact, Gombrich was not summarising Spiro's conclusions. The two authors were writing so nearly simultaneously that neither cites the other, nor indeed shows any awareness of his work. They were led independently to similar conclusions because they observed similar facts, and shared similar assumptions about Buddhism – and also I think because they shared similar views on the nature of religion, and especially of the place of belief in it.

The facts are indeed plain, and I observed them too. The conclusions that Gombrich and Spiro, and many others, have drawn from the bare facts seem also to be matters of fact, not of interpretation. I found them so when I was in Sri Lanka, as I am sure the reader would on the basis of a simple description. It seems plain that Gombrich did.

Spiro's interpretation is presented as a major conclusion of his work, and argued at length. The parallel view of Gombrich is not. The paragraph I cited is not presented as an analytical conclusion: on the contrary, it occurs as a mere aside, offered to illustrate what he means by 'changing aims'. This indicates that he took what he was saying not as a matter of controversy or analysis, but as one of plain agreed fact. So far from representing his analytical conclusion, what he says is actually inconsistent with conclusions he does offer. As I remarked in Chapter 1, Gombrich had earlier in his book taken up the common view that actual Buddhism is Buddhism in name only, and had expressed vehement dissent; he had covered it with ironic scorn, pointing out that it was based on comparison with an unreliable estimate of true Buddhism derived from Europeans.[10] By the end of his book he has come close to inverting the conventional judgement, endorsed in the paragraph I cited. The concluding sentence of the book is: 'If this is popular Buddhism, could it be that *Vox populi vox Buddhae*?'[11]

My practical problem was that while analysis of my data seemed inexorably to lead to the conventional judgement, my feelings and my intuition insisted that it was wrong. Since I supposed that I could not, as a social scientist, attach any public weight to emotion and intuition, I found myself paralysed. I needed to find a high road from the conventional judgement expressed in the longer passage I quoted from Gombrich, to the heresy he hinted at in his concluding sentence; though I did not see it that way, and indeed did not even notice what Gombrich was driving at until after I had myself achieved confidence in the same conclusion.

It will show how difficult the problem was if I set out the evidence from my own observations which gave the conventional judgement such a solid aura of factuality. Village Buddhists regularly say, when prompted by a suitable question, that they seek to attain Nirvana. Just as regularly, but with much less prompting, they say that they seek to be reborn in a happier condition, and seek to attain a long series of such rebirths. These two goals seem to be somewhat contradictory, in that Nirvana is defined, and very regularly by village Buddhists, as the ending of rebirth, of any further life. (Sinhalese Buddhists regularly do identify Nirvana with extinction, despite the fact that scripture states that this equation is definitely, though very subtly, wrong.)[12] When one asks a village Buddhist what Nirvana is, the standard and commonest reply is 'No suffering, no Rebirth'. So one wonders whether they are equally sincere in their statements of seeking the one goal and the other.

There seems to be no doubt that they really do seek and look forward to rebirths in happier conditions of life: not only when being interviewed by the anthropologist, but spontaneously in the ordinary situations of life, they speak frequently of this, and convey a lively interest and commitment. Often they talk about the conditions of the future life they hope they will attain if they can earn sufficient Merit, i.e. good karma, and sufficiently avoid incurring Demerit, i.e. bad karma: how they hope to be rich, of high status, perhaps powerful or at least not oppressed, to enjoy good health and a long life, and happiness in their families and more widely. It is impossible to mistake that they do desire these things, very much, and that they are animated even to entertain the hope of having them. And when one further reflects that these are just the things they plainly desire in the present life, strive hard if they can to get, and regret their actual lack of, one cannot doubt that their desire for a better rebirth is real, and that they are sincere in stating it.

But with Nirvana it seems very different. It is not uncommon to hear village Buddhists use the word (*nivan*), though usually in conventional and stereotyped phrases where one doubts if it carries much more than a nominal meaning. When questioned they will say that they hope, or seek, to attain Nirvana, though often only after some prompting; and I have never heard anyone readily admit that he did not want Nirvana. But it is striking how rare it is to hear such statements made spontaneously. When I interviewed Buddhist priests and novices I regularly asked them why they had decided to enter the Sangha (which is usually done between the ages of about ten and twelve). Only one, out of twenty-four, directly mentioned an aspiration to Nirvana among the factors. I asked several others whether this had not been a factor, and most replied, 'Of course not.' Similarly, what is striking about spontaneous references to Nirvana is how infrequent they are by comparison with what might be expected. On any definition Nirvana is what ultimately Buddhism is about, and village Buddhists acknowledge this, even if they rarely themselves proffer such a definition. More analytically, Ling is quite correct when he writes, 'Whatever is venerated for its "sacred" character is in Buddhism that which has a very close or special relationship to *nibbana* . . .'[13] And of course the phraseology of Nirvana is an approved conventional device for exhibiting Buddhist piety. Against this background, it is remarkable how rarely one hears Nirvana spoken of, and then usually in a way which suggests that the term carries little meaning or emotion. It is as if one found oneself living among people who claimed to be devout Christians, but did not often mention God, and then mainly in such conventional phrases as 'God knows', 'God will provide'; and yet were constantly speaking with animation of what they expected from Zeus and Aphrodite.

This impression that village Buddhists only pay lip service to the concept of Nirvana is reinforced when one asks them questions about it, e.g. why do you think Nirvana is so good? Why do you want to put an end to rebirth? Why do you say life is suffering, when there is so much else that is pleasant and happy about it also? They react to such questions with evident discomfort, even distress, trying to turn them aside or hold them at bay with downcast dogmatism. One gets a strong impression that they have never considered such questions before – which is to say they have never bothered to think seriously about the Nirvana which they *claim* to be the ultimate goal of their religious lives; and further that, being brought to consider them, they start to realise that Nirvana is not to their taste at all.[14] I felt sure that if I could only press them relentlessly enough they would have no recourse but to admit it. But this would have been such a callous and immoral thing to do that I could not do it. Except with one man, Banda, who kept on begging me to argue with him about Buddhism, until I felt that he had asked for it. So I did press him relentlessly until, in much distress, he did confess that really Nirvana was not what he wanted, he really wanted happier rebirths on earth or in the heavens. Understandably, this made me feel more confident that I could have extracted similar confessions from others if I had had the heart.

The conclusion seems inescapable: village Buddhists pay lip service to the declaration that Nirvana is the highest good, and claim it to be their goal, but they do not really believe the declaration nor seek the goal. Their real goal, and what they really believe to be good, is a happier rebirth. Hence they have practically abandoned the authentic goal of Buddhism, and have substituted for it a lesser, more worldly goal. *Ergo*, at the heart of the matter, they are not authentic Buddhists. This seemed the more certain because it appeared to be, and virtually is, the consensual conclusion of the literature on village Buddhism.

This, then was the nature of the *impasse* in which I was stuck when, having stretched procrastination beyond the limit of tolerance, I was determined to write my book. I had agreed first to write a paper on 'The concept of Nirvana in village Buddhism',[15] seeing in this an opportunity to limber up for the task; and I found myself stuck fast in the *impasse* I have described. A friend had written to me asking what I was working on, and I used my reply to muse upon my problem. I described the *impasse*, and diagnosed that the trouble must be that by starting from the concept of Nirvana we were entering the system at the wrong point. Better, surely, to start with what village Buddhists actually do say. And – meaning this as a sardonic joke – I said that since we get into such a mess by starting from the height of wisdom, perhaps I should do better to start from what impressed me as the daftest thing I ever heard them say. In the early days of my fieldwork, before I had much idea of villagers and their Buddhism, I had asked a number of people what, as a Buddhist, is it that one has to do? Vividly I recall the answer I had got from several seemingly unsophisticated rustics: 'Well, sir, not to kill animals.' I had had some difficulty in maintaining my composure. How preposterous, I thought, that a philosophy so noble, rich and subtle as Buddhism is reduced by these clods to the level of a childish, ludicrous taboo! In time, as I learned more, I was to realise that this reply was not half as daft as it had seemed, was even rather clever: but, in my conscious mind at least, its full wisdom still escaped me.

At that time I had been given as a present a very fine recording of Mozart's C Minor Mass.[16] I had long been familiar with the setting from this Mass of the words from the Credo, 'Et incarnatus est . . .'; I felt it so deeply moving that I found it painful, near to sacrilegious, to listen to it. I knew, of course, what the text meant: Et incarnatus est, de Spiritu Sancto ex Maria Virgine, et homo factus est: 'And was incarnate by the Holy Ghost of the Virgin Mary, and was made man'. But I had little time for the doctrine of the Incarnation, which seemed to me a cynical attempt to render Christ humanly irrelevant by presenting him as Principal Boy in an absurd celestial pantomime. I had no idea why a setting of this text should have moved me so deeply.

Now, I heard the music in the light of what I had learnt from Raymond Leppard's sleeve note.[17] Largely on the basis of musical intuition, he conjectures that this is the Mass that Mozart had promised 'in his heart of hearts' to write 'in memory of his much loved mother'. Now, as I listened to the *Et incarnatus est*, I knew the source of the profundity of feeling and melting beauty of the music. The making man that Mozart celebrated was his own. In his own incarnation came together all humanity, in Christ, in flesh, in God, and it was very good: of that he sang. And I heard, and knew.

Out of that dissolvement I found the pieces fit. I had, I now recalled, taken not killing animals extremely seriously. Not to kill animals, by which is meant all animate beings, mammals, birds and reptiles, fish and insects, is only part of the First Precept, by which a Buddhist undertakes to (try to) abstain from taking life; but since Buddhists suppose that all religions forbid the taking of human life, it is this part that they see as distinctively Buddhist. Now the First Precept is regularly cited as standing synecdochically for all the Five Precepts,[18*] which are the basic code of Buddhist ethics – and are also the greater part of the standard Buddhist profession of adherence or 'faith'. Thus my rustics had, with exquisite economy, summarised the whole basis of Buddhist ethics, which is indeed often presented as virtually the whole basis of Buddhism.[19*]

Now Buddhists are not daft: they do kill when they have to. They do, for example, use insecticides on their crops, though still with a certain remorse and sadness, knowing they must do it if they are to eat. Most village Buddhists will kill snakes of one particularly dangerous species, the *polanga* or Russell's Viper: they know that its bite is normally fatal, and that it is also aggressive, attacking unprovoked, and even chasing people. One young man told me a story of one evening when he had been at the temple and a snake had appeared: 'Kill it, kill it!' Sīlaratana had screamed at him. But the young man had only laughed, and said it was 'innocent'. 'Oh,' said Sīlaratana, 'I thought it was a *polanga*.' As some youths with whom, on another occasion, I was discussing Buddhist ethics said to me, 'Yes, it is sin (*pav*) to kill a *polanga*. But we have to do it.' I knew one exception even to this. Mrs. Rambanda was probably the most pious Buddhist in the village – and she was no fool. In her front garden, by the footpath, was a small ornamental pool, in which frogs lived, and this attracted *polangas* from far around. After dark the place seethed with them, I was told by our two research assistants, who, in fear and trembling, lodged with Mrs. Rambanda for a while. The *polangas* used to climb up into the thatched roof, and writhe and slither through it through the night. Sometimes one would fall down into the room below – there were no ceilings. But Mrs. Rambanda would not permit any member of her household – she had quite a large family, the youngest a boy of ten – to kill a *polanga*. They survived – the family, that is; one of her sons told us he did kill *polangas* when his mother was not around.

But most Buddhists would not kill any other kind of snake, no matter how venomous, if they could avoid it. I know of two occasions during our year in Polgama when a cobra was killed, most reluctantly. (There is clearly some sort of vestigial cult of the cobra, which is associated with numerous superstitions, as well as with the Buddha.)[20] On one, the man who had actually killed it explained to us that it had kept coming back to the houses although people had begged it to go away; after it had come the sixth time people had decided that someone would be bitten if this kept up, and there was no option but to kill it. The other cobra had developed a habit of taking a short cut at night through the room in which the family slept, and they too had decided it was too dangerous to allow this to continue. They had particular reason to be sensitive, having not long before lost a daughter by the bite of a *polanga*, which had been sent by the sorcery of her employer in the village, who had accused her of pilfering.

(He was a notorious sorcerer.) But to kill an 'innocent' snake was unthinkable. Even when I jumped at seeing one people used to laugh at me, and I know that to kill one would have been regarded as quite despicable.

It was somewhat the same with insects; as I have remarked, those that are definitely known to be harmful are killed. But most people will put up with a considerable degree of annoyance from insects rather than kill them. It is common when walking along with a Sinhalese to see him halt or step aside so as not to step on an insect. Middle-class Sinhalese have told me this is because for all you know the insect may be the reincarnation of one of your relatives. I did not hear this explanation from villagers, and rather doubt if they would think it, since it would imply that one's relative had been a dreadful sinner to be so reborn.[21*] And anyway, it comes to the same thing – which suggests to me that the Rebirth doctrine may be a way of transforming genuinely Buddhist principles into more apprehensible form.

My own conduct was very different: as an Englishman I thought nothing of swatting insects, and constantly did so, as they were a continual nuisance in our house, particularly at night when the pressure lanterns attracted them. As time went on I could not but notice the contrast between my conduct and that of the Sinhalese, and feel ashamed. We had one research assistant who was quite a pious Buddhist, and though he never reproved me, a number of times when he saw me swatting insects I saw him wince. There is something deeply impressive about people who really do try to abstain from taking life, and the more I felt it the less I liked myself. Besides, many years ago I had read Albert Schweitzer, and Tolstoy, who say that reverence for life is the basis of all true ethical sensibility, and I knew, really, that they were right. And, most shaming of all, there kept recurring to me that I owed my life to not killing insects, since, once in Uganda, it had spared me from a terrible death.[22*]

One day in Polgama I was at my desk, writing, and as usual being pestered by insects. I lifted my hand to swat a beetle. The sense of shame that had accumulated in me held my hand, and I let the beetle go. As I did so, I experienced the most extraordinary transformation of consciousness. Suddenly, I took delight in the life of the beetle I had spared, and in our world that had place for both of us as citizens. I felt myself to be living in a world that was good, a wonderfully intricate world of life, of which I was part and belonged as one of many infinitely varied members, at peace with one another and quietly rejoicing in their several occasions. Though I was not consistent, this feeling stayed with me for much of the rest of my time in Sri Lanka. I found the world wonderful and beautiful, found in myself a zest to be a part of it, smiled even to think of the snakes in the grasses winding along about their own affairs. It is a perception of the world that resonates with much that is most characteristic in Buddhist culture.

In the afterglow of Mozart's music all this came back to me, and I recognised, as I had not before, what it was about. The sense of peace and welcome in the world, the joy of belonging in community with other beings, recalled to me what I have read of Nirvana. I do not mean that my experience was Nirvana, which I understand to be perfection: but it was unmistakably of nirvanic kind. It was triggered by the simple act of not killing a beetle, but its cause lay deeper. Buddhists, including village Buddhists, regularly explain that it is not so much what one does that has effect, but the intention, the state of mind and being that issues in the deed. It was the piled-up remorse, the sense of shame that had gone deep in me, that had held my hand from killing, it was these, not the act in itself, that had set me free. I doubt if I could have come to that had I not been living in a Buddhist culture.

When I thought about this, I saw that it had dissolved my problem. I do not suppose that any village Buddhist ever experiences, as I had, as a revelation, the transformation of consciousness that I had when I spared the beetle. How could they? They have never known anything else which might be transformed. Growing up with and in the First Precept, the state of consciousness that so astounded me when I first came upon it must be their normal condition of life. What, then, are they going to make of the teaching about Nirvana that they are given? They are taught that it is immeasurably different from anything we experience in our ordinary lives. How then can they perceive it but as perfection, as I have suggested it to be: much as we Christians image to ourselves the nature of God? They cannot *think* of their everyday state of consciousness as like Nirvana, just because to them it is everyday. Yet what they actually do experience, without knowing what it is they experience, is very plainly nirvanic: its harmony with what they are told of Nirvana must make the concept meaningful to them, and, because it is meaningful, give them a lively grasp of how remote its perfection has to be. How tawdry, and how very sad, seem to me those who know so little of the nirvanic as to imagine Nirvana is little enough to be within their grasp – and that by cutting themselves off from the real world of their fellows, when the nirvanic is the fellowship of the world.

I saw now the wisdom of the remark that Dhammatilaka had thrown off at my wife: 'I am not in a hurry to attain Nirvana.' At the time I had thought he was merely teasing. He was well educated, and had a good idea of the nonsense that Europeans make of Buddhism, and with me he liked to throw off provocative remarks like this one, hoping to start an argument. My wife did not rise to the bait, and neither did I. I thought it too obvious an application of a dogma I had found standard among village

Buddhists, that no one will or can attain Nirvana until Maitrī, the next Buddha, is born, some time in the far, far future. Just when that will be, no one can say. I had heard Dhammatilaka, among others, estimate that it might be ten million births away – which would amount to some three-quarters of a billion years.

I saw, or thought I saw, now, very much more in the remark. If Dhammatilaka said it as a Buddhist priest, surely he was implying that one ought not to be in a hurry to attain Nirvana. The truth of that now seemed obvious to me. To be in a hurry to attain Nirvana is, on the one hand, to trivialise it, not to recognise the grandeur of the conception – and suggests that one has had no real experience of the nirvanic. On the other hand, it is hardly distinguishable from desiring Nirvana, which all Buddhists recognise, verbally at least, to be an absurdity, since Nirvana is without desire, and desire – explicitly including desire for Nirvana – is the principal obstacle to its attainment.

This actually makes it difficult to find out what a Buddhist's attitude to Nirvana really is, since if one seems to ask him whether he desires Nirvana he is bound to answer no. I think this may well be part of the reason why one gets the impression that village Buddhists do not want Nirvana: they have been so well schooled that to desire it is to miss it that it is not easy for them to know what to say. How does one handle a *summum bonum* which is by definition undesirable? There is here a paradox, inherent and not easily circumvented, as there is at the heart of other religions: or, to use a term preferred by the religious, a mystery. And how else does a religiously sensitive person handle a mystery but to be silent before it? By talk, at least: 'Whereof one cannot speak, thereof one must be silent,' as Wittgenstein wrote in the *Tractatus*.[23]

There seemed to me also something remarkably selfish about being in a hurry to attain Nirvana: to supposing it is something one can run off and grab for oneself, leaving other people mired behind. I have reported already the forthright view of Sīlaratana, and of some other people I knew, on the selfishness of those who do this, and my perception of the logic of his view (above, Chapter 5). Such self-absorption seemed to me in another world from the sense of community, of being part of an interdependent system of life, which is so strong in the nirvanic experience. I had also noticed for myself some observational grounds for agreeing with Sīlaratana. Among those Sinhalese I had met who were most emphatic that Nirvana-grabbing is the only true Buddhism, a significant proportion had seemed strikingly selfish, not to say nasty, people. If would be libellous, as well as unkind, for me to display my evidence; and in any case it is far too scanty and uncontrolled to carry much scientific weight. It acquires more significance from the way it chimes with the results of Spiro's more extensive and intensive investigation.

Spiro's analysis of the emotional characteristics of Burmese clergy[24] is based almost wholly on his sample of twenty-one monks selected for intensive study. As I pointed out in note 45 to Chapter 3, the sample cannot be typical of Burmese clergy generally, but probably is typical of those who conformed to Spiro's view of 'normative' Buddhism in which, e.g., 'Salvation can only be achieved by a total and radical rejection of the world in all its aspects.'[25] One of their distinctive characteristics he labels 'narcissism', and comments, 'One might, instead, use the colloquial "selfish," but this expresses a value judgement which I have attempted to avoid in this analysis, and which is obviated by the more technical term. By "narcissism", then, I mean an overriding preoccupation with self, regardless of its consequences for the welfare of others.'[26] Having illustrated his assessment from a variety of observations, he writes, justly:

The narcissism of [these] monks is seen in its most blatant form, however, in the process of monastic recruitment . . . A large percentage – perhaps the majority – . . . have already founded families when they decided to join the Order. For them to enter the monastery is to abandon wife and children. Often families are left not only without husband and father, but also destitute, with no one to care or provide for them. Nevertheless, such considerations do not serve as deterrents; their own needs, say the would-be monks, must take precedence above all others.'[27]

He illustrates this with statements made by three such persons. One is enough:

When *B*, a village farmer, decided to become a monk, he came to inform me of his decision. I asked him what would happen to his wife and children (who would be destitute). 'They will have to look after themselves,' he said. 'This is not my responsibility; I must think of my own nirvana. If they have good karma, they will be able to get along.'[27]

I was told, and can credit it, that in Sri Lanka such persons would not be admitted to the Sangha. In Burma they receive social approval.[28] Spiro further points out that their conduct is sanctioned by prominent precedents in scripture.[29] Avoiding value judgement, he does not consider whether these scriptures, or these interpretations of them, may be spurious.[30]*

Dhammatilaka, in fact, had not said any of this, though I know, from my various converations with him, that his own views are similar. Placed in its actual context, his remark implies the same connection between the urgency of Nirvana-seeking and selfishness, but inversely. I shall try to summarise the whole conversation, not only to contextualise the remark in which I had found so much significance, but also because it illustrates both the intelligent and concerned involvement in human affairs which is so characteristic of actual, especially village, Buddhism, and also the personality of Dhammatilaka.

The conversation was a long one – it lasted about three hours – but entirely unplanned. My wife, together with a research assistant, had called at Dhammatilaka's temple, meaning only to note the size of the congregation on Vesak day[31]* and then pass on, but they were caught by a downpour of rain. Dhammatilaka was evidently on good form, and Sarah was so impressed by what he said that she not only wrote her own notes but asked our research assistant to write his – at which he was very good. So I have two excellent accounts.

The conversation covered a wide range of topics, though the dominant themes seem to have been politics, ethics, and religion. Dhammatilaka, a supporter of the somewhat left-wing SLFP, said that it is the poor people who support Buddhism: without them it would die out, as the rich hardly give anything. This seems to have been a favourite theme of his, on which I have also heard him wax eloquent; within villages, at any rate, the facts seem to be with him.[32]* They then turned to talking about relations between teachers and students, and about 'ragging' in universities (a topic much discussed in Sri Lanka at that time). Agreeing with Sarah's suggestion that the immaturity of the students was a factor, Dhammatilaka attributed this immaturity to excessive parental control and too much segregation of the sexes. This led to a discussion on the upbringing of children, and Sarah asked him if people came to him with family and marriage problems. He said that many did, and in fact it took up most of his time.

Then, in Sarah's notes, 'He went on to say that nibbana is a long way off. So he takes his time to help poor helpless persons'; in our assistant's notes, 'He is not in a hurry to achieve nibbana. It is good to help people.'

In answer to a question: you can achieve Nirvana in this way. After some discussion of ways to attain Nirvana, Sarah asked him if a layman can attain it. Dhammatilaka replied, in the style I know so well:

If I tell you, then you'll ask me, why did you become a cleric? It can be achieved by both; but it is easier for a cleric. For example, when a pretty girl gets on the bus, a layman will want to talk with her and get to know her better; but a cleric can only look at her. A cleric is protected from temptations, for example pursuing the woman, or getting into a political argument in a shop, or with liquor. If you do not use liquor you do not need it.

Notes to Chapter 6

1 Page vii.
2 Evans-Pritchard (1965), p. 121, quoting Schmidt (1931), p. 6.
3 Part of the difficulty is that much of the evidence is negative, the things I did not observe. Thus I never saw a villager of Polgama drunk; I was rarely told a deliberate lie; no one ever attempted to steal from me, although, for example,

when I travelled on buses I was easy prey for a pickpocket. These, at least, are matters where comparison with my experience in Africa seems appropriate.

4 Gombrich (1971), pp. 16–17.
5 From *nibbana*, the Pali form of the word *nirvana*.
6 Spiro (1971), pp. 6–7, 12, 66.
7 *Ibid.*, p. 73.
8 *Ibid.*, p. 67, etc.
9 *Ibid.*, p. 79.
10 Gombrich (1971), pp. 50–6.
11 *Ibid.*, p. 327.
12 Smart (1964), pp. 34–5; cf. Rahula (1967), p. 41.
13 Ling (1973), p. 235.
14 Cf. Spiro (1971), pp. 76–9; Davy (1821), p. 216, quoted in Gombrich (1971), p. 318.
15 In Burghart and Cantlie (in press).
16 EMI ASD 2959.
17 Leppard (1973).
18 These are to abstain from (1) taking (animate) life, (2) taking what is not given, (3) wrong conduct in sexual desires, (4) telling lies, (5) intoxicating liquors which occasion heedlessness (Gombrich, 1971, p. 65). Rahula renders them into more idiomatic English, which loses some of their subtlety (1967, p. 80).
19 My claim that Sinhalese Buddhists do take the First Precept seriously seems to be challenged by the fact that Sri Lanka has a notoriously high homicide rate. I can here only outline a few points on this complex issue (on which see Strauss and Strauss, 1953; Gunasekera, 1951; Wood, 1961a, 1961b).

1. A homicide rate is high only in relation to that of other societies. Since a homicide rate is determined by a number of factors, to estimate the effect of religion one should compare the rate for Sri Lanka with that of otherwise similar societies. When this is done, one suspects that the rate for Sri Lanka seems high largely because cases are better reported, Sri Lanka having a rather efficient administration.
2. Within Sri Lanka the homicide rate varies considerably between different areas: a high overall rate is consistent with a moderate rate in typical rural Buddhist areas (cf. Gombrich, 1971, pp. 259–60).
3. A homicide rate reflects the behaviour of a very small minority of exceptional persons, and does not directly bear on the behaviour of the majority. Even with a high homicide rate, the great majority of people may be notably non-violent – as I think they are among Sinhalese Buddhists.
4. Various indications suggest to me that even among rural Buddhists the homicide rate may be somewhat high. I can suggest two ways in which Buddhism might contribute to this:

   (a) Buddhist morality concerning violence, sex, and other matters, does lead to considerable repression of human emotions, which may then, in some persons, break through in uncontrolled violence.
   (b) Since the First Precept abjures the killing of animals and men without distinction, it may obscure the special enormity of homicide. Some

persons who kill animals may feel themselves already to be irredeemably condemned, so that homicide hardly makes matters worse. This may have some bearing on the fact that homicide, and violence generally, is particularly prevalent in fishing communities.

20 Cf. Gombrich (1971), p. 167; Obeyesekere (1981), p. 134.

21 Though Sinhalese often say that the karmic consequence of various kinds of sin is to be reborn as an animal, and do speak ill of specific relatives, living and dead, I never heard anyone suggest that a specific dead relative might now be an animal. It is my impression, that is, that attitudes to dead relatives and karmic theory are not normally articulated in that way.

22 I was bothered by a nest of wasps in a hut I was living in. I felt moral compunction about killing the wasps, so instead rearranged my furniture to avoid them. Shortly afterwards, a large viper came unseen into the hut, on a spot where I should probably have trodden on it if the furniture had not been moved.

23 Wittgenstein (1922), 7.

24 Spiro (1971), pp. 337–50.

25 *Ibid.*, p. 65.

26 *Ibid.*, p. 344.

27 *Ibid.*, p. 345.

28 *Ibid.*, p. 346.

29 *Ibid.*, pp. 346–8.

30 One is the story of Prince Vessantara, supposedly the Buddha in an earlier incarnation. It is, of course, legendary. Sinhalese Buddhists do not regard the conduct of Vessantara as entirely admirable (Gombrich, 1971, p. 267). The other is the Canonical story of Gotama, before he had achieved Buddhahood, leaving his wife and child to seek his own salvation. This derives from the early biography of the Buddha, on the authenticity of which Frauwallner (1956) writes somewhat severely (see below, Chapter 10). In any case the story does not clearly legitimate the conduct Spiro describes, since it belongs to the period of Gotama's life when he sought salvation by various means which he came later to understand as unsound.

31 Vesak, which falls on the full-moon day which usually occurs about the end of May, is supposedly the anniversary of the Buddha's birth, and of his Enlightenment, and of his death. It is thus the most important day in the Buddhist liturgical calendar.

32 At least in the villages I knew, many of the more prosperous people did not give lavishly to village temples; when they did give lavishly they tended to prefer to do so at more prominent centres such as the sacred city of Anuradhapura.

7

Theology

I cannot remember how I got to this understanding from the experience of seeing the meaning of Mozart's Mass: my recollection of that period is of a convulsive frenzy of mind in which I was overwhelmed by a torrent of ideas new and suddenly recalled, and, as they settled into a pattern, of a quite extraordinarily firm sense of peace. But the link between where it began and what came from it is clear enough. What I divined as Mozart's understanding of the doctrine of the Incarnation is, I believe, quite orthodox; I read it somewhere long ago, though just where I can no longer recall. Perhaps in the same place that I read that the doctrine of the Incarnation is a recapitulation, a modulation, of the doctrine of the Creation. Once one has heard of this, it is exceedingly plain in the Bible. In our pictorial imagery of the Incarnation we regularly depict a dove descending to conceive the Christ. This is quite valid, since in the Bible the dove is a common symbol of the Spirit of God; and, as we know, the angel Gabriel declared to Mary, 'The Holy Ghost shall come upon thee, and the power of the Most High shall overshadow thee: wherefore also that which is to be born shall be called holy, the Son of God.'[1] Now, as is well known, this doctrine of the Incarnation, found more prosaically also in Matthew's Gospel, is not to be found in the earliest of the Gospels we have: in Mark the Sonship of Christ is not by birth inherent, but by adoption in adulthood.[2]* Jesus was baptised of John in the Jordan, 'And straightway coming up out of the water, he saw the heavens rent asunder, and the Spirit as a dove descending upon him: And a voice came out of the heavens, Thou art my beloved Son, in thee I am well pleased.'[3]

Now the imagery here plainly – and designedly – echoes that of the Old Testament story of the emergence of the earth from the waters of Noah's flood; and this[4] is very plainly, even to verbal repetition, a retelling of the story of the Creation in the first chapters of Genesis – one recalls, for example, 'and the spirit of God moved upon the face of the waters'.[5] Of course the link between Incarnation and Creation is made more plainly and directly at the beginning of St. John's Gospel – but there is point in exhibiting the somewhat less plain link in the Synoptic theologies by way of the imagery.

All of which helps only if one understands the doctrine of Creation. We usually understand it as a way of inferring to the existence of God from the character of the world. This is a misreading. To those who made it up, the existence of God was not at issue (see below, Chapter 8): but the character of the world was. They were not asserting that God partakes of the reality that the world has – an impertinent notion – but that the world partakes of the divinity that God has. They were asserting that the world as the creation of God is of its inherent nature good and right – the very same thing that I had come, by a different route, to see in Sri Lanka. Clearly the doctrine of the Incarnation is saying the same thing but with more particular reference to humanity – for Christ, the new Adam, is taken to be the epitome of humanity, and all that follows in the Gospel serves to image what epitomal man should be, and in a sense essentially is.

These are profound religious concepts. They assert, on the one hand, that the world and humanity are already divine, and thus perfect as they are; yet they clearly acknowledge also that this is not so – were not, for example, those who denied Christ and put him to death also human? This apparent paradox is handled through various imageries, which we need not now go into, in the New Testament. The underlying idea is that there are two sorts or levels of truth,[6]* of how things are, and these are both contrasting and interpenetrating. On one level, the more profound and ultimately true, the world and the divine are at one; on another, and more superficial, they are in conflict. These two levels of truth are two ways of apprehending how things are, and the religious message is that the latter is false and wrong: in Christianity it is commonly referred to as 'sin' (a term with much larger meaning than is commonly understood),[7] and in Buddhism more often as 'ignorance' or 'delusion'. What has to be done is to see that what is asserted on the former level is true, profoundly, but not yet fully manifested: it has to be unfolded,[8]* brought to full realisation, through seeing, acting, and wholly living in and by its truth. Christ by his first coming manifested and exhibited the truth, which death and the evil powers of the world could not overcome, for he, the Word, rose from the dead and lives for evermore; but the truth will not be fully realised and brought to completion till he comes again, when the world – that is, how things are as shaped by sin, the false level of truth – will of course pass away: for the three events are one and the same event.

My village Buddhists – or at least a good many of them – recognised the same ideas through their use of the words *lōkōttara* and *laukika*, which I briefly touched on in Chapter 1. As we also saw, the word *'Buddhāgama'* is commonly used to signify Buddhism. The word '*āgama*' is used to refer to (some of) what we would call a 'religion', e.g. to Christianity, Islam, or Hinduism. Though the word is foreign, it has become naturalised; for Buddhists, at any rate, it does not mean just what we mean by 'religion', since its sense is shaped by what is, for them, its primary application, to *Buddhāgama*. When I asked people to say what an *āgama* is, a common reply was that an *āgama* is concerned with *lōkōttara* matters as contrasted with *laukika* matters. Similarly, when I asked them if the cults of the gods and so forth were an *āgama* they said no, because these were concerned with *laukika* matters – and for the same reason they were no part of *Buddhāgama*. Similarly Buddhism, and elements of it, such as Nirvana, were often referred to as *lōkōttara*. Now these terms, *lōkōttara* and *laukika*, both derive from the word '*lōkaya*', 'world'. *Laukika* means 'worldly', and seems to be used very much as the English word is used, mainly evaluatively: worldliness is to perceive and evaluate reality as a man normally does who has not been enlightened by religion. The way my informants usually glossed the word '*lōkōttara*' was a little odd, and would require lengthier explanation than I wish to give at this point (I take it up below, Chapter 14). However their usage of the word corresponded to the meaning given in Carter's Sinhalese–English Dictionary, which is: 'pre-eminent in the world, the opposite of *laukika*',[9] and indeed a number of my informants did gloss it as 'the opposite of *laukika*'. In that sense one is tempted to translate it as 'sacred', with Ames (1964a); this is not necessarily wrong, but if the sacred is understood as too radically distinct from the world, it can be misleading. For the first phrase that Carter gives also expresses a necessary part of the meaning. Simply in evaluative terms, the *lōkōttara* refers to those values most radically contrasted with worldly, secular values; but at the same time the place of the *lōkōttara* is to be pre-eminent *in* the world. The religion which is *lōkōttara* must be in the world but not of the world.

I must, however, point out that it is uncertain how far the contrast between *lōkōttara* and *laukika* is standard in Sinhalese village Buddhism. Because Ames (1964a) implied that the terms were freely used by the people among whom he worked in southern Sri Lanka, I was not surprised when I encountered them in Polgama. Gombrich, however, who worked in villages near Kandy, reports that 'these terms are pure Sanskrit, and purely learned; I have never heard them used in conversation, and to most villagers they are not even intelligible'.[10] While I did not systematically test my informants for knowledge of these terms, they were certainly in common use in Polgama, and I do not know why my experience should have differed from that of Gombrich. Mine was not an area renowned for its learning; indeed, a senior Buddhist ecclesiastic described it to me as one in which 'religion is undeveloped'. The currency of the terms could well have been the product of the teaching of an

influential priest, or even schoolteacher, in which case there would be no
way of predicting whether they are or are not in use in other areas.

The terms are used in the village Buddhism of which I have first-hand
knowledge, and probably in that of some other areas. In considering how
far I may generalise from my observations, I would suggest that the
currency of terms is less important than that of concepts. If the pair of
terms '*lōkōttara*' and '*laukika*' is pure Sanskrit, there is another pair,
'*paralova*' and '*melova*', which is pure Sinhala (Elu). I registered these
terms on only one occasion, in a sermon I tape-recorded, in which they
were freely used and with the evident expectation that they would be
familiar to the audience; they may have been used more commonly
without my noting them. '*Lova*' is the Elu (non-Sanskritic Sinhala) form
of '*lōkaya*', 'a world', and '*melova*', meaning 'worldly, earthly, mundane,
secular', is synonymous with '*laukika*'; '*paralo*', which I take to be a
variant form of '*paralova*', means 'pertaining to the other world or next
life', as does '*lōkōttara*' in common usage.[11] Thus the contrasting pair of
concepts is not purely Sanskritic, but anciently established in Sinhala.
Moreover, as I argue with different reference below, when we know that a
concept is established in a culture, we may, and sometimes must, assume
it to be implicit in the thought of people formed in that culture, even
without direct evidence that they know it consciously.

In practice and in thought, in Buddhist and in other cultures, it proves
very difficult to maintain the balance between these two sides of the
concept: that is, on the one hand that the *lōkōttara* or holy is radically
contrasted with and opposed to the worldly, yet on the other hand that it
is pre-eminent in the world, mastering and transforming the world. These
two sides are termed in Christian theology Transcendence and
Immanence: which helps to focus on the need for both. In practice all too
often the balance slips, so that one gets overstressed at the expense of the
other. When Transcendence is overstressed, unduly emphasising the
separation between the holy and the mundane, then two bad
consequences follow: the world, God's creation, is degraded and despised,
while the holy is worshipped in a way which makes it irrelevant to our
lives in the world. That is the Manichaean tendency.[12*]

It seems to me marked, or at the very least insufficiently guarded
against, in Durkheim's conception of religion. The major part of his
definition of religion is: 'A religion is a unified system of beliefs and
practices relative to sacred things, that is to say, things set apart and
forbidden. . . .'[13] A little earlier he had written: 'But the real
characteristic of religious phenomena is that they always suppose a
bipartite division of the whole universe, known and knowable, into two
classes which embrace all that exists, but which radically exclude each
other.'[14] Even more extremely, he had written:

there is nothing left with which to characterise the sacred in its relation to the profane except their heterogeneity. However, this heterogeneity is sufficient to characterise this classification of things and to distinguish it from all others, because it is very particular: *it is absolute*. In all the history of human thought there exists no other example of two categories of things so profoundly differentiated or so radically opposed to one another.[15]

There do seem to be *some* religious phenomena which at least approximate to this description; I propose that they are, in terms of what I have argued, pathological. Moreover, they appear to me to be associated with pathological states of society, in particular situations where, as in exilic and post-exilic Israel, or in India, an arrogant priesthood is too sharply separated from the real centres of political power. If, which I doubt, Durkheim was correct in finding such absolute heterogeneity in the religion of the Australian aborigines, I would associate it with the extreme form that the sexual division of labour tends to take in hunting-gathering societies.

It is not to be doubted that such tendencies, of a broadly Manichaean kind, have been manifested in Buddhism. I find them not only in the exaggerated normative celibacy of the clergy, but also in the temptation, to which some have yielded, to indulge in isolated meditative self-cultivation, letting the world go hang.[16*] I sense it in the term which directly follows '*lōkōttara*' in Carter's Dictionary: *lōkōttara-vittaya*: 'the mind exalted above the world by religious meditation and attainments'. In my observation, this distortion of Buddhism seems to be notably associated with English-speaking, middle-class Sinhalese; when I offer a few remarks about their socio-cultural situation it will, I think, be evident enough in what relevant ways it is pathological (Chapter 10). On the other hand, I found little trace of this disorder among typical village Buddhists – indeed, it was the integration in their lives of the spiritual with the earthy, a religion thoroughly in the world, which I found so attractive. As we shall see (Chapter 9), this has been predominantly characteristic of actual Buddhism throughout history – one aspect of which is nicely exemplified in the next entry in Carter's Dictionary: '*lōkōttaraya*: the world's chief or most exalted one, viz. king'.[17]

On the other hand, in religion the Immanent also may be unduly stressed. The sense of peace and community of beings that marks the nirvanic experience is false if it leads to evasion of the reality of conflict, and to quietism; just as, 'we know that to them that love God all things work together for good' (Rom. 8, v. 28) can become the 'All is for the best in this best of all possible worlds' of Dr. Pangloss.

Perhaps the most emphatic statement of Immanence in the Buddhist tradition is the much-quoted aphorism of the great Mahāyānist philosopher Nāgārjuna: 'There is nothing whatever which differentiates

samsāra (existence in flux, the phenomenal world) from Nirvana; And
there is nothing whatever which differentiates Nirvana from *samsāra* . . .
There is not the slightest bit of difference between these two.'[18] This can
be said truly – much as Durkheim's contrary overstatement might be
justified – and no doubt Nāgārjuna himself understood the necessary
counterpoint. But it is not entirely a coincidence that the Mahāyānism
which produced such statements was also the Mahāyānism which lost its
fibre in antinomianism. In Sinhalese village Buddhism at least, though it
has some traits more usually associated with Mahāyāna[19] – several
educated Buddhists told me it was Mahāyāna in large part – the heavy
stress laid on ethics as the basis of religion is a bulwark against this.

Between these extremes a middle way must be found. I thought it was
found by Sārānanda, the priest about whom I remarked that I always felt
a certain aura of saintliness. He was Principal of the *pirivena* (seminary)
at Dodangola, a few miles from Polgama. I knew he was very busy as a
priest and administrator, as a teacher and in social service – at his temple
he cares for boys who have been convicted in the courts and placed on
probation – but I felt he would have liked to have more time to devote to
meditation. I asked him if he had ever thought he would like to go and live
at an *āranña* – a monastery for meditating monks. He replied that he did
have an idea to do so (*adahassak tiyenavā*), but that if he did all the
laymen would complain that they had no one to attend to their needs. He
explained to me the difference between the two recognised vocations for
clergy, the vocation of meditation, which is followed by the meditating
monks, and that of teaching, which is followed by the teaching priests
such as himself (see below, Chapter 9). More tolerantly than Sīlaratana,
he said they were both equally good roads to Nirvana,[20]* but the first is
like a man travelling with a light pack, and the second like a man with a
heavy pack: both will arrive together, but the latter will be more tired. I
asked him if he would agree some analogy between a cleric's life and
higher education, with meditation compared to research. Yes indeed, he
said, the best course is to combine meditation with teaching: then you
really know what you are teaching about.

The last sentence in Evans-Pritchard's *Nuer Religion* reads: 'At this
point the theologian takes over from the anthropologist.'[21] I have heard
my anthropologist colleagues sardonically say, and more often imply,
that it would have stood more justly as the first sentence. I have laid
myself open to the same condemnation. There are two separable issues
here. Is it appropriate to draw upon the theology indigenous to a given
religious tradition to interpret the empirical religion of ordinary people
within that tradition, who are probably quite unfamiliar with its
theology? And, even if it is, can it be appropriate to use the theology of one
religious tradition to interpret empirical religion in a different and

effectively independent tradition?

I am not the first to have drawn upon philosophical Buddhism in interpreting empirical Buddhism, but the precedents are not wholly encouraging. On the contrary, I agree with Leach that failure to distinguish clearly enough between 'philosophical' Buddhism and 'practical' Buddhism has led to serious distortions.[22] But if it is a perilous enterprise, I suggest that this is because it is easy to go wrong, not because it is impossible to go right. The real issue is one of basic theoretical and methodological importance: is it legitimate, in analysing what ordinary people – here villagers – do and say, to bring into account philosophy and doctrine of which they are probably unaware? Until recently I should have been fairly clear that it is not. But I have now too often had the experience of reading Buddhist materials of which I am virtually certain my villagers have no knowledge, and finding that what I read there makes clear sense of what otherwise seemed trivial or incomprehensible in actual village Buddhism. For example, I pointed out above (Chapter 3) that I found incomprehensible Silaratana's claim that his commitment to social service was warranted by the Buddha's charge to his disciples to go out and teach the Dhamma to the multitudes. When I read the Edicts of Asoka it became clear, even obvious, to me, as did some other features of actual Buddhism (I explain this later, Chapter 12). Now I am virtually certain that Silaratana has never read the Edicts of Asoka, and quite certain that never once in conversation with me did he as much as mention them. If he ever mentioned Asoka at all, it was not in a way significant enough to have seemed worth noting. From village Buddhists generally I did occasionally hear the name of Asoka mentioned. I imagine they have all heard of him, since they often talk of the Mahinda who brought Buddhism to Sri Lanka, and he was in fact sent by Asoka, whose son he is normally claimed – in Buddhist literature – to have been. Gombrich shows that a book on the 'History of Buddhism' was used in teaching in the Buddhist Sunday school in the village where he lived,[23] and this cannot have failed to deal with Asoka; probably the same is true of the courses in Buddhism which younger villagers have taken in the Government schools; it may well be true of the teaching that novices in the Sangha receive from their Teachers. But if much of this is remembered, I saw little sign of it; and I think it improbable that any text of the Edicts is studied by pupils or indeed by their teachers.

Now to suppose that the harmony between the Edicts and what one actually observes in village Buddhism is purely coincidental, and therefore cannot be invoked in explanation, seems to me quite implausible. But, if the connection cannot be attributed to conscious knowledge by the villagers, how else can it be thought of? I am very much aware of the perils of unduly reifying, or mystifying, the concepts of 'culture' or 'collective representations'. However, it cannot be doubted that a language, any language, exhibits exceedingly complex, rich, and subtle structures and patterns of which most, even all, speakers of the language have no conscious awareness: so much so that even intelligent and educated persons, as I found in Buganda, may be unable to recognise the most obvious grammatical 'rules' of their own language when they are put to them. Yet they very certainly 'know' these 'rules' in the sense that their own speech regularly conforms to them; further, they could and did at once recognise an infringement of these 'rules', as by me, and told me what I should have said – without being able to explain why one usage was correct and the other not, or even to make sense of the applicable grammatical rule when I stated it. (This is less obvious among ourselves because we are taught English grammar in school: but it is only necessary to take up some 'rule' which is not included in such teaching to see that the same is true of us.) It is thus entirely plausible to make similar assumptions regarding culture: that there are all manner of assumptions and structures implicit in a culture which are known to those who live that culture in the same kind of unconscious but very real way that the grammatical 'rules' of their language are known to them. Just as grammarians and linguists may make explicit the otherwise implicit 'rules' and structures of a language, so may philosophers and theologians the implicit bases of the culture; just as the students of a language may take as texts the works of celebrated authors in the language, so may we utilise – with due caution – in our study of a culture the acts and edicts of its statesmen. It matters little whether Asoka learnt his concept of Dharma formally from teachers, or whether he formulated it for himself from his own understanding of the Buddhist culture; it is not even crucial to determine what causative effect Asoka's ideas had, through his acts and Edicts, on the further development of Buddhist civilisation, large as this seems to have been. It is proper, even necessary, to think of a culture, and indeed an historical civilisation, as having a large enough distinctive character, identity, and organic unity to warrant our using one element of it to assist in our understanding of another, although no direct causal connection is demonstrable or even conceivable. One can indeed make many mistakes in applying this method, but this does not show that all applications are mistaken. The test must be by the results, and in principle an explanation which shows actual Buddhists to be authentic Buddhists and intelligent people is to be preferred to one which too hastily assumes them to be ignorant, disloyal, or foolish.[24]* It is by a broadly similar principle that I have, with I hope due caution, drawn upon my own Buddhist experience to illuminate village Buddhism.

To go further, as I have, and use Christian theology in analysing empirical Buddhism, cannot be justified on this basis, and may perhaps appear altogether indefensible in an anthropologist. It appears so because the anthropological tradition has tended to assume that religion is, in the end, nonsense, and Theology the elaboration thereof. I dissent. In my view, while religion and Theology are at least as much rife with error as any other branch of human activity, they are not inherently and essentially erroneous. I see religion as a response to genuine experience, and a valid mode of cognition; and take Theology to be as relevant and useful to the analysis of religious behaviour as, say, Economics is to the analysis of economic behaviour, or Political Science to that of political behaviour. Seeing religion as a human response to genuine realities, I expect to find that in different parts of the world similar human beings will respond to a similar reality in similar ways, whatever the superficial differences of cultural idioms through which these responses are mediated, just as we find basic similarities in human responses to common problems of political organisation. As few would reject political theory, formulated mainly with respect to our own polities, as necessarily inapplicable to the analysis of other polities, so I consider it unreasonable to assume *a priori* that Christian Theology can have no applicability to the analysis of religion in other traditions. This in no way guarantees that my own application of it has been sound – it must be judged on its merits; it argues only that attempting such an application is not necessarily unsound.

Notes to Chapter 7

1   Luke 1, v. 35 (R.V.).
2   On another interpretation, at his baptism his sonship was recognised. But in the stories, if not also the theology, what Luke attributes to the conception of Jesus Mark presents in the account of his baptism.
3   Mark 1, vv. 10–11 (R.V.).
4   Genesis 8–9.
5   Genesis 1, v. 2 (R.V.).
6   This is explicit and important in Buddhist philosophy: see, e.g., Rahula (1967), p. 55; Gudmunsen (1977), p. 37.
7   See, for example, Richardson (1957), pp. 226–9.
8   Cf. Bohm (1980). I recognise a considerable debt to Bohm's book, which does not emerge from specific references.
9   Carter (1924), p. 555.
10   Gombrich (1971), p. 58.
11   Carter (1924), pp. 554, 511, 358.
12   Manichaeism was a religion of the Ancient World. It was radically dualistic, holding that God and the good were opposed by an independent principle of evil essentially associated with matter: hence its adherents tended towards a rigorous asceticism seeking freedom from the material, fleshly, aspects of humanity (see Flew, 1979, p. 202). Here and elsewhere I use the term 'Manichaean' to denote and disparage a tendency to similar dualism in any religion.

13 Durkheim (1915), p. 47; (1912), p. 65.
14 Durkheim (1915), p. 40; (1912), p. 56.
15 Durkheim (1915), p. 38; (1912), p. 53; italics in original.
16 These seem to me largely variations on a single theme. The same is implicit in Spiro's analysis of the emotional characteristics of his untypical sample of monks (1971, pp. 337–50).
17 On the importance of kings, and more generally the political order, in actual Buddhism, see especially Ling (1973) and Tambiah (1976).
18 From the version quoted in Gudmunsen (1977, p. 43); I have slightly rearranged the wording, and added the phrase 'the phenomenal world'.
19 There are some suggestions of this also in Gombrich (1971): notably pp. 64, 222–3, 321.
20 This was said to me by several village clergy, and is probably a standard formula.
21 1956, p. 322.
22 Leach (1968a), p. 1.
23 1971, p. 336.
24 Gellner has argued at length that anthropologists are motivated to show the ideas of the people they study to be sensible, and that their techniques for doing so by suitable selection of contexts are too powerful, so that what is actually absurd or incoherent is not recognised as such (Gellner, 1973). I cannot fault his argument. I do think, however, that it is too easy and common to dismiss what we cannot understand in other people by attributing it to their incapacity rather than our own; that more is lost by underestimating than by overestimating the good sense of other people; and that when we have difficulty in understanding another culture it is more likely to be because we have failed to grasp its structure than because it actually is incoherent. I have been impressed by the intelligence I have found in people of other cultures, which is only superficially obscured by their relative ignorance and lack of sophistication: indeed, I have often felt they are wiser than we. Hence I consider that the burden of proof should lie with those who propose the folly of other peoples rather than with those who assume their good sense. At worst, if I have exaggerated the good sense of village Buddhists, it is a useful corrective to more usual assumptions.

8

Existence, symbolism, and belief

It may also seem odd that Christian theology played so large a part in enabling me to make sense of my experience when, as I wrote above (Chapter 4), 'for me He simply does not exist'; the more so as it functioned not just as a cold intellectual theory, but as revelation I warmly endorsed as true. I believed in God while believing He does not exist. As this seems quite paradoxical in terms of our ordinary understanding of belief, it may serve as an entry to an important aspect of the concept.

I am aware that the question whether God – or for that matter any comparable religious posit – does or does not exist is not, as it is so often taken to be, a theological problem about God, but rather a philosophical problem about 'exists'. It should be resolved, both because our naive use of the latter concept seriously confuses our understanding of belief, and because notions of existence are closely related to those of factuality, which we have already seen to be entailed in what we call 'belief'.

Russell cleared up much of the logical confusion when he pointed out that 'exist' must not be taken, as it so often had been, as a predicate or attribute (like 'bald', 'good', 'swims', etc.) but as a quantifier.[1] There is, however, more to be said. In the normal sense of the words, to say that something 'exists' is to say that it is an 'object'. It is not a mere pun to say that an object is basically that which objects: objects, that is, to being messed about by our minds in perception and, to a lesser extent, in conceptual thought. Objectness (could we not say 'objection'?) is, in Durkheim's terminology,[2] registered by us as 'constraint'. In its philosophical senses, the dictionary (SOED), derives the word 'object' from the medieval Scholastic Latin '*objectum*', literally 'thing thrown before (the mind)', which is nice.

If it is meaningful to say that something exists, it must be meaningful to say that something does not exist: hence these 'somethings' are not themselves objects but rather concepts, mental constructs. 'Exists', then, links a concept to a recognised constraint, a postulated object in the world of 'reality', the world out there, the 'object world'. Normally we call this the material or physical world. These terms once supposed, and may still suggest, that the world out there is constituted of matter or bodies, which is to assume too much.

There are three philosophical questions to be asked, which too often are not clearly enough distinguished. The first is whether there actually is any world out there, independent of our minds but throwing up constraints upon them – as against supposing instead that our experience, our phenomenal world, is entirely generated by our minds. The second, assuming that there is such an independent reality, is of how best we should represent it in our minds. The third, again assuming an affirmative answer to the first, is of how we should conceive of the relation between the world out there and our mental representations: can we take it to be one of correspondence and reflection, so that the world out there is, in structure at least, just like the mental representation that we have of it?

In our own philosophical tradition, at least as it is commonly understood by non-philosophers, there are two main positions. Idealism answers no to the first question – there is no independent world out there – and hence the other two questions do not arise. Realism – sometimes, Materialism – answers yes to the first question and to the third, and thus effectively dissolves the second: obviously we should represent the world so as to reflect its actual structure.

The position adopted by some of the schools of Buddhist philosophy lies between these two, and is more interesting. The answer to the first question is yes, there is a constraining reality beyond our minds. The answer to the third question is no, at least for normal thought: there is no isomorphic correspondence.[3*] Hence it is the second question, neglected by both the main Western positions, which becomes the one of principal interest. Two of the greatest of the Buddhist philosophers, Dignāga and Dharmakīrti,[4*] with others of their school, maintained that the character of what is out there – the existent – is thoroughly unlike the way we normally represent it in our minds: it is made up neither of matter nor of bodies, but of quanta (*kṣana*) of energy in constant flux. The concepts of objects, etc., by which we represent the existent in our minds are hypotheses we construct to account for the constraints we experience from the existent: they respond but they do not correspond to it. Whether, as Stcherbatsky implies, these philosophers really had worked out the basic picture of quantum physics more than a millennium before we did is a question of some interest, but not our present concern. It is more important to remark that their position, in more or less sophisticated form, is basic to most of Buddhist thought and goes back to its earliest philosophical presentation: if the role of the Buddha in creating the system has not been grossly exaggerated, to the Buddha himself. The view of the existent as a flux, without permanence, is that expressed by *anicca*, philosophically the basic Buddhist concept – and actually encountered in village Buddhism today.[5]* Necessarily with this goes the view that the shape and form, the array of objects in terms of which we see the existent, is a mental construct, hypothetical, which responds but does not correspond to it. There is no point in arguing about this: as a consequence not only of quantum physics but also of research into the physiology and psychology of perception[6] it is clearly established as correct. The practical consequence for life that Buddhists drew was that since our mental representation of the existent world was simply a hypothetical construct, by no means guaranteed by correspondence (isomorphism), it might well be improved by substituting better hypotheses. But more: our conventional representation was not merely fallible but false, and in its assumption of stable enduring separate entities – 'objects' – and in particular, selves, was the source of all that was wrong: it not only might but must be changed for a representation which more adquately represented the flux, the impermanence of the existent – *anicca*, impermanence, which when applied to the nature of ourselves is *anatta*, no enduring self.

Now from this point of view questions about existence turn out to be no longer as straightforward as we take them to be: they confuse the two questions, whether the concept responds to constraints in the existent, and whether it is an adequate representation for our purpose. If it is asked whether such everyday objects as chairs and tables exist, the answer must be in two parts: yes, the concepts (percepts) do respond to genuine constraints; and, yes, they are an adequate representation for everyday mundane purposes – but not for all purposes. If now we ask whether God exists, we have to interpret the question in the same way – that is, as asking about the relation between the concept and the physical world (giving 'physical' the wider sense which covers quantum physics). The answer is evidently dubious. Yes, the concept does respond well enough to constraints from the existent – but not so well as to single it out as the uniquely preferred hypothesis – as chairs and tables are uniquely preferred hypotheses – even for mundane purposes. It is usable but not indispensable. For more sophisticated purposes it is even less well-favoured: as Laplace famously replied when asked why he did not mention God in his system of celestial mechanics, 'I had no need of that hypothesis.' Laplace, however, was no atheist, but a religious man.[7] This might remind us that the principal use of the God-hypothesis never has been in physics even of the most commonsense kind; hence nothing of significance is lost by deciding to regard Him not as a physical object, i.e. as not existing in the ordinary sense.

The basic sense of 'exist', then, is to express the fact that we consider ourselves more or less obliged to use a concept because it best responds to a constraint originating from the physical world. But there are other ways in which a concept may come to seem more or less obligatory, and this also may be registered by talking of existence – in a different sense, though this may not be noticed. A very striking and important case is that which might be termed 'cultural existence'. If a concept – say, that of God – is established in a culture, and if everyone in that culture believes it and acts on that belief: then for all purposes involving people it is virtually as if God existed, in the first sense. If one lived among such people, in order to interact with them one would need constantly to refer to the concept: and the obligatoriness of the concept, deriving from the constraint rooted in the expectation and assumptions of others, would not easily be distinguished from that deriving from physical constraint, as in the first and main sense.[8]*

Similarly, a concept may acquire a quasi-obligatory character from the fact that it has become so axiomatic in our thinking that we can hardly think without it. This may happen with religious ideas, such as God or Nirvana; but what is much more characteristic of them is a comparable process which is best described in other terms. Such ideas function more usually and importantly less as intellectual concepts than as what may be loosely termed 'symbols'. Most often we think of a symbol as something which stands for something else, whether as index, sign, metaphor, substitute, or however. No doubt that is a legitimate application of the word 'symbol', and no doubt religious ideas function in that way, among others. But I am arguing that the principal function of major religious ideas is that of 'symbols' in a very different sense, namely that of Sperber (1975). Sperber argues that such a symbol functions mainly in the organisation of cognition. It seems to me that Sperber's account of this suffers from an undue weighting towards intellectual and rational matters: in truth it is not only, or even mainly, cognition, conceptual representation, that such symbols serve to organise. They organise, in addition to conceptual representation, all that field of representation and expression which Langer covers by her term 'presentational symbolism',[9] which covers at least the whole field of the arts, not least the active arts such as dancing, and its extension or analogue in what we more usually call 'ritual'. Further, they organise the emotions, moods, and dispositions, evaluation, conation and conduct; still more widely they organise what may be somewhat loosely gestured at as life and being. I cannot think of any simple term which specifically and precisely refers to this vast area: it is something of which we may apprehend the identity without having available an adequate terminology to describe or designate. Because of this, any description which is sufficiently comprehensive will be loose and open to misunderstanding. With that caution, it may be constructive to say that a symbol of this kind functions in the interpretation of experience. I have very much in mind the way Lienhardt (1961) analyses the functions of Dinka religious symbols, or 'figures' or 'images' – without implying that he has exhausted the possibilities of this very fruitful approach.

Most insightfully, Sperber keys his view of symbolism to what is implicit in the way the Ndembu speak of these matters:

> Moreover, to take the view suggested here is merely to follow the metaphorical expression that the Ndembu use to designate symbols: the word *chijikijilu*, which means 'a landmark'. A landmark is not a sign but an index which serves cognitively to organise our experience of space. This Ndembu metaphor seems much more apposite and subtle to me than the Western metaphor which compares symbols to words.[10]

I wholly agree; to me it seems that Sperber has here made a fundamental breakthrough in our understanding of the functions of religious ideas. He is saying that just as a landmark is a point of reference by which we orient ourselves in space, by which we impose upon our perceptual representation of the terrain an order or structure by means of which we can interpret and plan and organise our relevant activity (here chiefly locomotion), so is a symbol a point of reference, an anchor for imposed or imputed structure, for our organised interpretation of experience and our plans for acting on it: for our model *of* and our model *for* 'reality' (better, 'experience'), in Geertz's admirable analysis.[11] I suggest that since the word 'symbol' is, legitimately, used in several very different senses, it would be useful to specialise a term to signify just this one, critically important, sense. I shall, following the suggestion of the Ndembu metaphor, use the term 'Mark' for this purpose. In my usage, then, a Mark is a religious idea which functions as a basic or crucial anchor for a scheme or system of interpreting experience (in the very wide sense gestured at above). Its role is not unlike that of an axiom in conceptual thought.

There is in fact more to be extracted from the Ndembu usage of their term *chijikijilu* than Sperber has utilised. Curiously, Turner, who has reported the facts, seems himself to have misunderstood them; of the Ndembu application of the term he writes, 'Its ritual use is already metaphorical. ... It makes intelligible what is mysterious, and also dangerous.'[12] To suggest – if that is what these words were intended to mean – that a *chijikijilu*, a 'symbol', is like a metaphor is to miss the much more important point that Sperber has grasped.[13]* However, Turner does tell us that another, and apparently more original, sense of the Ndembu word is a hunter's 'blaze'. There is an interesting difference here: whereas a landmark is normally something given in the perceptual field and then *selected* for the purpose of organising it, a hunter's blaze is something deliberately created by a man for just this purpose. The first metaphor, of the landmark, suggests that the idea was already present before it came to be used as a Mark. In many cases this may well be the best analogy for the actual historical process of the development of the religion: thus it seems to me probable, at least, that the idea of God had been present for the early Hebrews on a quite crude basis, having the factuality perhaps of physical existence, certainly of cultural existence: and it was then taken up and elaborated as a Mark in the ways of which the Bible is testimony. But it is useful also to consider the possibility that some ideas may be created – analogously with a hunter's blaze – primarily in order to serve as Marks.

A third Ndembu meaning for their word, cited by Turner, is also suggestive: a 'beacon'. Although this does *not* seem to be the Ndembu sense, 'beacon' in the ordinary English sense strikes me as a valuable metaphor for part of the way a Mark may function, especially when Transcendence is stressed. A beacon is, or at least may be, something towards which we travel without expectation or even intention of actually arriving there. A still clearer metaphor is that of a 'lodestar', the 'Pole-star'. When mariners steered by the Pole-star it certainly was not with any expectation of reaching it – rather of reaching some sublunary but accessible destination, such as a port, which they could not attain by steering directly towards it. I think this is a very important aspect of the idea of Nirvana in Buddhism: no right-minded person expects to attain it, in normal circumstances, but it is important to set one's course by it in order to reach attainable destinations.

Now when we regularly and with commitment utilise and rely upon a Mark to interpret experience we come to feel constrained to do so: we feel we could not do without it. And such constraint too may be felt as a kind of existence, which we might perhaps term 'interpretative existence'. It is mainly in this sense, to the extent that I do use Christian symbolism, that God 'exists' for me. I had better point out that I am not advocating that we should frequently use such expressions as 'cultural existence' or 'interpretative existence'; on the contrary, it is more prudent to use the word 'exist' only in the sense in which it is normally understood, that of physical existence. The expressions I have coined are useful only as a way of noting that our sense of existence may derive from different kinds of factor.

A Christian might say that while what I have said about the function of the idea of God as a Mark is true as far as it goes, when he asserts or implies that God exists he means more than that this Mark has become indispensable for him. When he says that Jesus Christ was Son of God he is not only indicating his commitment to this particular myth: he means what he says as a truth about history. Quite so; the point of the doctrine of the Incarnation is not merely to entertain the Marks, it is to apply them: it is not only to consider and reverence divinity, it is to say that mankind partakes in divinity. Indeed; but as we saw, this is primarily a statement about humanity rather than about God. The function of such a statement is to make an unshakable commitment to applying this Mark to all our experience of humanity. The result looks exactly like an historical statement, but it is not, it is a theological statement applied in wholeness and commitment to the world. If it were an historical statement its basis would have to be historical evidence (of which there is virtually none); but as it is a theological statement its basis is Faith, i.e. commitment to taking this view of the world. This distinction is hard to grasp but fundamentally important. A Christian who knows what he is about is not asserting the physical existence of God, as one might that of a chair: but he is maintaining that God is real, though he has arrived at this position by a quite different route.

Since the Christian idiom is credible and attractive to me, it may seem odd that I converted to Buddhism although, for the sake of the objectivity of my research, I resisted doing so, while I have never been able to identify myself for long as a Christian, though I have tried to do so. As this is not a matter of public interest I shall not review the various factors involved. I would, however, draw attention to one, which is evident enough in the account I have given. I was drawn to Buddhism because I liked and admired the Buddhists I knew. For the most part I cannot say the same with respect to the Christians I know, but rather sympathise with the remark attributed to Mahatma Gandhi: 'We should all be Christian if it were not for the Christians.'

This illustrates a more general point which, if it is sound, has a large bearing on the way we should understand a range of religious phenomena. I suggest that a person converts to a religion mainly because he wishes to associate with its adherents, and stays converted to the extent that he finds such association gratifying. That a person deconverts from a religion because he wishes to be dissociated from its adherents – and/or associated with its non-adherents. And that a person remains in a religion in which he has grown up largely, but not entirely, because he wants or needs to associate with his co-religionists.

This hypothesis seems to me to explain – though it is not the only explanation – the remarkable stability of religions in traditional societies. I found that a fair number of village Buddhists were extremely sceptical of a variety of tenets which were not central in their religious culture,[14] and I wondered why none of them revealed, even to me privately, radical scepticism about Buddhism as such. It seemed quite clear to me that in communities such as these, where a man is highly dependent on his kinsfolk and neighbours, he could have little motive for dissociating himself from them, and powerful motives for not doing so; hence he was virtually obliged to participate at least outwardly in Buddhist practices; and since if one acts as though one believes . . . , there was no practical possibility of sustaining scepticism.[15*] On less central matters, a number of people told us plainly that, for example, they did not believe in the gods, or did not believe that it was necessary to have Buddhist clergy at funerals; but when I asked them whether they engaged in the cult of the gods, or would invite priests to a funeral in the family, they regularly said they did, or would, 'because of what other people would think'.[16*]

There are two points involved here. The first is that participation in religious forms of life is largely determined by social factors: by one's need, or wish, to associate or not with other participants, which itself is more or less restricted by the availability of practicable alternative fields of association. The second is that belief or unbelief, so far from being the independent variable in determining religious adherence which we commonly take it to be, is itself largely determined by religious participation, which in turn is largely determined by constraints on association. The more one is led or obliged to associate with 'believers' the more 'belief' becomes inevitable and scepticism impossible.

In a notable, and noted, passage in his *Nuer Religion* Evans-Pritchard remarked that one hears every day among the Nuer the affirmation '*kwoth a thin*', 'God is present'. He commented: 'The phrase does not mean "there is a God". That would be for Nuer a pointless remark. God's existence is taken for granted by everybody.'[17]

The situation was evidently similar in the societies which produced our Bible. Nowhere in all that book is the question – that is, what we perceive as a question – of God's existence ever discussed. So inconceivable was it that God might not exist that merely to mention the proposition it was necessary to attribute it to the insane: 'The fool hath said in his heart, there is no God.'[18] This is why I remarked (above, Chapter 7) that we misapprehend the original significance of the doctrine of Creation if we take it as a way of proving that God exists: that would have been for the Hebrews a pointless exercise.

Most probably, this is the normal situation in societies in which we encounter living religions. I remarked, for example, that for Sinhalese Buddhists the reality of rebirth rather plainly has this kind of unquestionable factuality; and, in the same context, that for us the unreality of rebirth has the same kind of factuality (above, Chapter 4). As this illustrates, it is not only religious tenets which may acquire such an aura of factuality as to make their truth axiomatic. What I have called the conventional judgement on village Buddhism, for example, tends to appear in this light (see above, Chapter 6).

As I shall argue at some length later, it is misleading to speak of tenets, of which the truth is taken for granted in this fashion, as 'beliefs'. Though their adherents hold them as true, to describe this as 'believing' is to suggest an inappropriate image of the cognitive attitudes involved. Evans-Pritchard indicated this when, after the observation quoted above, he remarked that the Nuer attitude to God must be understood as one of 'faith', in the Old Testament sense, not of 'belief' in its modern sense; and by his remarkable forbearance from using belief-terms throughout his account of Nuer religion. It was, however, in an earlier work that he had more centrally and seminally analysed the bases of belief and scepticism in the magico-religious system of another culture.

The central problem of Evans-Pritchard's *Witchcraft, Oracles and Magic among the Azande* (1937) is why it is that the Azande do not become radically sceptical of their 'mystical', i.e. magico-religious, notions. In a passage which amounts to a synopsis of the whole analysis, he lists no fewer than twenty-two reasons,[19] many of which apply to the persistence of mystical notions, or indeed any kind of dubitable notions, in any culture. It would be absurd for me to attempt to present his whole analysis here; the book itself is indispensable reading for anyone interested in these matters. I shall, however, take up a few of his points which are of immediate relevance.

Azande certainly do have experiences which conflict with the established notions of their culture; we might suppose that this would lead them to infer that the notions must be wrong, which Azande certainly have the intellectual capacity to do.[20] But logically it is also possible to reason to a different conclusion, and Evans-Pritchard tells us that this is what Azande normally do: 'An individual experience when it contradicts accepted opinion does not prove accepted opinion to be untrue, but merely that the individual experience is peculiar and inadequate.'[21] There are several factors which lead Azande to take this course of inference; in my view the most important is that the accepted opinion has so much force of cultural factuality that it is harder for a Zande to suppose it could be wrong than it is for him to suppose his experience is peculiar. And it seems to him to have such force because he supposes all his fellows believe it without reservation. Understandably he does not care to tell other people about his experience that he has judged 'peculiar and inadequate'; and the same will be true for any other individual who has a similar experience, 'for one does not discuss matters of this kind with one's friends'.[22] Hence no one ever finds out that such experiences, so far from being peculiar, are common, almost universal.

There certainly are instances where individual Azande reason from their own experience that there is something wrong with what (they suppose) everyone else believes. But in such cases a wise man keeps his opinion to himself so as not to antagonise his fellows.[23] This is because they see perfectly well that someone who objects to received conventional beliefs is far more likely to be regarded as discrediting himself than the beliefs. In consequence, scepticism on important beliefs is never expressed by people whose views would be respected by others; hence an individual never realises that his own private scepticism may be shared by many others whom he would respect. There are of course many other reasons, which Evans-Pritchard sets out, why scepticism about the mystical notions does not develop to the point where it might challenge the whole system. Here, I am only drawing attention to the fact that scepticism tends to remain private, and hence does not coalesce into an alternative viewpoint shared, and known to be shared, by a significant minority; and that because of this, individual sceptics mistakenly suppose that everyone else accepts the conventional beliefs more wholeheartedly than in fact they do.

Now the intellectual capacity to reason from experience right through to the conclusion that the system of beliefs in which one has been reared might well be wrong – this is rare; rare too is the courage it needs to accept for oneself such a demoralising conclusion about one's own culture, and to stand up against one's fellows and publicly declare one's own conclusion. My own assessment, based on my own impressions of people in two societies other than our own, is that these gifts may be no rarer among them than among ourselves. Suppose we assume that they are found in only one or two per cent of the members of a normal human population. Now in a small-scale society in which people live in relatively isolated communities numbering at most a few hundred people, the public scepticism of the rare individuals will appear to be a matter of the oddity of one or two eccentric individuals, easily to be dismissed as such – which of course will further discourage them from speaking their minds. But in a society where communications are better it will be much more apparent, to the sceptics and to others, that such scepticism, rare as it is in any local community, is significantly common in the wider-scale society.

As this suggests, analysis of the reasons why scepticism fails to develop in traditional societies not only helps us to understand their cultures better, but also, by contrast, draws attention to factors which have propelled the history of our own culture in a different direction, towards the dissolution of faith. Robin Horton has discussed these issues with much insight, and has termed traditional cultures 'closed' and scientifically oriented cultures 'open' in this regard.[24] His claim that in traditional societies there is no possibility of questioning established tenets because of the 'absence of any awareness of alternatives' has been criticised; it requires to be defended by a more careful consideration of what may serve as alternatives. I found in Buganda that people were sometimes well aware that Europeans had different views on, for example, sorcery from those that they held, but that these different views were not seen as alternatives *for them*. Quite correctly, they saw that views on such matters are conditioned by ways of life, and that their way of life was sufficiently different from ours that it could not meaningfully accommodate ideas current within our own. This was true also of Sinhalese, though to a much smaller extent, since they see more affinity between their way of life and ours.

We commonly suppose that among ourselves religious belief broke down because it was undermined by scientific thought. I suggest that this view is largely mistaken, both historically and theoretically. The growth of science was more symptom than cause. The main reason why scepticism developed so much further in Europe than in most other parts of the world was because communications were more effective: the availability of waterways facilitated transport, while literacy further facilitated the communication of ideas. As a result, effective awareness of alternative ideas was common.

The history of Buddhism provides a valuable test of this hypothesis, since it flourished not in primitive societies but in a socio-cultural environment rather similar to that of Christendom. Awareness of alternative religious ideas was probably more marked: indeed, early Buddhism evolved in a setting of notable religious and philosophical pluralism.[25] But agnosticism, and the more definite rejection of religious tenets which in our culture registers as atheism, are very much less common than they are with us. Except among a small minority of Marxists, irreligion seems to be rare among Sinhalese; indeed, apart from adherents of other religions, I did not meet anyone, villager or not, who seriously questioned the truth of the basic tenets of Buddhism. I suggest that the apparent invulnerability of Buddhism to scepticism is a product of its lack of dogmatism. Contemporary Buddhists boast, with much reason, of their religious tolerance.[26]* It has deep historical roots, being manifest, for example, in the Edicts of Asoka;[27] it is probably a product of the context of religious pluralism in which early Buddhism was formed. As a consequence Buddhists, unlike Christians, have never insisted on purity of belief as essential to religion, but have instead seen practice, especially ethical practice, as the touchstone. When village Buddhists asked me if I was thinking of becoming a Buddhist, I sometimes tried to keep my distance by telling them (falsely) that I could not become a Buddhist as I was already a Christian. Many of them found this incomprehensible: some of them told me that one can perfectly well be a Buddhist without ceasing to be a Christian. Malalgoda reports that Christian missionaries encountered similar attitudes among Sinhalese, both laymen and clergy, in the nineteenth century, and were much frustrated by them.[28] Hardy, who like others mistook this tolerance for apathy, was otherwise correct in explaining why belief, such as it is among Buddhists, is largely immune to scepticism: 'The carelessness and indifference of the people among whom the [Buddhist] system is professed are the most powerful means of its conservation.'[29]

Notes to Chapter 8

1 Russell (1905); cf. Quine (1961), pp. 5–6. A similar point was made by Frege, and was in part anticipated by Kant and Hume.

2 Durkheim (1895).

3 Isomorphism is similarity of structure: two structures are isomorphic when to each element in the one there corresponds just one element in the other, and to each relation in the one there corresponds a similar relation in the other. A map is normally an isomorphic representation of the relevant features of the terrain.

4 These were Mahāyānist philosophers, but I consider that their epistemology makes more explicit what is implicit in views accepted in Theravāda Buddhism. My account is derived from Stcherbatsky [1932] (1958).

5 Spiro reports that everyone in his Burmese sample understood the term, and it is constantly on the tip of the tongue (1971, p. 89). I could not say as much of the Sinhalese I knew. But as Gombrich points out, the words *Aniccā vata samkhārā* ('impermanent indeed are compounded things') are printed prominently on all funeral notices, 'and their general purport is probably understood by everyone' (1971, p. 241). People sometimes referred to these words when I commiserated with them on a death.

6 See, for example, Gregory (1970); Ornstein (1975), chapter 2.

7 Toulmin and Goodfield (1963), p. 278.

8 This is perhaps the major sense in which gods do exist. Durkheim wrote, 'Sacred beings exist only because they are represented as such in the mind. When we cease to believe in them, it is as though they did not exist ... Of course men would be unable to live without gods, but, on the other hand, the gods would die if their cult were not rendered' (1915, pp. 345 and 346; 1912, pp. 492 and 494; I have corrected the translation of the first sentence). This is what is meant by those theologians who endorse Nietzsche's statement 'God is dead'.

9 Langer (1951), p. 97 and *passim*.

10 Sperber (1975), p. 33, drawing upon Turner (1969), p. 15.

11 Geertz (1966), pp. 7–8.

12 Turner (1969), p. 15.

13 It is not clear that by these words Turner did mean that an Ndembu symbol is a metaphor. Nevertheless, in his analysis of Ndembu ritual he does usually interpret Ndembu symbols as metaphors, rather than on the more insightful model which Sperber sees in the Ndembu term *chijikijilu*.

14 Contrast Nash (1965), p. 293 (on Burma).

15 A striking illustration of this is related by Lévi-Strauss, from data obtained by Boas. Quesalid, a young Kwakiutl, did not believe in the pretended power of the shamans and, seeking to expose them, became an apprentice. But he became a very successful shaman and, despite himself, lost sight of his

original radical scepticism (Lévi-Strauss, 1963, pp. 175–8).

16 I knew only one man who, to the best of my knowledge, stuck to his guns: this was Appuhamy (see Chapter 14).

17 1956, p. 9.

18 Psalm 14, v. 1; 53, v. 1.

19 1937, pp. 475–8; 1976, pp. 201–4.

20 1937, p. 338; 1976, p. 159.

21 1937, pp. 120 and 476; 1976, p. 202.

22 1937, p. 120; 1976, p. 57.

23 1937, p. 124; 1976, p. 60.

24 Horton (1970), pp. 153–71.

25 Ling (1973), chapter 5.

26 Tambiah writes of the intolerance of contemporary Buddhists (1976, p. 520). It is true that, in Sri Lanka for example, Sinhalese Buddhists sometimes behave intolerantly towards other communities, notably the Tamils. But the criteria for intolerance and even persecution are ethnic rather than religious, despite the fact that these two kinds of category are empirically combined. I sometimes heard people express dislike or resentment of Tamils or Muslims, but never with the least implication that their religion as such was objectionable.

27 Notably in Rock Edict XII: Nikam and McKeon (1959), pp. 51–2.

28 Malalgoda (1976), pp. 209–13.

29 Hardy (1850), p. 262, quoted in Malalgoda (1976), p. 212.

9

Ministry and Meditation

Running through the account that I have given has been a distinction, more or less explicit, between two notably different kinds of Buddhism, or interpretations of Buddhism. Though the distinction is real enough, it is difficult to find a way of characterising it which fits closely enough the differences in empirical reality.

I have used the term 'village Buddhism' because it, or similar terms, were so commonly used by my informants, and in the literature, that it became habitual. But I have come to see it as misleading in its implications. Sinhalese, both villagers and non-villagers, regularly referred to the reality I was studying as *gamē Buddhāgama*; those who spoke English regularly used the literal English translation, 'village Buddhism'. The word *'gamē'* is the genitive form of *'gama'*, and therefore literally means 'of the village'. It is used to form numerous other compounds, notably *'gamē minissu'*, 'village people', i.e. 'villagers'. In all of them it refers to some aspect of the supposedly distinct sub-culture of a supposedly distinct category, or class, of people, namely villagers. Hence the sense of *'gamē Buddhāgama'* is more exactly conveyed by the translation 'the Buddhism of villagers'.

Now these commonplace usages imply that the Buddhism of villagers is a recognisably distinctive variety of Buddhism; that there is at least one other variety of Buddhism from which this one is to be distinguished, and with which it is contrasted; and that as this is associated with villagers, so the other or others is associated with non-villagers. These implications are all misleading in one way or another, though because they are not often made explicit, and because to a large extent they seem to be confirmed by observation, this is very far from obvious.[1]

Villagers normally spoke of *gamē Buddhāgama* as their own religion, without disparaging it, and did not seem to be thinking consciously of some other specific kind of Buddhism with which they were contrasting it. People who spoke English to me were *ipso facto* not villagers, in their own estimation or that of others; fluency in English is an index of membership of the somewhat loosely defined 'middle class'. Such people, as I remarked earlier (Chapter 1), almost invariably did disparage village Buddhism. When they said it was corrupt they implied that there was another, purer form of Buddhism, and this was still plainer when they said that village Buddhism was not true Buddhism. It was not usually explicit what true Buddhism was, for this was taken to be common tacit knowledge between us. A few people, however, did go so far as to tell me that I was making a bad mistake in studying village Buddhism, and that if I meant to persist I ought at least to find out what true Buddhism is. When I asked how I might do so I was referred either to Buddhist clergy of a particular kind, or to typical publications of the Buddhist Publication Society.[2]* From both sources I got expositions of 'Buddhist modernism' (see above, Chapter 1) which, as Gombrich notes, is very characteristic of English-educated Sinhalese.[3]

It was evident, too, from most of my English-speaking informants, that they were disparaging village Buddhism by contrasting it with positions characteristic of Buddhist modernism. Since someone presenting himself as a Buddhist, and as a superior kind of Buddhist, would hardly refer to 'true Buddhism' without implying that he professed it, I understood my informants to be implying that Buddhist modernism was both true Buddhism and their own Buddhism. Since 'untrue' Buddhism was characterised as that of villagers, I took the implication that 'true' Buddhism was characteristic of non-villagers, especially themselves. Hence I came to think of it as 'middle-class Buddhism'.

This categorisation does not exactly fit the facts. As Malalgoda has pointed out, elements of Buddhist modernism have seeped into the Buddhism of most villagers.[4] Some people who by most objective criteria are villagers speak of village Buddhism in the same disparaging terms that English-speaking, middle-class people do. I did notice that many of these were socially ambitious, and held or at least aspired to occupations that might be described as lower middle-class; but I also noticed that there were other people, objectively similar, who did not disparage village Buddhism in contrasting it with Buddhist modernism. 'Village Buddhism' is therefore a somewhat elusive construct. There is a fairly systematic variety of Buddhism, which in most important aspects is contrasted with Buddhist modernism, and which is practised and professed by most villagers, both lay people and also the clergy who are incumbents of village temples. It is this that I, together with the Sinhalese, refer to as village Buddhism.

I was too hasty also in identifying Buddhist modernism as the Buddhism of the (English-speaking) middle class. My pupil, Dr. Mark Hodge, has since made a study of varieties of Buddhism and their association with social class in the southern Sinhalese town of Matara.[5]

He found there that the actual Buddhism of members of the urban
working class was, unsurprisingly, similar to that which I and others
found among villagers. He also found that the actual Buddhism of
middle-class people was not very different, particularly in the respects I
had thought significant, and that most of them did not manifest
Buddhist modernism to any large extent.

There may be a regional difference here. Matara is a traditional centre
of Buddhist learning, and it may therefore be that the Matarese are less
inclined than others to learn their Buddhism from Europeans. But I had
noticed, even though it was not part of my business to study them, that
my middle-class informants, and others like them, did engage in
practices very similar to those they disparaged among villagers. My
middle-class informants were not a true sample: they were people I met in
and around Polgama, and elsewhere, most of whom chose to talk to me
about my work. Like others, they were concerned that I should report
favourably on Sinhalese Buddhism, and assuming that I would, like other
Europeans and themselves, regard village Buddhism unfavourably, they
sought to exempt themselves and their national religion from that
unfavourable judgement. No doubt sincerely, they presented themselves
as adherents of Buddhist modernism because they expected me to
approve it; they did not see how far their actual religion resembled village
Buddhism because they saw themselves as altogether superior to
villagers. Their adherence to Buddhist modernism was largely a matter of
profession, exaggerated in encounter with a European. Their practice, I
think, was largely similar to that of village Buddhists, except that many
of them took meditation seriously and tried to practise it.

If this is correct, what is termed 'village Buddhism' is in reality the
greater part of the actual Buddhism of most Sinhalese, and is not, as it is
misleadingly taken to be, peculiar to villagers. There are some Sinhalese
Buddhists who practise Buddhist modernism exclusively, shunning the
'corrupt' practices attributed to village Buddhism; what evidence I have
suggests that they are few, and many of them unusual in other ways. The
'true Buddhism' to which people allude is not primarily an actual
Buddhism of practice: I think some of my informants spoke more truly
than they intended when they told me, 'the true Buddhism is found only
in books'. To the extent that this is so, the contrast being offered is most
misleading: though people speak disparagingly of the Buddhism of
villagers as though villagers peculiarly are bad Buddhists, they are in fact
contrasting actual Buddhism, Buddhism as practised by real people,
with an essentially literary, idealised phenomenon. It is, at best, trite to
remark that the latter is purer than the former: for books of that kind are
written to give expression to dreams of purity. At worst, it deceives us
both about people and about religion, which has its true function in life,
not in dreams.

The distinction we are driving at is therefore skewed when one pole of it is taken to be the Buddhism of villagers. Spiro comes closer to comparing entities of like kind when he contrasts 'nibbanic' with 'kammatic' Buddhism, where the latter is taken to be the system of Buddhism found in practice among villagers.[6] However, Spiro seems not to recognise how far his 'nibbanic' Buddhism is in fact a literary phenomenon, and biased by the Western interpretation of Buddhism; moreover his contrast is markedly in terms of 'ideology'[7] or belief-system, which I am arguing is an erroneous approach to religion; and his plain implication that the one is concerned with Nirvana, but the other with Rebirth and karma, misrepresents the true state of affairs, as we shall see.

It is better to begin with a pair of distinctions that the clergy often make explicitly.[8] Some of the priests I spoke to told me that they were *granthadhura* as contrasted with *vidarsanadhura*; some also said that they were *grāmavāsin* as contrasted with *āraññavāsin*. These are standard terms of very ancient lineage; though only some of my informants used them explicitly, I have little doubt that all clergy, at least, would have done so if occasion had arisen, since they simply describe the plain facts. The first pair of terms label a distinction between two kinds of clerical vocation; the second pair label a distinction between two patterns of residence for clergy.

'*Granthadhura*' means literally 'having books as their burden', and it refers to those clergy who see their vocation as primarily one of learning and, especially, teaching the Dhamma (doctrine). '*Vidarsanadhura*' means literally 'having meditation as their burden' and it refers to those clergy who see their vocation as primarily one of practising intensive meditation.[9]

'*Grāmavāsin*' means literally 'those who reside in villages (or towns)'. '*Āraññavāsin*' means literally 'those who reside in forests (or jungles)'. Those who do the latter sometimes go to very wild and remote places indeed, living perhaps in caves, but trying to live as alone as possible, as hermits. Most of them, however, live in communities with like-minded fellows, in permanent buildings which may well be termed 'monasteries'. Hence the term *ārañña* has come to be specialised to mean such monasteries, which are ideally, and more or less really, in the forests and distant from the settlements of laymen.

It is wholly understandable that the terms of these two dichotomies have come to be linked.[10] Those who see their vocation as primarily one of teaching, which is largely teaching the laity, naturally live among them, in villages and towns. Those who are more concerned to devote themselves to meditation naturally prefer to separate themselves from the distractions that involvement with the lives of laymen brings, and to retreat to the forests (as we would say, in Christian terminology, to 'the wilderness').

The real meaning of these contrasts is obscured if we stick too closely to the etymology of the terms. The teaching vocation is not simply that, as we would understand the terms. As we noted with reference to Sīlaratana (Chapter 3), 'teaching the Dhamma' may be understood as including social service, and for most priests it certainly means more than just instruction in doctrine. The Christian term 'ministry' seems to me apt: such clerics see themselves as 'ministers', in which their activity as teachers is certainly very prominent, but they seek to minister also to other needs of the lay people. For example, we noted that Dhammatilaka said that the greater part of his time was taken up in giving advice on family and marital problems, and all priests seem to do this to some extent at least. It is apt, too, to borrow another Christian term, and to refer to these as the 'Secular clergy': they are those who pursue their vocation in the world. They are the people I usually refer to as 'priests' (see Appendix); more explicitly, I would call them the 'ministering, secular clergy'.

To refer to the others as the 'meditating' clergy may seem clear enough, though the term is ambiguous.[11]* Sometimes I term them 'forest-dwelling',[12] as the Sinhalese often do. They may be called the 'Secluded' as contrasted with the 'Secular' clergy, since they try to cut themselves off from the world, i.e. the society of lay people. Most often I refer to them as 'monks', with or without further qualification.

These two patterns, of secular priests and secluded monks, are ideal types, or poles of what is actually a continuum. It is not the case that priests generally only minister and never meditate, nor that monks generally only meditate and never minister; the distinction is rather one of relatively greater or lesser emphasis on two aspects of the ideal life of a cleric.

All clergy ought to meditate, and it is therefore unsurprising that I found, as did Gombrich,[13] that every cleric one specifically asks claims that he does so. In some cases the claim does not carry conviction. When I talked to laymen about priests in the locality they would sometimes specify some (notably Sīlaratana) as never meditating, most as meditating moderately, and a few as unusually devoted to meditation. Meditation (*bhāvanā*) is usually understood as a special activity set apart from others: it may be a matter of thought and contemplation, or it may be a matter of more strenuous mind-training, yoga, 'spiritual exercises' as Christians say. Laymen often say or imply that such 'meditation' is a euphemism for sleeping, which no doubt it sometimes is. But since it is an essentially private activity, normally conducted behind closed doors, there is no way of knowing. When I asked Dhammatilaka if he meditated he said yes, he was meditating all the time whatever activity he was engaged in. This may have been an evasion, but in fact such an interpretation has good scriptural warrant.[11] In short, I cannot know; but I guess laymen are broadly right, that most priests meditate to some extent, though probably less than they like to claim.

Among the secluded monks, a few of the more fanatical hermits are said to subsist on fruits they gather in the jungles, and to avoid all human contact.[14] Most, however, depend on the alms (*dānē*) of laity for support. When lay people visit a monastery bringing donations, notably food which they cook and present as a meal, the monks normally reciprocate by preaching a sermon. In my own limited observations, some of the monks at least are willing also to talk to lay visitors less formally. Some of them at least will also travel away from their monasteries to minister to lay people, notably by teaching them the techniques of meditation.

Clerics may also move from one vocation to the other. Some secular priests may leave their parishes to go and live as monks; some monks leave their monasteries and settle as ministers among lay people. Some clerics are ambivalent or divided between the two vocations. Temples/monasteries are not always clearly of one kind or the other. Most temples I know are in the midst of villages and very open to the lay people. Some, however, are outside the villages they serve, often built atop high rocks, which certainly makes access more difficult: I know of at least four such within about ten miles of Polgama. Clergy are not entirely free to choose where they reside, since their major entitlement to residence is acquired through their Teachers; but I can see various processes by which priests more inclined to meditation might gravitate to the more isolated temples, and those more inclined to ministry to the less isolated. I have only scanty data on this; but I think it not entirely coincidental that the two most overtly Secular priests that I know, Sīlaratana and Dhammatilaka, both have temples which are bus stops.[15]*

A balanced view might be that meditation and ministry should both be components in the life of a Buddhist cleric: indeed, this was stated to me by some of the priests I talked to, and implied by others. Then it would seem that we are dealing merely with natural and slight differences in inclination and emphasis along a continuum. However, there are factors which make the contrast much sharper, in practice and in ideology, than this would suggest.

In the first place, differences in location, though they do not wholly determine the orientations and practices of clerics, do strongly influence them. It is difficult for a cleric in a village temple to devote a great deal of his time to meditation at the expense of ministry; if he attempts to do so he is likely to be met with the disapproval of the villagers, and sanctions in the form of withdrawal of support. It is difficult, too, to be active in ministry if one resides in a remote monastery, and therefore unlikely that one so inclined would continue to stay there.

Both parties, the Secular and the Secluded, tend to be pulled apart by what might be regarded as their extreme wings. There is an unmistakable tendency for Secular clergy, who are in the world, to become worldly (*laukika*), of the world, and where this happens they are widely condemned. The more extreme of those inclined to meditation tend to become ascetic (*tāpasin*), to adopt extreme austerities, and often to live as wandering beggars rather than as settled monks. They claim, with some reason, in this to be following the way of life of the earliest *bhikkhus*, and are regarded with great veneration by some. Most actual Buddhists, both clergy and laymen, regard them rather with contempt and even loathing.[16]

The two vocations seem to be markedly associated with two different judgements on a matter of fact which does not easily allow of middling judgement. We noted that, with Dhammatilaka, the view that Nirvana is attainable only in the far future was directly connected with his inclination towards ministry. In my experience most people who place more than average stress on the importance of meditation also maintain that Nirvana can be attained in the present, or at worst the near future. I shall explain later the logic of this association (Chapter 14). It probably is the case that some people first have a view on whether Nirvana is near or far, and this then affects their preference between the vocations; it is also possible that an inclination towards one vocation or the other influences judgements about Nirvana.

It is unsurprising that the two vocations, the two interpretations of Buddhism found among the clergy, are paralleled by a similar division among the laity. I shall call one of these two divisions, or parties,[17*] the 'Meditation-Buddhists'. Its members regularly say that the best Buddhists are the meditating monks; usually they say that the priests, just because they are less committed to meditation, are traitors to their calling. So far from finding anything good to say for the acts of ministry of the secular priests, these people tend to treat such acts as evidence of unworthiness. They also regard meditation as important for lay people; many of them take trouble to learn the techniques of meditation and to practise them. Very commonly they will assert that Nirvana is attainable in the present: a person who is well qualified in terms of intellect and virtue, and who applies himself diligently, could expect to attain in his present lifetime. Even more ordinary people such as ourselves, if we apply ourselves diligently, can expect to attain after only a few more rebirths. They value application to meditation precisely as the means to attain Nirvana rather soon. These people are characteristically, but not invariably, middle-class.

I refer to the other party as that of the 'Ministry-Buddhists'. Its members consider the activities of the ministering clergy valuable and important; often they will say that they are essential for the preservation of Buddhism. Such people do indeed often condemn the priests almost as scathingly as members of the other party do; but their grounds are typically different. They do not condemn them simply for not meditating enough: they regard complete failure to meditate as a blemish in a priest, but one which can be compensated for by other virtues. They condemn them rather for being too worldly, inadequate in their actual vocation. Their ideal of what a cleric should be is so unrealistically high that in order to preserve the ideal they have to be unduly hard on the actual human beings who fail to live up to it.[18*] But in fact most laymen of this party are more realistic most of the time: they wish the clergy were better than they are, but accept the realities of life. Some of these people are as vehemently condemnatory of the meditating monks as Sīlaratana was. Others speak of them with irony and more or less evident derision (I quote an unusually scathing comment on them below, Chapter 14). Most, in my experience, seemed to be more or less indifferent to them.[19*] These people show little interest in practising meditation themselves, and tend to speak of its alleged practice by other lay persons, and even clergy, with irony tending towards derision. They regularly say that no one has attained Nirvana for a very long time past, that it is virtually certain that no one now can, or will until the next Buddha, Maitrī, is born in the distant future. Most villagers are firmly of this persuasion, though there are significant exceptions.

One would not expect real human beings to sort themselves neatly into just these two parties: one does encounter people whose position is intermediate or mixed. Nevertheless there does seem to be a high degree of association between the variables. If one registers in a person one element of either kind of Buddhism there is a high probability that he will also manifest the others. Again the kind of Buddhism that a person will favour is largely predictable from his class characteristics – and also vice versa.

Most Western people who know, or think they know, something about Buddhism, having been indoctrinated by the Western interpretation of Buddhism, are likely to take it for granted that Meditation Buddhism is the same thing as Buddhism, the only genuine article, and that any other interpretation is some kind of deviation, defalcation, or corruption. They may even have been surprised, perhaps affronted, that I have chosen for the alternative interpretation the label 'Ministry-Buddhism' which plainly has rather favourable connotations. If so, they are likely to be still more surprised to learn that their value judgement is not endorsed by most real Buddhists either at the present time or in the past.

The Rev. Walpola Rahula is an exceedingly able and erudite Sinhalese Buddhist cleric, with a high international standing in the world of scholarship. I should share with the reader the fact that as a young priest in the late 1940s he was very active in the politics of the left, apparently supporting the Trotskyite LSSP.[20] He was one of the founders in 1946 and leaders of the Ceylon Union of Bhikkhus (LEBM), and two decades later he told Phadnis, 'We initiated the movement with a view to help the suffering masses, for us it was based on compassion. It is the legitimate right of the Bhikkhus to protect the rights of the toiling masses.'[21] His *History of Buddhism in Ceylon* between the third century B.C. and the tenth A.D. is based on study of the Sinhalese chronicles and other sources; it is a standard authority on this period.

Rahula tells us that the Pali names for the two clerical vocations are first found in literature of the fifth century , though the basic distinction goes back several centuries earlier.[22] He continues:

Out of the two vocations [that of Teaching] was regarded as more important than [that of Meditation]. Examples found in the Commentaries show that almost all able and intelligent monks [clerics] applied themselves to [the Teaching vocation] while elderly monks of weak intellect and feeble physique, particularly those who entered the Order in their old age, devoted themselves to [the Meditation vocation].[23]

This was not altogether an innovation. At the earliest period for which the scriptures yield us sound historical evidence, that of the first few centuries after the Buddha's death, the distinction between the two vocations was not explicit, but the parallel one referring to type of place of residence was. Dutt tells us that once the clerics had begun to settle in one place, rather than live as wanderers, most of them settled in towns and villages;[24] further he remarks:

It was not, as we have observed, the purpose of a monastery to shut out the world, but only its distracting evils. One class of monks shunned the world – those called *Āraññakas* (Forest-dwellers) in the *Vinayapitaka* – and they are not regarded in it as necessarily the best specimens of monkhood.[25]

The distinction between the two vocations, which originated in Sri Lanka, was carried thence to Thailand. There today, at least in the town in which Bunnag worked, meditation and its vocation are held in very low regard. Less than one third of the clerics whom Bunnag interviewed claimed to meditate at all, and then only occasionally. They regarded it as an activity more appropriate to members of the Sangha of low status: nuns, magical practitioners, and *thudong* monks. The latter are those who adopt, at least temporarily, the way of life I referred to as that of ascetics (*tāpasin*), in order to go on pilgrimages. The meditation vocation is strongly associated with these ascetics, and compared most unfavourably with the ministry vocation: 'By comparison, the [ascetic] is regarded as selfish and lacking in public spirit.' Moreover, the ascetics 'are frequently regarded as being on a par with tramps, beggars and other kinds of social derelicts'. Bunnag's own observation of some of them at a place of pilgrimage showed this assessment to be fairly accurate: the 'ascetics' seemed to belong to two types, 'either elderly men who had retired into the Order, or younger *bhikkhus* out on a spree'.[26]

The evaluation in contemporary Sri Lanka, so far as I could estimate it, was more moderate than that, though not very different from what it had been some 1,500 years earlier. There are about 20,000 clergy, of whom only some 800 live in secluded monasteries;[27] so it is clear that most clergy follow the ministry vocation. Those few men who choose to enter the Sangha in middle age are always steered to the meditating monkhood – which is not to say that all or most monks are of that kind.[28*] One might surmise that the overwhelming majority of clergy who follow the ministry vocation consider it superior, and a few told me they did; but it is uncommon to meet a priest like Sīlaratana who scathingly condemns the meditating monks. To me at any rate, most of the priests with whom the topic came up expressed a judgement similar to that of Sārānanda. As we saw earlier (Chapter 7), he told me that both vocations were good ways to Nirvana. The way of meditation is easier, for the burdens of ministry are heavy: but it is no more rapid, the meditators do not attain Nirvana any sooner. Superficially this is broadminded and tolerant, but implicitly it is less so. Many of those who favour the meditation vocation do so because they see it as an 'express route' to Nirvana, which they expect to attain rather soon. To say that they are mistaken about this, that they too cannot attain before the next Buddha comes, is seriously to undermine their position: if this were accepted the meditation vocation would lose much, though not all, of its appeal.

From time to time this relative devaluing of the meditation vocation seems to be reversed. It is said that the secular clergy have a marked tendency to become worldly, and in fact so corrupt as to endanger the health of the *Buddha Sāsana*. When they did, it was expected that the king would intervene to reform and purify the Sangha. Such interventions were notably frequent in the histories of Sri Lanka, Burma and Thailand.[29] Naturally, since the corruption was seen as too great a compromise with the world, purification was spoken of as a return to and renewal of the contrary ideal, that of the secluded meditating monks. This was at least the standard rhetoric, and rhetoric is not insignificant socially. But a measure of scepticism is in order. Tambiah has detected 'an unmistakable correlation' between purifications of the Sangha and the stronger kings, that is, those who were most effective in centralising their kingdoms and maximising their own control over them.[30] He also asks 'to what degree was purification ... in certain instances a euphemism for victimisation for political reasons rather than a moral cleansing dictated by a decline in the monks' ways of life?'[31] There is certainly the possibility that these purifications were essentially political acts which were legitimised by false accusations of depravity: just as in other societies (and indeed Sri Lanka too) rebellions have been legitimised by false accusations, before and after the event, against the victim king, e.g. Richard III of England.[32] It may well be that the kings who sorted out the Sangha praised the secluded monks just because kings seeking to centralise power in their own hands have obvious reasons for preferring clergy who emasculate themselves politically by withdrawing from the world. I cannot of course say that clergy never did become corrupt in point of fact; but I incline to scepticism also because I know that today many laymen disparage the clergy in ways that seem not at all warranted by the facts.

I remarked that not only in Polgama but also in each of the four near-by villages that I knew best the village priest was strongly, and it seemed unjustly, criticised (Chapter 3). A village priest is expected to act in some ways as a leader of the village, and indeed must do so to some extent whether or not he has, as Silaratana did, a dominant personality. It is not an empty idiom that the priest is a *hāmuduruvō*, 'lord'. We were very struck by the fact that when we asked people in Polgama who they thought were the leaders of the village, nearly always they replied either that they could think of none, or by naming one or both of two prominent persons who had recently died. It was evident too from the history of the previous few decades that every time a layman had tried to exercise leadership this had provoked such jealousy as to render his efforts ineffective. This was one of the main reasons why the repeated attempts to raise the funds necessary to build a new presbytery had always failed (above, Chapter 2). It seems an obvious inference that individual priests may be disparaged just because their status imposes on them a leadership role.

My tentative conclusion is not only that the secular ministry is the overwhelmingly most common role pattern for clergy, but also that it is normally more highly esteemed. This tends to be obscured by the fact that, largely for reasons of political jealousy, the ideal of the secluded monk may be used as a stick with which to beat the secular clergy.

In writing of the origin of the two clerical vocations, Rahula is interestingly ambivalent. The first century B.C.[33]* was a time of chaos in Sri Lanka, to such an extent that the very continuance of the *Buddha Sāsana* was thought to be in peril. In response, several hundred clerics met in conference to debate what was the basis of the *Sāsana*: learning – which in fact very much meant teaching – or practice – which meant mainly meditation. The party of the teachers was victorious. This was the basis on which the formal distinction between the two vocations came to be evolved. Rahula writes of this as a 'radical' and 'vital change', a 'new attitude' forced on the clergy by circumstances: for, as he says, it was 'not in keeping with the original idea as found in the Dhammapada', a Canonical scripture.[34] That, I suggest, is the voice of Rahula the orthodox scholar.

Some thirty pages later, Rahula is writing about the general situation in the period his history covers:

There were two classes of monks: One class of monks devoted themselves only to meditation, with the sole purpose of saving themselves, without taking any interest in the welfare of the people. The other class of monks seems to have taken an interest in the welfare of the people – both spiritual and material – in addition to their own salvation. This attitude seems to be healthier than the first one, and is in keeping with the spirit of the Master.[35]

There I hear the voice of Rahula the actual Buddhist, politically involved.

Apart from one anecdote from Canonical scripture, Rahula here cites no evidence for his assessment of the spirit of the Master. There is in fact a great deal. I cannot go into it here without prematurely raising a very large problem which lies before us. Suffice it to say that there is ample scriptural warrant for both views of the clerical vocation. The favourite passage of those who prefer the ministry vocation is the one that Silaratana cited: it is the charge that the Buddha allegedly delivered to his first sixty disciples:

Go forth, O Bhikkhus, on your wanderings, for the good of the Many [*Bahujana*, the masses, the common people] – for the happiness of the Many, in compassion for the world – for the good, for the welfare, for the happiness of gods and men. Let not two of you go the same way. O Bhikkhus, proclaim that Dhamma which is gracious at the beginning, at the middle, and at the end.[36]

On the other hand a favourite passage of those who rather esteem the secluded meditators is the one which has verses like the following:

Having left son and wife, father and mother, wealth, and corn, and relatives, the different objects of desire, let one wonder alone like a rhinoceros.

Spiro quotes this, together with three similar verses having the same rhinoceros refrain.[37] He evidently regards them with high esteem; referring to Gotama Buddha he terms these '. . . His explicit words'.[38] Moreover, in at least two passages crucial to the structure of his argument, where he is declaring that the only true Buddhist is the world-renouncing secluded meditating monk, he again quotes with evident approval the phrase about wandering alone like a rhinoceros.[39] It seems an odd similitude.

These two passages are radically contradictory in spirit, and hardly reconcilable even in letter. It seems unlikely that the Buddha uttered both, and quite likely that he uttered neither. But, without combing the scriptures for passages parallel to each, it must already be evident that the scriptures do not speak with one voice in support of the secluded meditator ideal.

Notes to Chapter 9

1 I have discussed some aspects of this in Southwold (1982).
2 Its publications are mostly in English, and are distributed in seventy countries; at least half of them are by English or German authors. See Gombrich (1971), p. 55; Peiris (1973), pp. 142–3.
3 Gombrich (1971), pp. 51, 55.
4 Malalgoda (1972), p. 163.
5 Hodge (1981).
6 Spiro (1971).
7 E.g. 1971, p. 66.
8 Cf. Gombrich (1971), p. 320 f.
9 Cf. *ibid.*, p. 269.
10 Gombrich denies this, writing that the *grāmavāsin/araññavāsin* dichotomy 'has for the most part lapsed into meaningless scholasticism' (1971, p. 270). The scholastic sense of the terms to which he alludes was not used by my informants.
11 Most Western people, and I think also most Sinhalese, think of meditation (*bhāvanā*) as a special kind of secluded activity. Rahula terms this *samādhi*, and says that it is not purely Buddhist nor essential for the realisation of Nirvana. The essentially Buddhist meditation, he says, is rather the practice of mindfulness (*sati*) in all the activities of life (cf., in the Christian tradition, George Herbert's poem 'The Elixir'). On this, see especially Rahula (1967), chapter VIII, to which I am indebted. Of my informants, Dhammatilaka at least understood this, for when I asked him if he meditated he replied that he was meditating all the time whatever he was doing. Most people, however, seemed to be thinking of meditation as a special activity (Rahula's '*samādhi*'). Only in this latter sense could it be assumed that the *vidarsanadhura* clergy are specialists in meditation as the *granthadhura* are not. This is the sense in which I normally use the term.
12 Translating *araññavāsin*.
13 1971, pp. 280–1.
14 Carrithers (1977).
15 Dhammatilaka's temple in Henagala was actually the terminus of a bus route, and it was common to see the bus parked in the temple compound.
16 On the *tāpasin*, see Carrithers (1977, 1979).
17 This dichotomy is mine, and I do not think it is clearly perceived by the Sinhalese; the term 'parties' may therefore be too strong.
18 I have applied here part of Gluckman's analysis of the frailty in authority: that in rebelling against a 'bad' king the rebels are sustaining the ideals of kingship which, in fact, no king could ever attain (Gluckman, 1956, chapter II).
19 It did not occur to me to ask people systematically what they thought of meditating monks, so I am not sure what they did think. Simply from the fact that the topic did not often arise I infer that most people did not have very strong opinions. The few forest monasteries I know of in the area were practically inaccessible to most of my informants, and would therefore have

hardly impinged on their lives.

20 Phadnis (1976), pp. 162–72; Rahula (1974).
21 Phadnis (1976), p. 169 n. 28.
22 Rahula (1956), pp. 158–60.
23 *Ibid.*, p. 160.
24 Dutt (1962), pp. 54, 57.
25 *Ibid.*, p. 161.
26 Bunnag (1973), pp. 53–7.
27 Carrithers (1980), p. 196; no doubt some clergy pursue the meditation vocation outside these monasteries.
28 Obeyesekere (1981, p. 41 and n. 15) implies that most forest monks have taken up that vocation in middle age, coming to it sometimes from lay life, more often from following the ministry vocation as priests. Carrithers, however, tells me that this is not so (personal communication).
29 Tambiah (1976), chapter 9, Carrithers (1979), p. 298.
30 Tambiah (1976), pp. 170, 173 n. 13.
31 *Ibid.*, p. 174.
32 Gluckman (1956), chapter II.
33 This would be about 500 years after the beginning of Buddhism at the Buddha's Enlightenment. The Buddha lived from 563 to 483 B.C., and attained Enlightenment in 528 B.C. – or it may be that each event occurred three years earlier (Gombrich, 1971, p. 19).
34 Rahula (1956), pp. 157–9.
35 *Ibid.*, p. 193.
36 *Mahāvagga*, I, 11, 1; quoted as the epigraph to Dutt (1962, p. 17).
37 *Sutta-Nipāta, Khaggavisāna Sutta*, 4, 10, 26 and 30; quoted in Spiro (1971), pp. 347–8.
38 Spiro (1971), p. 347.
39 *Ibid.*, pp. 64 and 279.

10

The quest of the historical Buddha

How then is it, in the face of such evidence, that we are most of us so confident that the way of the secluded meditating monks is true Buddhism, uniquely: so confident that even someone as learned and talented as Spiro, and an anthropologist to boot, could be so mistaken? It is because of the way that we in the West came to study Buddhism.

Before the nineteenth century a little was known about Buddhism from travellers' tales, but it was largely inaccurate and seems to have aroused little serious interest. Beginning in the 1830s, several scholars began publishing or translating Buddhist scriptures or sending manuscripts of them to Europe. In the latter part of the century it became evident that the scriptures in Pali – that is, those of the Theravāda Buddhists – were generally older than those in Sanskrit, and to that extent more reliable as historical evidence; and scholars seem to have fallen into the trap of assuming that because they were more reliable they were simply reliable. From around 1880 onwards Buddhism was intensively studied through the Pali scriptures.[1]

This unfortunate bias is at least understandable. Scriptural texts could be sent to Europe for study, as actual Buddhism could not. Some of the scholars, however, did reside in Buddhist countries, notably Sri Lanka; but beyond talking to some of the most erudite clerics, they made very little attempt to study actual Buddhism. Social science hardly existed at that time, and social anthropology, in anything like the modern sense, not at all. Outside the natural sciences, scholarship and research were identical with the study of books and texts. Even if, anachronistically, it had occurred to anyone that it might be more useful to study people, he could hardly have profited. This was the heyday of imperialism. Actual Buddhists appeared, at any rate in Sri Lanka and Burma, as colonised, coloured, and superstitious: in a word, inferior. It would have been quite anachronistic to perceive them otherwise. In any case the study of religion had not progressed to the point where it is possible to make good sense of what appears to be crude superstition. On the other hand, there was much in the scriptures which evoked respect and even admiration.

A more fundamental reason lay in the way that religion was understood at that time, and largely still is. The term 'Buddhism' is used in any or all of four senses, referring to four distinguishable kinds of thing:

1. Buddhendom, Buddhist civilisation, society and culture as a whole.
2. What within this appears to be specifically a religion.
3. The doctrines of that religion.
4. The teaching of the Founder, the Buddha himself.

Now Buddhists themselves appear to relate these in reverse order. The origin and core of Buddhism is the Buddha's teaching; this is the basis of Buddhist doctrine; this is the basis of the religion; and this is the basis of Buddhist civilisation. I am not clear how far Buddhists do say just this – nor, to the extent that they do, how far they have been influenced into doing so by European ideas. No matter; this is what nineteenth-century Europeans would have 'heard' them saying, because it precisely corresponded with their understanding of the structure of their own religious civilisation, of Christendom.

This having been assumed, it was obvious that the most important thing to do in order to know and understand Buddhism was to get to know its essential basis, its core and origin, the teaching of the Buddha. Buddhists say that this is contained in the scriptures; there are virtually no other reliable sources; and these the scholars, mainly philologists, were well qualified to study. So the programme began. Its inspiration is expressed, with charming naivety, in a letter written to a Sinhalese in 1893 by the great Professor Max Müller:

You should endeavour to do for Buddhism what the more enlightened students of Christianity have long been doing in different countries of Europe: you should free your religion from its later excrescences, and bring it back to its earliest, simplest, and purest form as taught by Buddha and his immediate disciples.[2]

There was of course a practical problem: the sources present a great variety of accounts of the teaching and the deeds of the Buddha. It was easy, and fairly justifiable, to weed out the plainly later and less authoritative sources, the Commentarial literature. But even when one got down to the bedrock of the Canonical scriptures, there was no clear picture: inconsistencies and indeed contradictions abounded, not only on the rhinoceros issue but on virtually every other of significance – or, where the sources did agree in attributing a certain doctrine to the Buddha, its meaning was variously interpreted to the point of gross obscurity.[3*] Critical method was needed. Virtually nothing was known about the circumstances of composition of the various scriptures, except that they were composed by monks several centuries at least after the Buddha's death, on the basis of received traditions which were, in considerable part at least, undeniably legendary. Nothing daunted, the scholars resorted to internal criticism. That is to say, the scholars read the scriptures as everyone normally does, because he must, because this is what scriptures are actually for: they selected the bits which suited their fancy, which is to say their preconceptions, and treated these as authentic; and then found excuses for explaining the rest away as later excrescences, or evident superstition or invention. They gazed into the magic mirror, and saw themselves. They fell into the same trap as did their contemporaries engaged on a similar task with the Christian scriptures: of whom Albert Schweitzer wrote, 'The so-called historical Jesus of the nineteenth century biographers is really a modernization, in which Jesus is presented in the colours of modern bourgeois respectability and neo-Kantian moralism.'[4]*

The students of Buddhism were not all of one kind:[5] among them, for example, were some Christian missionaries seeking to know their enemy. But prominent, and I think dominant, among them seems to have been a particular kind of person. He was, of course a scholar, even if, like T. W. Rhys Davids, his career was not wholly academic. He was interested in religion – or he would not have bothered. But he was disaffected with Christianity – or he would not have bothered enough with Buddhism. He was influenced by the humanistic, rationalistic, scientific – or rather, positivistic – ideas of that period, and was doubtless attracted to Buddhism by the traces of similar ideas which actually are present in the scriptures. So he came up with a picture of the historical Buddha as a civilised intellectual gent like himself, teaching an enlightened philosophy which would pass muster with his latter-day student.[6]

Apart from the rationalism of this nineteenth-century Buddha, his teaching does seem to have had a strong leaning towards secluded meditatory monasticism of the rhinoceros kind. This bias may also owe something to the predisposition of the scholars who found him: though they were not monks themselves, it is evident from our own cultural history that there is a marked affinity between the temperaments of the monk and of the scholar. The idea of wandering alone like a rhinoceros may be thought not altogether alien to the spirit of middle-class individualism.

Now that the scriptures have been re-examined by other scholars, perhaps more objective or perhaps simply with different biases, it is plain that the account of the scriptures which was given by the nineteenth-century scholars was selective, and that in a tendentious manner. They set the basic framework for the Western understanding of Buddhism, and set it so firmly that most of their successors, both scholarly and more popular, have been imprisoned within it, and their work has reinforced it. Those who have had evidence that it is seriously defective – and

Gombrich is an excellent example – have in general been unable to break free of its trammels. And the statements of those who have more or less clearly challenged it have had little impact, having been mainly ignored or too hastily dismissed.

There is no suggestion that the scholars were in any useful sense dishonest: given their historical situation they could not have been expected to have acted otherwise than they did. The scriptural material is so inconsistent,[7] not to say chaotic, that it offers only two possible options. If one is to extract from it a coherent account of the life and teaching of the supposedly historical Buddha, one has to be highly selective, and hence in fact biased. The only alternative is to recognise that the whole programme is incurably futile. Obviously the scholars could not have recognised that. It would, in the first place, have put them out of a job. In the second place, and perhaps still more distressing, it would have required of them a radical revision of their whole view of the structure and nature of religious phenomena.

I have suggested that the Western misinterpretation of Buddhism was shaped by the selective and biased way in which the scholars read the scriptures. This may not have been the only factor: I suspect that the scriptures themselves already presented a selective and biased account of Buddhism. I cannot be sure that this is so, since I have neither the time nor the ability to read all the scriptures and form my own assessment of their overall tendency. But from my reading of the work of those who have immersed themselves in the scriptures I get the definite impression that the bias of the Western scholars was by no means wholly imported by themselves. It is the more useful working hypothesis that the scriptures are, quite objectively, misleading.

The Buddhist scriptures were not composed by a representative sample of Buddhists. They were composed by clerics, a religious élite. And not even by typical clerics such as the village priests that I know. The scriptures were first produced as oral compositions, and then handed down for many generations, indeed centuries, through very formal oral transmission from teacher to pupils.[8] This could only have occurred in the larger monasteries, and the work would have been entrusted to the clerics of the most eminent, and best endowed, of the monasteries. Thus the scriptures were the product of an élite among the clerical élite. It does not follow that such clerics were themselves involved in monasticism of the secluded meditatory kind; but we can be rather sure that they were little involved with ministry to the common people. It is not in the least surprising that the view of religion propagated by such authors should have had a distinctly élitist tendency.

It is, at first sight, more surprising that any contrary tendency should have found a place in the scriptures. But on second sight, not surprising but predictable. The clerical authors, in the better endowed monasteries, were probably not themselves significantly dependent on the support of the common people. But the more astute of them, at least, must have been very well aware that the *Sāsana* as a whole was critically dependent on such support. Scriptures are composed primarily in order to legitimise the religious views and practices of the authors and their clients. It is natural, then, that some clerics took care to compose scriptures legitimising the actual religion of the common people.[9]* It is also natural that the clerics collectively, however much disdain many of them may have felt for the popular religion, took care to see that such scriptures received the authorisation of inclusion within the Canon. If they had not, scripture would have failed to authorise the religion of the peasants and would have implicitly condemned it.[10]* This would hardly have motivated the indispensable support of the peasants, but would rather have inclined them to adhere to an alternative, more indulgent religion. And then Buddhism would have died out long ago.

In point of fact, Ministry-Buddhism was carried and practised mainly by people other than the learned clerics, and transmitted by means other than scriptures. Its principal bearers were the ordinary people, and I suspect rather more the less privileged than the more privileged among them: the peasants or villagers, and their immediate pastors the village clergy, who presumably then as now were drawn mainly from their own stratum.[11]* As is observable now, it was surely transmitted from generation to generation by example and by the teaching of the village clergy, who were probably as indifferent to the minutiae of scripture as their present-day representatives seem to be (see Chapter 3). Such people rarely write books, even at the present day; hence it is inevitable that study of literary sources alone must grossly underestimate the incidence and importance of their kind of religion in any religious civilisation.

Ministry-Buddhism was also commonly carried by kings. Like peasants, kings also live in the world and have more use for a form of religion that is relevant to real life. It is rather evident from the history of various civilisations that there is a certain community of interest between kings and the common people, since both have a common foe: the élite, of barons and the like, who are the principal oppressors of the people and the principal obstacle to the king's exercise of power, and threat to his retention of it. Even when it is more latent than evident, this community of interest may generate a certain harmony of outlook between king and commoners, which is likely to find religious expression.

There are two basically different kinds of situation in which kings may find themselves. One is where the boundaries of the kingdom have been fairly stably established for some time, and where the king can best increase his power, his control over his domain, by weakening that of his rivals, the members of élites. It is in such a situation, as I suggested earlier, that the king might find an interest in emasculating the clergy politically by defining their vocation as an unworldly, secluded one. The contrasted situation is one in which there is little real possibility of exercising centralised political control over the domain. Very commonly this is found where a kingdom has recently expanded to incorporate hitherto independent peoples and/or where its extent is too large for it to be tightly controlled with the political, economic and technical resources available to the king. In such a situation control over the domain must be largely in moral and symbolic, which is to say religious, terms. A king so placed will emphasise the more religious aspects of kingly office. In a Buddhist society he will have much use for the clergy as propagators of the religious legitimation of his sovereignty. And of course it will be those who follow the vocation of ministry who will be of most service to him. Since these are obviously those who are also of most use to the common people, in this situation the always latent community of interest between king and commoners is here realised.[12]

Kings do not usually write books, though their more or less loyal servants do. It is extraordinarily fortunate that probably the first, and certainly the greatest and most influential of all Buddhist kings, the emperor Asoka, was the man he was. His situation was very much of the second kind we have sketched; he was a man of profound religious understanding; and he had an urge to record his thoughts in writing, imperishably, mainly on rock. The text of his Edicts did indeed become lost to Buddhist consciousness for millennia; but it has now been recovered and published, and is an invaluable guide to Buddhism.

There are now several books which explain, more or less clearly and fully, what Buddhism really is and always has been. One of the best that I know is Emmanuel Sarkisyanz's *Buddhist Backgrounds of the Burmese Revolution* (1965). Characteristically, the author had great difficulty in getting his work published; and so well received was it that it has been allowed to go out of print, despite the fact that the analysis is warmly endorsed in a Preface by one of the most eminent scholars of Buddhism, Professor Paul Mus.[13]

A central passage, entirely sound, is this:

There *are* Buddhist social ethics – no matter how widespread the notion that Buddhism is anti-social and *only* negative. Yet it is true that this Ashokan social emphasis was not identical with the ethos of the Buddhist order of monks striving out of the world of Impermanence towards Nirvana, but it is nevertheless Buddhist ethos: the ethos of *lay* Buddhism acting with the world of Impermanence, in pursuring Nirvana by creating the outward social conditions for such a striving towards the overcoming of Attachment. It was *this* social ethos that the Ashokan tradition of historical Buddhism transmitted, a political lay tradition within Buddhism. This 'political Ashokan Buddhism' of historical rulers is less widely known than the philosophical canonic Buddhism of the monastic Order.[14]

In his Preface, agreeing with this judgement, Mus points out that most of Western scholarship on Buddhism has been the study by philologists of texts, unduly overlooking the historical and sociological background, and that this runs the risk of 'finding finally in history just the shell of what once filled it'. At one point he even refers scathingly to 'the die-hards of Theravâda monachal orthodoxy'.[15]

I remarked that the quest of the historical Buddha is incurably futile. From this it follows that the product of that quest must be worthless, at least for the purpose intended. There was, however, at least one set of people for whom it was invaluable.

Colonial society in Sri Lanka, and probably everywhere else, was basically a three-class society. At the top was the colonial British expatriate élite. At the base the great mass of natives, mainly villagers. Because some kind of indirect rule is the most economical way of running such systems, there evolved an intermediate group, from the natives by origin but towards the British by orientation.[16*] Its members in nineteenth-century Sri Lanka were referred to as 'the middle class', as their successors commonly are today. The term was structurally accurate.

Their situation was a difficult one:[17] as their modern descendants sometimes say, 'between two worlds'.[18] Their position and privileges depended on holding the approval of the British, which meant assimilating British customs and values, externally at least; in large measure these were also internalised. This was facilitated, and betokened, by language. English was established as the official language; for many middle-class occupations mastery of English was essential, and for all it was most advantageous; in itself it became an emblem of privileged status. Middle-class Sinhalese sought to become British, and many of them were highly successful in this, both linguistically and culturally. In a third respect, that of race, they had no chance. Many sought to compensate by becoming more British than the British culturally, and by overstressing how very different they were from the unsophisticated peasantry whom they superficially resembled. But with rare exceptions the British rejected them as social equals. Denied the British identity they sought, they could only identify themselves as Sinhalese. But this was tricky. The last thing they wanted was to be identified with the inferior villagers; they still needed the approval of the British reference group, not least as internalised within themselves. It would have been folly to come out as Sinhalese nationalists in any political sense; so, like groups similarly placed in Europe, their nationalism was expressed in religious idiom. This was particularly easy since for millennia Buddhism and Sinhalese national identity had been virtually identified. But it was difficult, since they did not want to lumber themselves with actual Buddhism, village Buddhism, which all right-thinking persons condemned as gross superstition.

The Western misinterpretation of Buddhism, which was just coming on to the market at that time, was ideally adapted to their needs. Here was a Buddhism, warranted as authentic by Europeans, no less, which was not only purged of vulgar and degrading superstitions, but was actually 'scientific', and admired by (some) Europeans, of whom a number actually converted. The emphasis on secluded meditatory Buddhism also spoke to their condition. It was Manichaean.[19]* Just as some of their European near-contemporaries were enormously godly on Sundays, and diabolical the rest of the week, so here it was possible to pay homage to non-self when one visited the forest monasteries, and self everywhere else.[20]* It may be that the sharp separation between the domains of the sacred and the profane symbolised for them the two worlds, British and Sinhalese, between which they saw themselves painfully suspended. An emphasis on meditation, a solitary activity, as the principal religious activity to be expected of laymen was congenial to individualists. They had no need of the ministry priests, for they were largely self-sufficient, not dependent on neighbours and community as villagers are; and they could read the Dhamma for themselves, even in 'its earliest, simplest, and purest form as taught by Buddha and his immediate disciples' as well as by Professor Max Müller and other European scholars. This was the basis, then, of the form of Buddhism they evolved, strongly under Western influence, which Bechert and Gombrich call 'Buddhist modernism', and I, too crudely, 'middle-class Buddhism'.

When I remarked that the quest for the historical Buddha was incurably futile, I allowed that the nineteenth-century scholars could hardly have been expected to see this. It should be quite obvious to us, but since evidently it is not, I had better enlarge a little on the considerations which compel this conclusion.

1. It has generally been accepted by scholars of Buddhism that the earliest of the scriptures were composed, on the basis of traditions, several centuries after the Buddha's death. This is doubtless true of most of them. Frauwallner has argued, rather convincingly, that the first was probably composed between 100 and 160 years after the Buddha's death.[21]

2. The author of that work, the *Skandhaka*, was about as close in time to the Buddha as we are to Karl Marx. It is notorious that much of what passes as Marxism diverges markedly from Marx's own views. One need only read 'The Poverty of Theory',[22] a demolition by the Marxist historian

E. P. Thompson of the Marxism of Althusser: even without taking sides, it is plain that at least one of these two Marxists has seriously misunderstood Marx's thought. Yet Marx published his views in print, and his works have been widely circulated. Ours is an age, as his was, of extensive literacy, in which standards of objective empirical enquiry are strongly established and somewhat widely diffused.

3. Suppose now that Marx had published never a word in writing, nor had anyone else written a word about his life and doctrine until the present day. Suppose further that those who transmitted traditions about him were credulous and uncritical, and had not the least inkling of scientific, objective historical method. Can anyone imagine that it would be possible now to reconstruct a reliable account of Marx's views, and to have justified confidence in its reliability?

4. The situation regarding the Buddha is even worse than this. If we accept, as I do, and Gombrich[23] and some other Orientalists do, the soundness of Frauwallner's work, we had better attend to what he tells us of this *Skandhaka*, the earliest known scripture, composed a century after the Buddha's death:

> [The author's] working method is clearly recognizable. He deals quite freely with the tradition, gives it another meaning and completes it through inventions of his own. And everything is subordinated to a unitary plan . . .
> The biography of the Buddha, which forms the framework of the old *Skandhaka* text, is not authentic old tradition, but a legendary tale, the work of the author of the *Skandhaka*.[24]

This 'biographical' material contains some of the most often quoted 'sayings of the Buddha', as well as alleged events which are much relied upon in forming interpretations of Buddhism. Frauwallner has already told us that most of the later 'lives of the Buddha' are derived from the *Skandhaka*;[25] what is not is based on traditions and inventions with even less claim to be taken seriously as history. Hence Frauwallner concludes:

> What we know and are able to know about the person and the life of the Buddha is therefore even less than we have hitherto believed; we must prepare ourselves to relegate in the realm of fable many things which were believed to be trustworthy tradition.[26]

5. If we reject, as some scholars[27] do, Frauwallner's conclusions, then we have no knowledge of any scripture having been composed earlier than several centuries after the Buddha's death; and in any event this goes for most of the alleged discourses of the Buddha in the *suttas*.

6. We are considerably better placed to give a scientific historical account of the life and teaching of Jesus than we are to do so for Gotama Buddha. The earliest 'biography' that we have, St. Mark's Gospel, was written little more than *forty* years after the death of Jesus;[28] we have a little evidence from the still earlier Epistles of St. Paul; and we are far

better placed to make a critical evaluation of the materials. If, despite these advantages, we can know very little about the historical Jesus, it is an inevitable conclusion that we can know even less about the historical Buddha.

7. It is not as widely known as it should be that we can know very little about the historical Jesus. This is largely because most of those who are motivated to read about the matter are Christians, to whom such a conclusion is, understandably if mistakenly, distressing; and hence most of those biblical scholars who write about the matter are reluctant to express themselves as plainly in print as they often do in talking to their colleagues. But despite the obscurity, if not evasiveness, of much of what they write, one cannot read much New Testament criticism with an open mind without recognising a near consensus that we really know, in the scientific sense, very little about Jesus.

8. James M. Robinson, for example, in *A New Quest of the Historical Jesus* (1959), argues that while we may know much about 'Jesus of Nazareth as he actually was' on the basis of Faith, and that this is a valid form of historiography, the quest of the historical Jesus as this was conceived in the nineteenth century was largely futile.

It is in this sense that one must correctly understand statements which might seem shocking if used in the other sense of the term: 'We can know very little of the historical Jesus'. If by this one means that we can know very little about Jesus of Nazareth by means of the scientific methods of the historian, so that a modern biography of him is hardly possible, such a viewpoint need not trouble the believer, although it could be a topic of legitimate discussion among historians.[29]

He goes on to maintain that 'the kind of quest of the historical Jesus envisaged by the nineteenth century not only *cannot* succeed but . . . *ought not* to succeed'.[30] It ought not to succeed because it was an attempt to evade the real need for Faith by providing human knowledge. In support, he quotes from Karl Barth, writing in 1923: 'The man who does not yet know (and that *still* means all of us) that we know Christ *no* longer according to the flesh, can learn it from critical biblical scholarship: the more radically he is shocked, the better it is both for him and for the cause.'[31]

9. The reasons why we cannot learn much about the historical Jesus by the means of objective scientific historical scholarship are commonplace in New Testament criticism; I summarise them from Nineham (1963). By the time our primary sources – mainly the Gospels, especially that of St. Mark – were composed, it is doubtful if their authors had available material which would have enabled them to write scientifically sound biographies: it was already too late to separate historically sound from legendary material in the traditions with which they worked. But the point is merely academic, since it is clear that they had no idea of writing

such biographies. Our scientific notions of historiography did not exist at that time, at any rate among such people, and their primary purpose was to write not history but theology. Like the other Evangelists, St. Mark sought to proclaim the saving truth; and since he believed that Jesus had completely proclaimed it, whatever he knew to be true he thereby knew that Jesus had taught. And he knew something to be true because he found it saved. Hence the religious experience of the author, and of the Church out of which and for which he wrote, was projected on to Jesus. This was admirable, but it does not produce reliable history, of Jesus.

In addition, the Evangelists had other purposes. Already different local Churches had formed somewhat different interpretations of Christianity; scriptures were written in part to legitimise the local version, to some extent in contention with rival views. There was also a common purpose, resulting from the common historical situation in which the Evangelists wrote. In the latter part of the first century A.D., and indeed for a considerable time thereafter, the Church was in great danger because the Romans tended to identify the Christians with the Jews, and to see them as the followers of a seditious Jewish prophet. As a consequence of the Jewish revolt of 66–70 A.D., which the Romans had suppressed only with difficulty, this was a perilous identification which invited persecution. A major purpose of the Evangelists was to present an account, almost certainly fictitious, of Jesus in opposition to Jewish leaders, and of his execution by Pilate, not as a result of supposed sedition against the Romans, but as a result of Pilate's acquiescence in Jewish hostility to Jesus.[32]

10. Robinson summarises the situation thus:

The *possibility* of the original [i.e. nineteenth-century] quest resided primarily in its view of the oldest sources as the same kind of objective, positivistic historiography which the nineteenth century itself aspired to write. The basic reorientation [in the twentieth century] consisted in the discovery that the Gospels are the devotional literature of the primitive Church, rather than the products of scholarship ... The Gospels are primary sources for the history of the early Church, and only secondarily sources for the history of Jesus.[33]

11. We know of no notable historical event, still less crisis, which occasioned the composition of the Buddhist scriptures,[34]* nor does their content suggest any. In other respects the purposes and procedures of their authors were similar to those of the Christian authors. It would be prudent to assume as much in the absence of evidence; but in fact scholars – e.g. Frauwallner – have produced ample evidence of it.

12. The conclusion is inescapable: we have no scientific means of determining with confidence what the historical Buddha did or said, except in barest outline.[35]* The Buddha – or rather Buddhas – that the scriptures present to us are essentially projections of the religious

understanding of their authors and the communities within which they composed. The scriptures are good evidence for the religion of the early *Sāsana*,[36]* but at best hypothetical evidence concerning the objective historical Buddha.

13. They are none the worse for it. As the Gospels tell us the religious meaning that the early Christians saw in their apprehension of the life and teaching of Christ, already largely legendary and essentially mythical,[37] so too the Buddhist scriptures tell us what early Buddhists made of their traditions. This is of real historical value; and it is arguably of more religious value to consider what ordinary men, much like ourselves, understood, than it would be to have the original words of a genius which we are less well placed than they were to understand.

Though these critical conclusions are plainly recognised, in some contexts at least, by scholars of Buddhism, their implications for the understanding of Buddhism are insufficiently appreciated. Even such excellent scholars as Gombrich or Ling write with great assurance of the views of the Buddha, as if these were known historical data.[38] The reorientation, which should have resulted from recognition of the fallacy of positivistic historiography, has been far less developed in Buddhist than in Christian studies.

In part this is a result of the very uneven distribution of resources to the two areas of study: progress in Buddhist studies is so much slower because many fewer able scholars, in the West at least, apply their talents to this area. In larger part, I suspect, it is because those who are attracted to Buddhist studies tend to be 'humanists' who have by no means thrown off the positivist bias, whereas interest in Christian studies is in large part religiously motivated, and thus more responsive to the profound religious understanding of men such as Karl Barth.

These are not the only, nor even the principal, causes of the persistence of the conventional Western interpretation of Buddhism. One does not need to be learned to recognise, if one chooses, the futility of attempting to know the historical Buddha from the scriptures. Even among Christians, with our relatively restricted scriptures, it is an ancient popular proverb that 'The Devil can cite Scripture for his purpose'.[39] This is to recognise that scripture is open to a wide range of interpretations: hence it does not yield us unambiguously one consistent picture of the historical Christ, about whom we have therefore little certain objective knowledge. This is even more true of Buddhist scriptures and the historical Buddha; and I suggest that village Buddhists come close to recognising as much, at least implicitly. I remarked that both clergy and laity were notably unspecific and relaxed in their allusions to scripture, to the point that I wondered whether Silaratana was not inventing some of the anecdotes about the Buddha which he retailed with evident amusement (above, Chapter 3). Such an attitude to scripture is sounder, both scientifically and religiously, than that of positivist scholars and their uncritical readers.

The Western interpretation of Buddhism persists in part through inertia and conservatism. It suits our vanity to assume that we are the people who understand Buddhism. On the other hand, to recognise that our understanding is fallacious would require us, as I shall show, to undertake a distressing revision of our estimate of how, and with what sources, religion must be understood.

Whatever may be the case among the scholars themselves, interest in Buddhism among a wider educated public is often derived from quasi-religious motivations, and the Western interpretation of Buddhism maintained for its religious, or sub-religious, value. It is not unknown among religiously inclined people to seek an infallible authority which will answer all their questions for them, and it is obvious how the historical Buddha, if we could know him, might serve this need. This craving to be exempted from responsibility for our own decisions seems to me escapist, an abdication from our human condition. It seems consistent that it is gratified by rhinoceros Buddhism, which is also escapist, and has a tendency to association with the most shocking abdication of human responsibility, as we saw from Spiro's evidence (above, Chapter 6).

As I have presented it, village Buddhism, and Ministry-Buddhism generally, is quite different: it is rooted in a sense of responsibility for the affairs of the world, and recognition of the need actually to help other people. Consistently, village Buddhists display little anxiety to determine exactly what the Buddha said, or misgivings in discounting what others allege he said (as in the rhinoceros verses) when it does not make good sense to them.

When I asked villagers what an *āgama* (roughly, religion) is, some of them replied – obviously having *Buddhāgama* primarily in mind – by defining an *āgama* as that which teaches us the difference between right and wrong conduct; some of them said that anything else in an *āgama* is subordinate and even inessential. Though it was only some people who stated this flatly, a similar understanding appears to be implicit in the views of village Buddhists generally – with the qualification that ethical action is valued primarily for its effect on the state of mind (and being) of the actor, and its figurative extension as his future state.

Logically this raises the further question of how we can know that a given *āgama* is true, and this was not lost on village Buddhists. Pragmatically they often stated that we know the truth of Buddhism on the basis of Faith (*visvāsa*). This is directly contrary to the claim, much vaunted by Buddhist Modernists, that Buddhism, unlike Christianity, does not appeal to Faith, but solely to reason. Analysis shows that Buddhist Modernists are mistaken in this, for their reasoning appeals to premises the truth of which is not rationally demonstrable. Indeed, they are necessarily wrong: in so far as a religion is a matter of propositional 'truths' – which I argue it is not, primarily – it is necessarily based on beliefs which cannot be demonstrated by reason. It is either based on rationally unwarranted beliefs, or not based on beliefs at all.

But Faith (*visvāsa*), though it can produce assent, cannot warrant the objective truth of its object, for faith may be misplaced. The best objective test of the truth of an *āgama* is that proposed by the *Kālāma Sutta* (see above, Chapter 5), the test of good conduct. Though they reveal no direct awareness of this scripture, village Buddhists imply a similar view. They will say that one can be a Buddhist without ceasing to be a Christian; they go further and say a person may be a good Buddhist whatever his religious, or non-religious, adherence: he who does well is *ipso facto* a good Buddhist. With this highly ecumenical view, questions concerning the reliability and foundations of Faith are not of critical importance to them. There is, indeed, an element of tautology in their position, and, in that of the *Kālāma Sutta*: if it is the function of an *āgama* to produce ethical conduct, its quality is best measured by its product.

As is explicit in the *Kālāma Sutta*, this position offers no infallible authority on to which we can shuffle off responsibility for judgement; it requires us to make our own decisions, as is stressed in other, familiar scriptural texts. But, in actual Buddhism at least, there is no suggestion that a man decides alone: otherwise there would be no point in teaching, no value whatever in the scriptures. Finally, a man decides for himself, but he reaches his decision in the light of guidance from his fellows. This is why, to Sinhalese villagers, and to ourselves if we seek in religion something of practical relevance to our lives, scriptures are really useful: they convey to us the considered judgements of our fellows, bygone men like ourselves, who authored the scriptures and projected their own judgements on to the supernatural, which is to say fictitious and symbolic, figures of Buddha and Christ. But our bygone fellows are not the most relevant to us, for they lived in rather different circumstances, and their judgements have been somewhat obscured in the process of transmission down time. Our contemporaries are more relevant, even though this has the consequence, unwelcome to some, that we have to take very seriously the actual religion of rustics, peasants, and unsophisticated peasants at that. For a start, we had better take care to understand it.

There is a still larger, if not more important, conclusion which is no less unwelcome. The analysis challenges, or rather demolishes, the whole basis of our usual understanding of religion.

I suggested earlier that, along one dimension, the term 'Buddhism' has four different senses, referring to four different elements or aspects of the whole. It seems natural to people with a Christian cultural background to sort these analytically into an order which makes the Buddha's teaching the core of the whole system: from it follow, in sequence, the doctrine, the religion, and the civilisation. This was the basic assumption which led scholars to seek to determine what the Buddha's teaching was, through study of the scriptures.

That ordering has a certain plausibility: at least, it is more likely than not that Buddhism did originate from the teaching of the historical Buddha, Gotama (*c.* 563–483 B.C.). But the programme of study and analysis which derived from this assumption runs into the insuperable obstacle that we cannot know anything, or at best not nearly enough, about the historical Buddha and his teaching. So, even if this approach is well founded and methodologically proper, we cannot usefully follow it, and must either find another or despair.

Our critical account of the scriptures, summary as it has been, suggests further that the traditional approach is not only futile but misconceived; and hence that the basic assumption from which it was derived was unsound. It would appear that the four elements to which the one term 'Buddhism' may refer should not be sorted in the order which it has seemed natural to suppose, but in just the reverse order: which is that in which I listed them. Thus the primary reality is Buddhist civilisation,[40*] Buddhist society and culture, a way of life of real men. This generates Buddhist religion, as a construction which orders and legitimises, in symbolic form, that civilisation. This in turn is systematised in Buddhist doctrine. And to legitimise the doctrine and the religion that lies behind it, these are attributed to Lord Buddha, who thus emerges as a projection of, perhaps an impersonation of, the prior and more basic elements of the system. No doubt the historical Buddha was the origin of the whole system; but he is unknowable. The Buddha we encounter in the scriptures, and other sources, is not that historical Buddha, the origin of the system, but a construction, a figure of fiction, though perfectly valid of its own kind, who is not the origin but the symbolic product of the system.

This seems to be true if we approach Buddhism historically, seeking it in its earliest knowable form, which turns out not to be the Buddhism of the historical Buddha, but the Buddhism of Buddhists a century and more later, who left us evidence of themselves in the scriptures they composed. But to prefer to study the Buddhism of the remote past, rather than that of the present, seems to derive from another peculiar bias of scholars. In the main, the further we look back into the past, the poorer the evidence we have about human reality. If we did know more about the character of the ancient Buddhist civilisation which generated the scriptures, we should be able to make more of them and understand them better; but we cannot hope for much in that direction.

If we did not, for various reasons, overrate the importance of the scriptures, but rather regarded them with the kind of lax respect that actual Buddhists do, we should be less obsessively concerned with the past, and would see that we can know most about, and therefore have the best chance of understanding, the actual Buddhism of the present. Epistemologically, indeed, it may be suggested that the actual Buddhism of the present stands to the actual Buddhism of the past much as the latter stands to the Buddhism of the Buddha. No doubt in the actual sequence of historical process what came earlier generated what came later, but in terms of what we can know the reverse order holds. This is not only because we can have more and better knowledge of what comes later: more basically it is because what we can make of the evidence of the past is inescapably shaped by our understanding of and in the present.[41]

It follows from this that ethnographic fieldwork, not necessarily conducted by a professional anthropologist, is the best way to learn about Buddhism; and its results, if the work has been competent, must be the canon of what is authentic Buddhism, against which the authenticity of everything else which is claimed to be Buddhist must be measured. I do not mean by this to assume that village Buddhism is the only canon, and that the actual Buddhisms of the middle class and other categories of people are *ipso facto* less authentic; that conclusion is based on other grounds, as I have shown. But, as a matter of methodology, it is actual Buddhism, of which village Buddhism is one variety, which must be the canon. It is a measure of how far our understanding of religion is distorted that we have regularly stated the opposite, confidently declaring village Buddhism to be deviant, not true Buddhism, by judging it against a less authentic canon, whether this be the scriptures (selectively) as with Spiro, or the views of the Buddha (imaginatively) as with Gombrich.

In asserting that the four elements of Buddhism should be sorted in just the reverse order from that in which they traditionally have been, I have assumed more than I have demonstrated. I have not proved that it is a society and culture which generates its specific religion, rather than the reverse. And I have not proved that religion as practised generates doctrine, rather than the reverse. These are standard assumptions of the anthropological approach to religion. Ideally I should like to go on to show that both assumptions are well warranted, but this book would become unwieldy if I were to attempt it. I shall therefore confine myself to presenting some basic arguments for the second assumption, while leaving the first unsupported, other than by reference to the quantity of anthropological and sociological studies which do lend it support. I do so partly because I have more to say about the second assumption, partly because some of the things I shall say in this context are relevant also to the other case. In particular, I shall be arguing that moral conduct is the fundamental basis of religion, or at least a fundamental basis of a religion such as Buddhism is; and it will be rather evident, I trust, that what moral conduct is is crucially related to the actual form of society.

But before laying aside the basic issue of how a society and its religion are related, I had better say a few words lest my assumption be misunderstood. The view that the form of a society generates its religion, as a construction which orders and legitimises it in symbolic form, has often been advocated in a context of belittling religion: as a reductionist argument that a religion is nothing but a reflection of social forms, but illusory because it is not recognised as merely this.[42]* That is very far from my intention. I do not see a religion as merely a reflection of actual social forms: it is also a proclamation of and commitment to new social forms, and hence a criticism as well as a reflection of actual society. I do not see it as only concerned with social issues, but also with various other issues of human life, which could hardly be called social without stretching that term close to the point of vacuity of meaning. I say simply that a religion is very much concerned with social issues, and fundamentally so because its basic message is concerned with fellowship; and since it is a thoroughly human construction, it is necessarily shaped by the particular social awareness of particular humans in their particular societies. I see nothing in this to demean religion. As the doctrine of Creation asserts that the world partakes of divinity, and the doctrine of the Incarnation asserts that humanity partakes of divinity, so I assume, and with the same qualifications,[43] that society partakes of divinity, is holy. My assumptions that religion is natural, human, and social, so far from being intended to imply that it lacks divinity or holiness, are meant to recognise that it has these qualities in their most genuine form.

Notes to Chapter 10

1 I have summarised Thomas (1975), pp. xiv–xvii.
2 Quoted in Gombrich (1971), p. 54.
3 We seem to encounter something analogous to Heisenberg's uncertainty principle in quantum physics: the more confident we are that the Buddha taught some doctrine the less confident we are of what the doctrine means. Thus we can be highly confident that his teaching was concerned with the concepts of nirvana and *anatta*: but the interpretation of both concepts is notoriously controversial. Davies (1982, p. 62) maintains that the Heisenberg uncertainty is not merely a product of the inadequacy of our means of investigation, but is 'an inherent property of the microworld'. The electron 'is an intrinsically uncertain entity'. I suggest that similarly our uncertainty as to what the Buddha taught has a deeper basis than the inadequacy of the

scriptures as historical sources: that it is inherently impossible to be sure what another man thinks, and seriously so when that other man is an original genius. Nineham seems to be making a similar point when he writes with reference to 'the historic Jesus', 'Seldom, if ever, can we distinguish with certainty and say: "This is pure history" and "that is pure invention or interpretation". Indeed it is not at all clear what "pure history" would be, for the history of any man comprises what he did and said and the impression it made upon those with whom he came into contact' (1963, p. 51). It may be implicit in those scriptural passages, as in the *Kālāma Sutta*, which have the Buddha asserting that every man must determine truth and salvation for himself, for no one else can do it for him.

4   Quoted in Robinson (1959), p. 32. Robinson does not specify the source, which I guess to be Schweitzer's *The Quest of the Historical Jesus*. It may be objected that I have fallen into the same kind of trap, in that the Buddhism and hence the Buddha I perceive is shaped by my peculiar prejudices. Of course; the difference is that I know it, and have indeed taken pains to warn the reader of it. The real fault of the nineteenth-century biographers was to have presented their perception as objective historical fact, with the implication that any different perception must be false. I make no such claims for my perception, but rather reject such claims for all perceptions, including my own.

5   Peiris (1973) brings together much of the data in brief.

6   This picture of the Buddha and his teaching is marked in Weber (1967), pp. 225–8, and in Ling (1973), e.g. p. 106, pp. 116–17.

7   Cf. Tambiah (1976), p. 402.

8   Thomas (1975), p. 252; Dutt (1962), p. 294.

9   It is likely that some of these clerics had been born into poor families and were sympathetic to the popular religion in which they had grown up.

10 I have remarked (Chapter 3) that villagers do not seem greatly concerned to produce scriptural warrant for their views and practices. This unconcern, I suggest, is conditioned by the confidence that such warrant is available if needed. I am arguing here that if there were no such warrant the attachment of villagers to Buddhism would have been fragile.

11 I asked all the priests and novices whom I interviewed about their family backgrounds. If they did not exaggerate, in nearly all cases their fathers were villagers of more than average prosperity and standing – broadly members of the local élite (Roberts, 1974). None came from the national élite or 'middle class'; and middle-class Sinhalese have told me that it is rare for boys from such families to join the Sangha.

12 This paragraph condenses analyses in Southall (1956) and Tambiah (1976).

13 Bechert also approves it: 1978a, p. 191; 1978b, p. 201.

14 Sarkisyanz (1965), p. 36.

15 Mus (1965), pp. xi, xii, xix.

16 'It was part of general British policy in their colonial territories to create an indigenous British-oriented élite to man local administration, a policy well expressed in Macaulay's minute on Indian education urging the need "to form a class of persons Indian in blood and color, but English in tastes, in opinions, in morals and in intellect". In this the British were eminently successful and

many facets of later Ceylonese history would be inexplicable without an understanding of this' (Seneviratne, 1976, p. 97).

17 For much of the material in this paragraph I am indebted to Hodge (1979).

18 The phrase was used as the title of a distinguished film by Lester James Pieris.

19 In the sense explained in Chapter 7, n. 12.

20 I do not suggest that all Buddhist Modernists were, or are, peculiarly selfish. I merely observe that quite often attachment to Buddhist Modernism is found in people whose conduct in business affairs is less than ruthful.

21 Frauwallner (1956), p. 54.

22 Thompson (1978).

23 Gombrich (1971), p. 42 n. 6.

24 Frauwallner (1956), p. 163.

25 *Ibid.*, p. 155.

26 *Ibid.*, p. 164.

27 E.g. Dutt (1962), p. 79 n. 1.

28 Nineham (1963), pp. 41–2.

29 Robinson (1959), pp. 31–2.

30 *Ibid.*, p. 43; italics in original.

31 *Ibid.*, p. 45; italics in original.

32 See especially Brandon (1971).

33 Robinson (1959), p. 35; italics in original.

34 There are traditions which relate the writing down of the scriptures to contemporary crisis; my statement refers to the earlier composition of the scriptures in oral form.

35 Cf. Thomas (1975), p. 251: 'In the present state of our knowledge we cannot in any instance declare that Buddha said so and so.'

36 Some reservations are necessary even about this. Scriptures are composed for controversial purposes among others, and their authors are not wholly typical of the people of their time. The views maintained in the scriptures may therefore not be wholly representative of all those held among Buddhists of the period.

37 Nineham (1963), pp. 17–25, 33–5.

38 E.g. Gombrich (1971), p. 16 (quoted above, Chapter 6); Ling (1973), *passim*.

39 Shakespeare had Antonio quote it in *The Merchant of Venice*, I, iii, 99.

40 This is a major thesis of Ling (1973), especially chapter 2.

41 Cf. Collingwood (1946).

42 This is the major drift of Durkheim's argument (1912, 1915). He is somewhat ambivalent and inconsistent; some of his followers have been less reluctant to suppose that religions are 'made up of a tissue of illusions' (Durkheim, 1915, pp. 69–70; 1912, pp. 98–99).

43 See above, Chapter 7.

11

Practice and belief

William Robertson Smith's *Lectures on the Religion of the Semites* (first edition 1889) is a comparative study of the rite of sacrifice among different branches of the Semitic peoples at different periods, with further reference to sacrifice among some non-Semitic peoples. It is based mainly on research on historical sources, notably the Old Testament, though Smith did do a little fieldwork among contemporary Arabs. He found that the rite itself was remarkably constant wherever it occurred in a variety of places and times, but that the beliefs, doctrines, and myths associated with it were highly variable. Most strikingly, he found that the form of the sacrificial rite changed very little over the long history of the Hebrews, although the beliefs by which it was explained were very different at different periods. He concluded that in actual religion practice, especially ritual practice, must be primary, and belief secondary: that beliefs are produced to explain ritual rather than, as had usually been supposed, ritual being the practical expression and consequence of beliefs which were prior. Though some of his evidence and his interpretation of it have since been rejected, his major points stand firm, and the logic of his argument is hard to resist. It would be astonishing if the various beliefs that the Hebrews held at various periods had each generated, by some strange coincidence, just the same form of ritual expression; but the facts seem quite natural if one can suppose a continuity of a fixed form of rite which gives rise to various kinds of belief, serving to explain and rationalise it, at various periods. The same logic applies when the comparison is of the relation between ritual practice and belief not at different periods of the history of one people, but among different peoples.

The same conclusion was suggested when he studied, in a range of instances, the relationship between belief and a particular ritual form in a particular society at a particular period. Here he found that the form of ritual practice was strictly fixed, and participation in the rite was obligatory; but the attached beliefs were vague and various, and people were at liberty to adhere to any, or indeed none, of them. (This has been confirmed by much subsequent anthropological research in other cultures.)[1]*

Thus Smith concluded that our habitual way of thinking about religion as primarily a matter of beliefs and doctrines of which religious, especially ritual, practices are the consequences, must be wrong, at least with reference to the religions of other peoples. Clearly it is the practices which come first, both chronologically and logically, and it is the beliefs which are derivative from them. Hence when we study other religions we should observe the same priority, attending first to the practices which are basic and then to the beliefs which have to be regarded as derivative from them.

Smith was well aware that this way of regarding and analysing religion was directly contrary to the understanding we have of our own religion, and to the way that as Christians we are taught to think of religion. He was not at all hostile to Christianity; on the contrary he was one of the leading theologians and biblical scholars of his age, and himself a devout Christian. The facts, however, and inescapable logic, drove him to the conclusion he stated. If the facts are correct, as they are, no other conclusion (except as I shall modify it shortly) is logically possible. This should be evident even from the brief summary of the case that I have given. Nevertheless, for all its logic, the conclusion is quite remarkably difficult to accept: even professional anthropologists, who regularly (but not invariably) profess adherence to it as a basic methodological axiom, experience great difficulty in remaining true to it in their actual research and analysis. Its truth is demonstrable but unpersuasive.

It is tempting to refer the reader who requires further persuasion to Smith's own work, especially the first chapter (Lecture) in which the argument is mainly developed. This may help, but often does not, since the logically crucial points are embedded in such a mass of erudition that they are easily missed. For this reason I shall pull out the passages which most merit attention, quoting them at some length in Smith's own words.

In this first passage I should point out that when Smith refers to some 'strange or antique religion' he means simply a religion of another culture, or of some past period of history: in effect the kinds of religion that anthropologists are most likely to study. Though it might suggest it, his phraseology was not intended to imply any disparagement.

And here we shall go very far wrong if we take it for granted that what is the most important side of religion to us was equally important in the ancient society with which we are to deal. In connection with every religion, whether ancient or modern, we find on the one hand certain beliefs, and on the other certain institutions, ritual practices and codes of conduct. Our modern habit is to look at religion from the side of belief rather than of practice; for, down to comparatively recent times, almost the only forms of religion seriously studied in Europe have been those of the various Christian Churches, and all parts of Christendom are agreed that ritual is important only in connection with its interpretation. Thus the study of religion has meant mainly the study of Christian beliefs, and instruction in religion has habitually begun with the creed, religious duties being presented to the learner as flowing from the dogmatic truths he is taught to accept. All this seems to us so much a matter of course that when we approach some strange or antique religion, we naturally assume that here also our first business is to search for a creed and find in it the key to ritual and practice. But the antique religions had for the most part no creed; they consisted entirely of institutions and practices. No doubt men will not habitually follow certain practices without attaching a meaning to them; but as a rule we find that while the practice was rigorously fixed, the meaning attached to it was extremely vague, and the same rite was explained by different people in different ways, without any question of orthodoxy or heterodoxy arising in consequence.[2]

These latter points are expressed still more strongly in the following passage:

... it is of the first importance to realise clearly from the outset that ritual and practical usage were, strictly speaking, the sum total of ancient religions. Religion in primitive times was not a system of belief with practical applications; it was a body of fixed traditional practices to which every member of society conformed as a matter of course. Men would not be men if they agreed to do certain things without having a reason for their action; but in ancient religion the reason was not first formulated as a doctrine and then expressed in practice, but conversely, practice preceded doctrinal theory. Men form general rules of conduct before they begin to express general principles in words; political institutions are older than political theories, and in like manner religious institutions are older than religious theories.[3]

He remarks that the analogy was not lightly chosen; and then continues with a passage which, though it diverts us a little from the main line of the present argument, is so true and important, and so relevant to our wider considerations, that it must be quoted:

... the oldest religious and political institutions ... were parts of one whole of social custom. Religion was a part of the organised social life into which a man was born, and to which he conformed through life in the same unconscious way in which men fall into any habitual practice of the society in which they live. Men took the gods and their worship for granted, and if they reasoned or speculated about them, they did so on the supposition that the traditional usages were fixed things, behind which their reasonings must not go, and which no reasoning could be allowed to overturn. To us moderns religion is above all a matter of individual conviction and reasoned belief, but to the ancients it was a part of the citizen's public life, reduced to fixed forms, which he was not bound to understand and was not at liberty to criticise or to neglect.[4]

Smith points out that not only were the rites more important than the beliefs which were developed to explain them, but also in most cases there was no such belief: 'The rite, in short, was connected not with a dogma but with a myth . . . In all the antique religions, mythology takes the place of dogma.'[5] His most forceful methodological point is made with regard to myths which purport to account for rituals; it may be seen that it is applicable also to beliefs or doctrines of similar purport:

So far as myths consist of explanations of ritual, their value is altogether secondary, and it may be affirmed with confidence that in almost every case the myth was derived from the ritual, and not the ritual from the myth; for the ritual was fixed and the myth was variable, the ritual was obligatory and faith in the myth was at the discretion of the worshipper . . . the myth is merely the explanation of a religious usage; and ordinarily it is such an explanation as could not have arisen till the original sense of the usage had more or less fallen into oblivion. As a rule the myth is no explanation of the origin of the ritual to any one who does not believe it to be a narrative of real occurrences, and the boldest mythologist will not believe that. But if it be not true, the myth itself requires to be explained, and every principle of philosophy and common sense demands that the explanation be sought, not in arbitrary allegorical theories, but in the actual facts of ritual or religious custom to which the myth attaches. The conclusion is, that in the study of ancient religions we must begin, not with myth, but with ritual and traditional usage.[6]

These words are very impressive, the more so when one recalls the great and well merited eminence of their author as a scholar and as a theologian. But I am rather sure that the reader will not have been wholly convinced by them; nor would he be if I were to lay out, as I have not space to do, the great bulk of anthropological evidence in their support which has been gathered since they were written. I suppose this because anthropologists, who learn about Robertson Smith as students, and who regularly pay obeisance to him, in practice have much difficulty in avoiding the way of thought which his words should have rooted out. Again I must forgo taking space to demonstrate that too many of us, too often, explicitly or implicitly, lay too much stress in our analyses on the importance of belief in religion. One remarkable illustration must suffice. Few if any anthropological writers on religion have been more thoroughly and expressly influenced by Robertson Smith than Durkheim was; yet, in a crucial passage of his *Elementary Forms of the Religious Life*, Durkheim wrote:

Religious phenomena are naturally arranged in two fundamental categories: beliefs and rites . . . The rites can be defined and distinguished from other human practices, moral practices for example, only by the special nature of their object . . . So it is the object of the rite which must be characterized if we are to characterize the rite itself. Now it is in the beliefs that the special nature of this object is expressed. It is possible to define the rite only after we have defined the belief.[7]

If we are to become thoroughly convinced of the truth of Robertson Smith's view, it is not more evidence that is needed. What is needed is first to diagnose the causes of our rooted reluctance to accept it, and second to show why it is not only true in empirical fact, but necessarily true, as I have already hinted in several passages.

The first obstacle to our fully accepting that belief is not the foundation of the religious life, but rather its dispensable by-product, is the one that Smith himself pointed to, the weight of our Christian tradition that the reverse is true. This is not, for individuals, simply a product of theology and religious instruction. The bias that belief is basic to religion is built into our culture, into our language itself, so that the very idiom in which we most easily talk about these matters itself sustains the bias. We commonly term an adherent of religion a 'believer', and an opponent an 'unbeliever'. It is common for a person to explain his rejection of religion by saying, 'I cannot believe that' (e.g. that God exists), as if believing and disbelieving were causes, and not consequences, of attitudes to religion (cf. Chapter 8). We call a religion a 'Creed' or a 'Faith', and regularly identify faith with belief. It is not easy to abandon so deeply rooted and axiomatic a pattern of thought.

Then, if one is tempted to embrace Smith's view to the extent of actually thinking within its frame, one rather rapidly encounters a consequence that is, apparently, most disturbing. People, ourselves included if we are religious, regularly do explain their ritual practices by reference either to associated beliefs or to associated myths. If, with Smith, we suppose that these are no explanations at all, but rather cultural products which themselves require explanation, we have to conclude that those who practise ritual have no explanation for their practice. Considering how much importance has been attached to ritual practice in so many cultures, including our own at least till recently, it may seem alarming that human beings generally have been so concerned to do things without having the least idea why they do them. And anthropologists, whose trade it is to offer explanations of human behaviour, have sometimes been reluctant to remainder their old stock of explanation by beliefs when they had little better to put in its place.

This has now changed. It is increasingly widely recognised that ritual behaviour is unlike many other kinds of behaviour, of the kinds that may be termed 'technical' or, better, 'instrumental', and that it is similar to what we call 'art' in being a form of presentational symbolism.[8] We do not find it odd that a musician normally cannot give an adequate account in words of what he expresses, and we respond to, in his music: on the contrary we find it rather obvious that if he could have expressed what he had to convey in words, he would have done so, and not hired a whole symphony orchestra.[9] Music, it seems clear, and probably presentational symbolism generally, is a product of a different set of mental processes – probably located in a different part of the brain[10] – from those which generate the matter-of-fact ('discursive')[11] use of language.

It is for the same reason that people cannot provide in matter-of-fact language a valid account of what they are doing in ritual.[12] This does not imply that ritual behaviour is, as has often been assumed in the past, 'irrational': it has its own kind of rationality, which is different from that of the matter-of-fact use of language, and which is largely untranslatable into the terms of the latter.

If this is so, then attempts by its practitioners to explain ritual behaviour in terms of statements of belief may be understood in either of two ways. Either those statements of belief are to be taken as expressions in the matter-of-fact idiom of language, as attempts to rationalise in such terms what inherently cannot be so rationalised, so that they are necessarily irrelevant as explanations because they are misconceived. Or, if we are less ready to assume that other people are as confused as they may seem to us to be, we may take their statements to be expressions not in the matter-of-fact idiom, but rather in another idiom which, like poetry, is a form of presentational symbolism. Instead of two different kinds of behavioural product, ritual and belief, which we have to relate in one order or the other, we then find ourselves with a homogeneous product. It then becomes rather easy to see that belief-statements are neither the precursors nor the successors of ritual practice, but part of it: that the ritual unit comprises not only the more obvious acts of presentational symbolism such as genuflection, libation, immolation, music and dance, but also the verbal behaviour, whether it takes the form of myth or of the proclamation of belief or doctrine.[13*]

At first sight this might suggest that Robertson Smith went too far in claiming that ritual practice has priority over belief: now it appears that neither has priority over the other, for they have been only arbitrarily distinguished. I think it might be better to say that he did not go far enough, since what this analysis really shows is that there is no such thing as belief, as that term has normally been understood. As Needham remarked in a contribution to a highly relevant controversy, 'Something that is believed by nobody is not a belief.'[14] But what we regard as statements of belief in a ritual context are, by those who make them, not believed as we ordinarily understand that term,[15] that is, not maintained as true statements of fact. Their import is not factual but symbolic.[16] Or, to be more exact, that is their proper import: it is not excluded that some of those who participate are confused about what they are saying, and naively suppose that the statements they utter are statements of fact.

Robertson Smith produced cogent reasons for thinking that religious practice is basic and primary, and religious belief derivative and secondary; and hence that 'we shall go very far wrong' in studying another religion if we 'assume that here also our first business is to search for a creed and find in it the key to ritual and practice'. I have now paraphrased, and perhaps somewhat extended, his views by claiming that, in matters of religion, people do not normally believe what they are reported to believe. Hence they do not normally have belief, of the sort we suppose them to have, and must suppose them to have if the hypothesis that religious practice follows from belief is to seem plausible. They may believe, and have belief and beliefs, in other senses of these terms; but in these other senses it is rather plain that belief could not be the basis of religious practice, but must rather be its product.

If these remarks appear contrary to common sense, and indeed paradoxical, it is because of the confused and unscientific way in which we regularly use belief-terms, i.e. the verb 'believe' and the noun 'belief'. No doubt people do not often misuse belief-terms with the deliberate intention of sowing confusion; but at the cultural level the usage is not unmotivated. In a variety of cultures one finds that key terms, crucial in important cultural complexes, are strikingly ambiguous or vague, and that this protects the values they convey from being too sharply confronted with discordant empirical reality. Axiomatic concepts and suppositions are made vague and ambiguous enough to accommodate any facts, and hence made immune to factual falsification. A critic can only say that what is unfalsifiable is uninformative, and to that extent meaningless.

This device, of protecting dogmas by making them too vague and ambiguous to be clearly falsifiable, is familiar to anthropologists[17] who consider the 'mystical' notions of other peoples – that is, roughly, the notions which are employed in religious thought and discourse, and also in such closely related phenomena as magic, witchcraft and sorcery. It is just such notions which are most often referred to as 'beliefs'. Because they are unfalsifiable they are factually uninformative, and *empirically* meaningless; but they are not wholly meaningless, or people would not go to such lengths to maintain them. The kind of meaning they do have is suggested by the following remarks of Pears, summarising Wittgenstein's views on religious belief:

A religious tenet is not a factual hypothesis, but something which affects our thoughts and actions in a different way . . . the meaning of a religious proposition is not a function of what would have to be the case if it were true, but a function of the difference it makes to the lives of those who maintain it.[18]

I am suggesting that our notion of 'belief', extended in our usage of belief-terms, is more like a mystical notion than a scientific concept: in itself it resembles a religious 'belief'. This is why one encounters such difficulty, and apparent paradox, in attempting to show that it does not adequately fit the facts. The bias of our Christian suppositions binds us even at this basic level of concept and terminology. If we are to describe and categorise the facts more objectively we shall need to break free from our customary question-begging usage. For the present, it will suffice to show that the use of belief-terms in ethnographic reports does not reliably convey what is usually understood, and that when the evidence is critically considered it provides no grounds for supposing that there really are religious beliefs of a kind which could be taken as prior to, rather than derivative from, religious practice.

Anthropologists have often used belief-terms with a freedom which implies they have regarded such usage as straightforward and unproblematic. In a few cases where the usage has given rise to puzzles there has been some more or less explicit discussion of some of the underlying conceptual difficulties, but this has normally been brief and unpenetrating. I know of only one full-length study specifically focusing on the basic problems involved in the use by anthropologists of belief-terms. This is Rodney Needham's *Belief, Language and Experience* (1972).

Needham's book is extremely erudite, abstruse, and difficult. Because it is both unique and important it deserves to be discussed, but a discussion which would do it justice must also be abstruse and difficult. I am reluctant to embark on this, because the issues which Needham tackles seem to me only a small part of those which need to be considered, and not in fact those most relevant to the problem as I have posed it. Needham does not refer to Robertson Smith at all, which in itself indicates that his focus is notably different from mine. It seems to me best, therefore, to give a brief account of the problems that Needham poses and the solutions he arrives at, as an introduction to discussion of the other issues I wish to take up. I do not suggest that this is an adequate account of Needham's work, merely an adequate account of the bearing it has on the present discussion; the reader who wants a fuller account of all that Needham says can, and should, consult the book itself.

Needham begins by remarking that although anthropologists do often use belief-terms, this usage appears to be ill-warranted:

If, however, an ethnographer said that people believed something when he did not actually know what was going on inside them, or if he simply reported nothing of their usual psychic states in association with presumed articles of belief, then surely his account of them must, it occurred to me, be very defective in quite fundamental regards.[19]

A little later he writes, of 'ethnographical statements referring to belief':

If they are assertions about the inner states of individuals, as by common usage they would normally be taken to be, then, so far as my acquaintance with the literature goes, no evidence of such states, as distinct from the collective representations that are thus recorded, is ever presented.[20]

For the sake of brevity, and clarity, let us define a term which Needham frequently uses and implies. A 'belief statement' is a statement which, by use of belief-terms, imputes believing to some person or set of persons. A belief-statement may take a variety of syntactical forms. It may use the verb 'believe', asserting, for example, 'they believe'. It may use the noun 'belief' in the sense of a 'thing believed'; or it may use the noun in the other sense which is nearly synonymous with 'believing'. These forms are intertranslatable: any reference to 'their' belief or beliefs implies that 'they' believe, and any statement that they believe implies that they have belief, and that what they believe are their beliefs.

All ethnographical belief-statements assert, explicitly or implicitly, that 'they believe . . .'. Are statements of, or reducible to, the forms 'he believes . . .', 'I believe . . .', 'we believe . . .' examples of the same kind of thing? Needham plainly assumes that they are, so I shall use the term 'belief statement' in that sense. But I shall have to go on to show that the meaning of belief-statements may be significantly different according to grammatical person: e.g. that the verb often has different meanings in 'they believe . . .' statements and 'I believe . . .' statements. When we take this up we shall have to recognise that the category of belief-statements must be further divided if we are to avoid serious confusion.

Now it is evident from the two passages I have quoted, as from innumerable others, that Needham's problem was posed by his taking it for granted that belief-statements are statements about the inner or psychic states of individuals. Or, at the very least, he takes it for granted that they will normally be understood in that way, so that an author who did not intend that interpretation is at fault if he uses belief-terms.[21] He further assumes that there is a unitary concept of belief,[22] so that those who use belief-terms are imputing some particular mental state; and further, that imputation of that mental state implies a common human psychological capacity, the capacity to have such mental states.[23]*

Needham's book is partly devoted to showing that anthropologists rarely have, and still more rarely show that they have, evidence to warrant their making such imputations and implications; and partly to showing that what he has read into the use of belief-terms is ill-founded in logic. Through closely wrought philosophical analysis he shows that there is no unitary concept of belief, and the notion of belief is merely a by-product of the use of the English verb 'believe' and its derivatives.[24] He also shows that whatever the word 'belief' does refer to, it cannot be taken to be a universally human state or capacity of mind.[25]. And he draws the important practical conclusion:

. . . since the possibilities of misunderstanding that are inherent in the notion of belief are so great, I do indeed urge that in ethnographical reports, or in comparative epistemology, the use of the word should be quite abandoned.[26]

Some readers may be as puzzled by all this as I was when I read Needham's book. It seemed to me that the problem he had expended so much effort in solving was a spurious one, or at any rate a merely private problem of Needham's, of no public interest. It had never occurred to me that belief-statements did impute mental states to individuals in such a way that one needed to 'know what was going on inside them' in order to be warranted in making the statements. On the contrary, it seemed to me that the facts to which belief-statements refer are of a much more readily accessible kind, namely what people say and do, and that people who make belief-statements commonly do have sufficient evidence of those kinds. As I shall make clear later, I was partly right about that.

Also, however, I was partly wrong. Needham's problem was not purely private and idiosyncratic, but is shared by others, perhaps many others; and it may be a major determinant of much of the puzzlement and uncertainty in anthropological literature concerning the nature and status of religious belief. This is difficult to demonstrate, since anthropologists rarely discuss such matters: normally they either use, or refrain from using, belief-terms without stating explicitly what they understand by them, or what misgivings they may have about such understandings.

There is, however, one quite clear piece of evidence, which emerged in discussion of an odd but highly pertinent topic. There are a number of reports in the ethnographic literature which state, or appear to state, that the people studied denied that there is a causal connection between copulation and pregnancy: allegedly the people were ignorant of the fact that insemination by a man is a necessary cause of a woman's becoming pregnant, they were ignorant of physiological paternity. Such reports raise a number of issues, some of which have been discussed at some length over the years. That which concerns us here is the bearing they have on questions of believing. Do these people believe what they say (or at any rate are taken to say)? And if they do, in what sense can they be said to 'believe' it?

This issue comes into focus only when one realises that the people in question are in fact well aware of physiological paternity. This fact has not always been obvious either to the ethnographers or to those who have read their reports; but it has sometimes been known, and sometimes assumed on the basis of circumstantial evidence. Where it has been known or assumed (correctly), we seem to have reports that people believe what they know to be untrue. This seems paradoxical, since 'to believe' means 'to hold as true':[27] how can people hold as true what they know to be untrue? This was how the issue appeared to Leach when he discussed it in his paper 'Virgin Birth'.[28]

Leach offered two alternative solutions to the problem. The first is indicated in the following passage:

When an ethnographer reports that 'members of the X tribe believe that . . .' he is giving a description of an orthodoxy, a dogma, something which is true of the culture as a whole. But Professor Spiro (and all the neo-Tylorians who think like him) desperately wants to believe that the evidence can tell us much more than that – that dogma and ritual must somehow correspond to the inner psychological attitudes of the actors concerned.[29]

This passage is obscure and confused. What Leach intended to say was that ethnographic belief-statements refer to a people's collective adherence to a dogma, but do not tell us that the people as individuals believe what the dogma asserts.[30] He did not put it like that because he assumed that 'inner psychological attitudes' is substitutable for 'beliefs'. Rather clearly he implies that it is absurd to imagine that an ethnographer has evidence about individual beliefs as inner psychological attitudes. He later confirmed that this was his view when he wrote, in a letter replying to his critics, 'I claim that the anthropologist has absolutely no information about what is inwardly felt by any professed believer.'[31]

It is therefore clear – and much clearer if one reads these passages in their original contexts – that for Leach, as for Needham, belief, at least in individuals, is a matter of inner psychic states. Leach draws the conclusion that we know nothing about such inner states, and consequently cannot say that, or what, an individual believes. Ethnographic belief-statements refer not to the beliefs of individuals but to the dogmas of a collectivity – what Needham correctly paraphrases as 'collective representations'.[32] (Presumably the implied argument is that people know the physiological facts of life as individuals, but deny them as members of a collectivity, so there is no direct contradiction.)

There are some grains of truth in this, but in the main it is nonsense. If a collective representation is a tenet, a proposition which could be believed in some sense, then either it is believed by the members of the collectivity singly, as individuals, or it is not believed at all, is not their collective representation. I do not mean that a real collective representation must be believed by each and every member of the collectivity, any more than a real custom must be practised by each and every member of the collectivity: it is normal for there to be some individual deviance from collective realities. But it is nonsensical to suppose that all individuals always deviate, because then what they are supposedly deviating from does not exist. The existence of a collective representation which can be treated as a belief is largely a function of the proportion of the members of the collectivity who do believe it; but also, to a small degree, of the extent to which believing it is held to be right, is backed by authority. When an ethnographer reports that 'members of the X tribe believe that . . .' he is describing a collective representation; but if he is not also implying that most individual members of the tribe believe it, he is talking rubbish. No competent ethnographer would make a report in these terms unless he had good grounds for supposing that most individuals did believe that . . .

Leach is assuming a disjunction between individual belief, which, because it is a matter of inner psychic states, is unknowable, and collective belief, which is knowable even without evidence that anyone believes. Such a disjunction does not correspond to the way that belief-terms are in fact used, and is unworkable if the reality of collective representations is to be given any factual basis. It derives from grave distortions in Durkheim's treatment of the concept of collective representations, and in particular his wish to define them as falling wholly within the province of sociology and outside the province of psychology.[33]* Those who have followed him in this – and it may well be that Leach is here typical of most social anthropologists – have thus been prevented from coming to grips with what religious belief really is. They have been inhibited from examining just how individuals believe because this has been considered a matter for psychologists, not social scientists; they have felt it proper to consider only collective representations, but without examining the evidence for their reality, because such evidence, the believing of actual people, has been assigned to the province of psychologists.[34] In consequence belief-terms have been used uncritically, and hence naively, because critical examination has been ruled out of order.

I cannot demonstrate how widespread this curious and gratuitous inhibition has been; but the conjecture that it may have been important is supported by Geertz, who wrote:

Just what does 'belief' mean in a religious context? Of all the problems surrounding attempts to conduct anthropological analysis of religion this is the one that has perhaps been most troublesome and therefore the most often avoided, usually by relegating it to psychology, that raffish outcast discipline to which social anthropologists are forever consigning phenomena they are unable to deal with within the framework of a denatured Durkheimianism. But the problem will not go away, it is not 'merely' psychological (nothing social is), and no anthropological theory of religion which fails to attack it is worthy of the name.[35]

If the influence of Durkheim, or at any rate of 'a denatured Durkheimianism', has indeed led social anthropologists to regard belief, in any but the most naive sense, as outside their proper province, this may have contributed to the esteem in which we hold Robertson Smith's views, which of course are highly consistent with a position which would treat belief as a matter of minor importance. It is not accidental that Leach, in another article,[36] has been outstanding in endorsing his views. But the same fact would explain why we rarely do more than pay homage to these views, doing little to advance or support them. Since we inhibit ourselves from considering 'just what does "belief" mean in a religious context?' we inhibit ourselves from producing the kind of evidence which would make the views seem more persuasive. And, at the same time, to the extent that we do find it necessary, or convenient, to use belief-terms, but uncritically, we actually connive at the prejudice that belief is more basic than it is.

Thus Leach's first attempt to explain how people may believe what they know to be untrue was unsound, and symptomatic of a grave and possibly common disorder. Perhaps he sensed this himself, for later in his paper on 'Virgin Birth' he let it drop and offered instead a far sounder explanation. 'There are different kinds of truth,'[37] and 'An alternative way of explaining a belief which is factually untrue is to say that it is a species of religious dogma; the truth which it expresses does not relate to the ordinary matter-of-fact world of everyday things but to metaphysics'.[38]

The problem that Needham tackled in his book was rooted in his assumption that belief-statements are 'assertions about the inner states of individuals'. We have seen that this assumption was not peculiar to himself, and may well be common among anthropologists. We have also seen that it is associated with other assumptions which inhibit critical consideration of the character of religious belief, and thus make it impossible to carry Robertson Smith's analysis further. Hence by showing that the assumption is fallacious Needham has performed a notable service.

It is, however, a narrow one: Needham has removed one impediment to discussing the real issues, but the task of actually discussing them remains to be done. I shall now embark on that task by showing that belief-terms are exceedingly ambiguous, imprecise, and confusing. In consequence, belief-statements are extremely misleading, so that we tend to interpret them as conveying information which cannot validly be inferred from them. Sometimes these invalid inferences are intended by the authors of the statements: through misunderstanding the meaning of belief-terms they supposed, mistakenly, that they had sufficient evidence for what they meant to assert or imply. Sometimes the authors seem themselves to have been innocent, but the invalid inferences have been mistakenly drawn by their readers. In the first kind of case the report, the ethnographer's belief-statement, depends on invalid inference from the evidence; in the second, there is invalid inference from the report. It is not always possible to diagnose at which point the mistake occurred, and it is not of first importance to do so: for in both kinds of case the reader has come to a mistaken and unwarranted judgement as to what the facts behind the ethnographic report are. I shall try to show that what can be reliably inferred about the facts is either nothing, or else something which strongly supports the view of Robertson Smith.

One of the chief obstacles to knowing what to make of ethnographic belief-statements is the sheer unreliability of anthropologists in these matters. If an anthropologist tells us unequivocally that 'members of the X tribe believe that . . .' should we believe him, or should we not rather doubt his capacity to interpret what the people he studied told him?

Much of the controversy about ignorance of physical paternity, at which we have already glanced, stemmed from and hinged on a brief report published in 1903. Leach refers to it thus:

One of the first detailed accounts of Australian aborigine attitudes to sex was W. E. Roth's description of the tribes of North Central Queensland (Roth, 1903). He concluded that his informants were ignorant of any causal connection between copulation and pregnancy. He described the beliefs of the Tully River Blacks on this subject in the following words . . .[39]

As I remarked, Leach went on to argue that in fact the aborigines were *not* ignorant of the facts of life; hence Roth's (supposed) conclusion was wrong. It is odd that he did not suggest the obvious hypothesis that Roth made a simple mistake through misinterpreting what his informants said, and still more odd that none of the other participants in the controversy thought of it either. It is more odd when one considers the circumstances in which the fieldwork was conducted. It was carried out before 1903, long before the modern methods of professional fieldwork had been developed: moreover, 'Roth can have spent at most a month or so altogether on the Tully river . . .'.[40] It seems to me quite extraordinary that so many serious scholars should have unquestioningly accepted the reliability of an improbable report on an elusive topic produced in such unfavourable circumstances.

It is perhaps equally extraordinary that Roth was right after all. In 1963–64, R. M. W. Dixon conducted ten months' intensive linguistic fieldwork among the Tully River aborigines, and confirms that Roth's report was accurate as far as it went. Roth correctly understood and reported what his informants told him, even though he did not know their language.[40] What is utterly extraordinary is that Leach, and the other anthropologists who discussed it, misunderstood and misreported Roth's report, printed in their own language. He did *not* state that, in Leach's words, 'his informants were ignorant of any causal connection between copulation and pregnancy'. Neither did he explicitly 'describe the beliefs of the Tully River Blacks on this subject': Roth did *not* use belief-terms in reporting the views of the aborigines on the subject. Both these errors are repeated, and indeed augmented, by Leach's principal opponent in the controversy, Professor Spiro: he both concludes that the aborigines are indeed ignorant of physiological paternity, and uses belief-terms lavishly in discussing the issue.[41]

What Roth actually wrote was:

Although sexual connection as a cause of conception is not recognized among the Tully River blacks so far as they are themselves concerned, it is admitted as true for all animals . . .[42]*

This does not state that the aborigines were ignorant of the causal connection between copulation and pregnancy, as both Leach and Spiro misread it. On the contrary, it puts it beyond doubt that they were not ignorant. As they kept no domestic animals, the aborigines could have observed only wild animals. It is not easy to observe wild animals so closely as to notice, repeatedly, that the *same* individual seen to copulate at one time can be seen as pregnant as a subsequent time; as hunters, aborigines in a position to make such observations would surely have killed the animals, thus frustrating the sequence. It is nearly impossible that aborigines could have inferred the facts about animal reproduction on the basis of observation of animals; and totally impossible that they could have done so without inferring similar conclusions about humans who were far more readily observable. Their knowledge of animal reproduction must have been extrapolated from knowledge of human reproduction. Leach saw this point and mentioned it very briefly;[43] astonishingly, Spiro confessed, 'it is rather difficult to divine precisely what the force of this argument might be'.[44]

To say that people do not recognise something – which is what Roth actually wrote – does sometimes mean that they are unaware of it; but at least as often it means that they are aware of it but choose not to acknowledge or speak about it. Since, as we have seen, the reference to animals rules out the first interpretation, Roth's words should have been read in the second sense. If Leach had noticed this, much of his discussion would have been superfluous. After a long discussion based on the first interpretation, Spiro grudgingly allowed that the second was possible: that 'the natives' procreative ignorance . . . is based not on the absence of biological knowledge, but on its rejection'.[45] If he had allowed this less grudgingly and more clearly – and if he had admitted that it was the most natural reading of what Roth actually wrote – he would have seen that most of his contribution to the debate was misconceived, and that Leach and he were agreed on the major issues of fact.

Needham wrote: 'Ethnographical literature in general is replete with allusions to belief, and the notion is so well accepted that it has even become a standard term of description.'[46] This statement is a premise for Needham's assumption that a long and taxing analysis of the notion of belief is relevant to anthropology; if it is false the whole enterprise becomes questionable. He produces rather little evidence for it. On a later page he remarks, 'The standard acceptation of belief as the distinctive feature of religion is commonly expressed also by ethnographers in their accounts of exotic religions . . .'[47] and he illustrates this by quoting belief-statements which have been made by a number of ethnographers, concluding with the observation 'Among the many peoples to whom the faculty of belief is thus ascribed are the Nuer' – he is of course referring to Evans-Pritchard's ethnographic account of them.[48]

If we count also quotations from Lawrence (1964) which had been cited in a similar context on an earlier page,[49] we find that Needham refers specifically to only six ethnographers, and only three of these are modern professional anthropologists writing in English. And of these three, he cites several belief-statements from Lawrence, just one from Geddes, and none at all from Evans-Pritchard. As evidence for the truth of his claims, this is cursory indeed.

Needham devotes a whole chapter[50] to a highly critical discussion of Evans-Pritchard's work on Nuer religion. He does not cite even one sentence in which Evans-Pritchard uses belief-terms in a way which would ascribe 'the faculty of belief' to the Nuer. Much of his discussion hinges on one brief passage in which Evans-Pritchard writes that while we can say that 'all Nuer have faith in God' this is not 'faith' 'in the modern sense of "belief"', and concludes, 'There is in any case, I think, no word in the Nuer language which could stand for "I believe".'[51] This is certainly not to ascribe any 'faculty of belief' to the Nuer, but more nearly to reject it.

Not only so, but Needham proceeds at once to misreport Evans-Pritchard's actual words. He paraphrases them as 'and he thinks that there is no Nuer word to express belief',[52] which goes beyond what he wrote; and confidently repeats this misinterpretation at least twice.[53] He cites numerous passages from the writings of missionaries among the Nuer to show that Evans-Pritchard was wrong: not one of them refutes what Evans-Pritchard actually wrote.

Although Needham cites Evans-Pritchard as a typical example of an ethnographer who, by his use of belief-terms, ascribes the faculty of belief, he is almost wholly wrong about that too. I went right through the book (*Nuer Religion*) counting instances of this usage. I counted thirteen, and a further seven which probably, though not certainly, should also be counted.[54]* On the other hand there are at least one thousand sentences where the meaning might naturally have been expressed by use of belief-terms, but in fact was not. So far from being a typical example of an ethnographer who used belief-terms as standard terms of description, Evans-Pritchard was plainly one who made strenuous efforts to avoid using them.

I do not like to pillory esteemed colleagues in this way, but the facts are too significant to be kept concealed. Needham devoted a great deal of time, and effort, and brilliance, to producing a book specifically on the topic of belief. But on quite critical points he misread the evidence, though he had it before him, in print, in the English language. He does little to substantiate his claim that 'Ethnographical literature in general is replete with allusions to belief . . .', and his prime exhibit tends to suggest that this is an illusion rather than a fact.

I do not know what the facts are. I found it very tiring to work through just one book counting and classifying the uses of belief-terms, and I am not disposed to repeat the drudgery on every book in the ethnographic literature. It would not have occurred to me to do it even once had I not been exasperated by Needham's misrepresentation of what Evans-Pritchard actually wrote.[55]* It would appear that Needham has not actually counted even once; *a fortiori* it is unlikely that other anthropologists, who do not share our special interest in the topic of belief, have done it either. Probably, then, no one knows what the facts are. Since Needham perceived Evans-Pritchard as a typical user of belief-terms, when in fact he is a remarkable non-user, it is rather likely that our common impression that belief is 'a standard term of description' in ethnographic literature is somewhat illusory.

I have a hunch, or prejudice, that use of belief-terms is inversely correlated with the quality of anthropological description and analysis of religious phenomena. Accordingly, when I have been particularly struck by the quality, good or bad, of a book I am reading I have marked the occurrence of belief-terms over a few pages. It appears that the correlation is real, though far from perfect; it also appears that modern ethnographers make belief-statements rather sparingly. But these are very tentative judgements.

More alarmingly, we have noted that Needham, and also Leach and Spiro, perceived belief-statements which were not there in the texts before them. If leading anthropologists can do this with texts in their own language, how much more likely is it that we do it with spoken statements in a language less familiar to us, that is, in doing fieldwork? In the first place there is little hard evidence that anthropologists do commonly attribute belief to those they study; in the second place, what attributions there are should be treated with suspicion.

I do not mean by this that all anthropological evidence on what other peoples believe is wholly worthless. As we have seen, Roth's report, though based on relatively flimsy evidence, has been confirmed by subsequent research. Other reports, too, have been confirmed by the work of other ethnographers on the same society. And what is thus confirmed is so similar to independent reports of beliefs in other societies that the latter are presumptively sound also. I do not dismiss the evidence out of hand: I simply urge that it be assessed more critically than it has been, even by those who have written at length on it.

Even where an ethnographer actually has made belief-statements, and where we are reasonably confident in his reliability, it is extremely difficult to determine what kind of facts are reported by such statements.

As we have already noted, ethnographic belief-statements are normally collective, in the form 'they believe (that) x'. Can we infer from these that it will be true of most members of the collectivity that 'he believes (that) x'? Leach denies it; but I have already argued that if the inference is false, the original statement was either false or meaningless, and is unlikely to have been made. I therefore stipulate that in interpreting ethnographic belief-statements we can take them as attributing belief to most individual members of the collectivity (commonly a whole society or tribe).

But what does this attributed 'belief' amount to? Very aptly, Gilbert Lewis writes:

The relationships we have to those things we assert or affirm can be most various – from unshakable faith, strong conviction, agreement, consent, through cool neutrality that sees it might be so, to uncertainty, half-doubt and then its willing suspension, and at last to a mere wish to think so and a measure of voluntary delusion.[56]

These various relationships are plainly very different, and notably with regard to the issue which most concern us. Some of them could be the basis of religious practice: if a person has unshakable faith or strong conviction that something is so, this might be sufficient to lead him to act in ways that otherwise he would not. But this is hardly likely with half-doubt or voluntary delusion, unless of course the alteration in practice is costless to him. If bare belief-statements can designate any of such relationships they tell us nothing to the point, nor indeed much of any kind. To be genuinely informative the ethnographer must, as some do, amplify bare belief-statements. But statements such as that which Needham cites from Geddes, that the Land Dayak of Sarawak 'believe ... that every object ... has in it a kind of force'[57] are, in themselves, nearly vacuous.

A related difficulty is raised by Gombrich when he remarks that it is normal usage to say that a person does not 'really believe' what he says he believes if his conduct is radically inconsistent with his holding as true what he claims to believe.[58] He cites in illustration the usual example of a person who says he believes that ghosts do not exist yet refuses to sleep in a haunted bedroom.[59] This suggests a serious problem: are the authors of ethnographic belief-statements reporting what the people studied say they believe, or what they 'really believe'? It is difficult by use of this criterion to be confident of what even one person really believes. People actually are inconsistent: all of us do things which are inconsistent with what we are strongly convinced, indeed wholly certain, is true. Further, it is well established that people hold inconsistent beliefs which they draw upon selectively in different kinds of situation.[60] It would seem to be virtually impossible to establish that each of many thousands, if not millions, of people 'really believe' what they say. Hence ethnographic belief-statements must be interpreted as reporting what people claim to believe, with perhaps a somewhat cursory check that their conduct is not grossly inconsistent. Some ethnographers do check, and report, that typical members of the society appear really to believe what they say. But bare belief-statements cannot be relied upon as reporting the kind of 'real belief' which could be taken as determining practice.

'To believe *that* . . .' is commonly understood as meaning 'to hold it as true *that* . . .': this indeed is the principal definition in the dictionary.[27] Thus 'John believes that smoking causes cancer' means 'John holds (or deems) the proposition (or statement) "Smoking causes cancer" to be true'. In our culture we normally interpet truth as a matter of empirical fact:[61]* hence we interpret believing as judgement of factual truth.

In reality, however, it is common for a person to assert something, or say he believes it, without intending any judgement of factual truth. Again Gilbert Lewis poses the question:

With statements of the type 'I must stay here in the village because my mother's brother wants to catch some bats roosting in a tree on his land. I must stay in the village now so the bats won't fly away' . . ., we are tempted to ask ourselves whether they believe it literally, or whether they are only talking symbolically. Is it a literal statement of magical belief in a mystical connection, or a statement intended to be understood symbolically?[62]

Let us consider a simpler case. Buddhists regularly say that Lord Buddha was eighty-eight cubits (40 m) tall. This has a ready symbolic interpretation: it expresses metaphorically that he was a giant in spiritual stature. I was astonished one day when a well educated friend assured me it was literally true. When I asked him how Lord Buddha got into people's houses, or under the Bo-tree beneath which he attained Enlightenment, he assured me that everyone and everything else in those days was more than twenty times larger than their modern counterparts. He appeared to believe it literally. Presumably many other Buddhists, less educated than he, also believe it literally. Probably others believe it only symbolically.

An ethnographer to whom it had not occurred that such assertions might be intended symbolically might well report, 'Sinhalese Buddhists believe that Lord Buddha was eighty-eight cubits tall.' Even if he knew that he was dealing with symbolic statements he might still report them in those terms. Christians at least appear to say they 'believe' symbolic statements. Leach, who was quite clear that the Tully River blacks did not regard their statements about human conception as literally true, nevertheless referred to them as their 'beliefs'. To make matters worse, it may be impossible to decide whether people are making literal or symbolic assertions, because the people themselves do not know. Lewis again:

> But if people are not always absolutely committed to what they say they think, if the relations they may have to their statements vary . . . then the answer about literal belief or symbolic statement need not involve an either/or choice.[63]

Hence we cannot be sure what an ethnographer intended by a belief-statement; and even if we are sure what he intended we cannot be sure that he was right to intend it. Unless he has been unusually scrupulous in investigating the matter, we do not know whether the belief-statement reports factual or only symbolic affirmation. But these may be two notably different states of affairs, particularly as regards the possible relation of the 'belief' to practice. On the other hand a great many readers, unless they have been specifically warned, are likely to interpret belief-statements in the literal sense, as reporting judgements of factual truth, because this is how belief-terms are commonly understood in modern English.[64]

This is closely related to another issue. Many belief-statements in English on religious matters actually employ the verb 'believe in', not the verb 'believe (that . . .)'. Though there is some overlap, these two verbs have different meanings. But the distinction is regularly overlooked and indeed confounded: even Needham cites and uses 'believe in' and 'believe (that . . .)' expressions as if they were interchangeable.

A crux is the common Christian expression 'to believe in God'. Most people understand and use this expression as synonymous with 'to believe that God exists'. But that was not its primary meaning originally, and is not today in the understanding of informed Christians. Its primary meaning is nearly 'to trust in, have confidence in, God'. For the sake of brevity we may risk some theological inexactitude in saying it means 'to trust God'. Now the two expressions, 'to believe (factually) that God exists', and 'to trust God' are not synonymous, equivalent, bi-implicatory. It is entirely possible to believe that God exists but not to trust him: this was in fact the supposed position of the Hebrews to which the Old Testament Prophets addressed themselves. It is harder to grasp that there is not even a relation of simple, unilateral implication between the two expressions. Nearly all of us take it for granted that it is impossible to trust God unless one believes that he exists; that is, we assume that the former presupposes and implies the latter. It may be so in secular logic, but it certainly is not so in religion;[65]* as Leach remarked, 'you won't get anywhere by applying canons of rationality [better, 'logic'] to principles of faith'.[66]

What does it actually mean to trust, to have confidence in God: if it were questioned whether someone really did, for what kind of evidence would one look? It seems to me that to have confidence in God is to have confidence in oneself, in the cosmos, in the Christian (etc.) religion, and in the relationships between these: it is to have confidence, and not dismay, however bad a situation appears, that it will be in the end, and is now in truth, for the best: it is the confidence of the nun in 'The Wreck of the Deutschland' who 'christens her wild-worst Best'.[67] I cannot distinguish it from what Buddhists call *upekkha*, equanimity.

It is therefore essentially a state of mind, or of spirit, a set of being. In Buddhist idiom it is treated as such. In Christianity, as in most other religions, what are really psychic states are figured as relationships with a posited supernatural entity (see below, Chapter 13); hence confidence, equanimity, is treated as confidence in such a being, God. Basically, God is the posit required to figure such psychic states, or dispositions – trust, confidence, love, respect, reverence, awe, and so forth – relationally. Analytically, therefore, the confidence is prior to the positing of God. Apart from the many situations in which God already has cultural factuality, or existence, this is also the sequence in individual experience. Through having confidence, and regularly figuring it as confidence in God, one finds that He comes to 'exist' for one, as an indispensable symbol or Mark (see Chapter 8). It could not be otherwise, since, apart from cultural factuality, there is no other way one could become convinced that He exists.

If this is the proper paradigm for 'believing in', it is quite different from 'believing that . . .', and does not necessarily imply any 'believing that'. Further, we have shown that such believing-in is, and must be, a product of religious practice rather than its prerequisite, as might plausibly be supposed of believing-that. To mistake believing-in as believing-that is thus a grave error, and prejudicial to understanding the truth of Robertson Smith's view.

It is a grave error that is frequently, even regularly, made. We have seen that most people, including many Christians, take it for granted that believing in God is synonymous with believing that God exists. The error is assisted by the fact that English linguistic idiom does not regularly correspond to and register the difference in sense, and that certain common expressions can, not implausibly, be understood in either sense. Thus 'believing in ghosts' is regularly understood as 'believing that ghosts exist', though close analysis of usage shows that it more directly means 'fearing ghosts'. 'Believing in the Common Market' must mean having confidence in it; but are 'believing in Communism' or 'believing in Relativity' simply matters of confidence, or of judgement of truth – or, still more confusing, of confidence in truth? And, on the other side, there are numerous Christian idioms and texts which use the simple 'believe' where the sense is 'believe in'.

No anthropologist has given closer attention to notions of belief than Needham has; it is depressing that he has quite failed to notice the difference in sense, or concept, between 'believing in' and 'believing that', and confounds them in numerous passages. He does so, for example, on each of the first four pages of his book; and again repeatedly, and most deleteriously, on pages 20 and 21. The clearest evidence of all is in his failure to understand the passage from Evans-Pritchard which he excerpts for severe, but misdirected, criticism. Evans-Pritchard had written:

... when we say, as we can do, that all Nuer have faith in God, the word 'faith' must be understood in the Old Testament sense of 'trust' (Nuer *ngath*) and not in the modern sense of 'belief' which the concept came to have under Greek and Latin influence. There is in any case, I think, no word in the Nuer language which could stand for 'I believe'.[68]

Unmistakably Evans-Pritchard is marking by 'faith' and 'belief' the distinction I have marked by 'believe in' and 'believe that'. Equally unmistakably, all Needham's comments presuppose a failure to recognise the distinction.

What hope is there, then, for other anthropologists who have given the matter of belief far less attention? Whenever an anthropologist writing about religion tells us that his people believe that such-and-such, we have to suspect that the reality was one of believing-in rather than of believing-that. Needham devotes a whole chapter[69] to the difficulty of finding words, in a variety of other languages, which correspond at all closely in sense to English belief-terms; it may be seen that many of the nearest equivalents carry the senses of 'trust' and 'confidence'. This is true of the two Sinhala verbs most often used in religious contexts, *adahanavā* and *visvāsa karanavā*. As Gombrich explains,[70] both of them mean mainly 'to have trust or confidence in'. Nearly always they should be translated as 'believe in' rather than 'believe that ...'. During my fieldwork, I must confess, I nearly always did mistranslate them as 'believe (that ...)' ...

There is still another, and major source of difficulty. It derives from peculiar, and largely unperceived, features of the sense of the verb 'to believe' as it is most usually understood, and its relation to the verb 'to know'. In this usual sense, 'to believe' means 'to hold as (factually) true', and 'to know' means this also. To use 'to know' correctly certain other criteria must be satisfied. These have been much discussed by philosophers;[71] but in nearly all cases of practical usage only one criterion is considered. A person can be said to know what he holds as true if and only if it certainly is true.[72]* In strict logic, knowing is a sub-class of believing, and the two words are sometimes used in this way. But then the situation is that the domain of holding as true (believing, in the strict sense) is divided into two areas: that of holding as true what certainly is true, and that of holding as true what is not certainly true. But cases in the first area will regularly be referred to as 'knowing' because that designation is more informative; hence 'believing' in practice comes to be applied only to cases in the second area. Hence it comes to be understood as applicable only to such cases, and the meaning of 'believing' comes to be understood as 'holding as true what is not certainly true'. This may seem strange, until we note how many other pairs of terms, whose meanings are basically related by inclusion, come by a similar process to be understood as having mutually exclusive meanings. Animal/human, man/woman, Sociology/Social Anthropology, are other familiar examples.

When believing is understood as a matter of holding as factually true, a paradigmatic form of a belief-statement is illustrated by our example 'John believes that smoking causes cancer'. A paradigmatic form of a knowledge-statement would be illustrated by 'John knows that smoking causes cancer'. Either of these two statements could reasonably be asserted: what is the difference between them? When 'believe' and 'know' are understood in the exclusive sense, as they usually are, the difference is this: the knowledge-statement is appropriate if the proposition 'smoking causes cancer' is certainly true, but the belief-statement is appropriate if that proposition is not certainly true. But who forms the judgement whether or not the proposition, held as true by John, is certainly true? Not John, who holds it as true in either case. It is the author of the statement, whether of knowledge or of belief, he who asserts it. Thus both belief-statements and knowledge-statements involve judgements on the truth of the proposition by two persons: one the knower/believer, here John, the other the author of the statement. The statement says explicitly that the knower/believer holds the proposition (here 'smoking causes cancer') as true, and also implies that the author of the statement does or does not hold it as (certainly) true.

For brevity and clarity, let us specialise some terms. Both belief-statements and knowledge-statements assert that someone holds something as true: that is the area of common meaning between statements of the two kinds. I shall refer to that someone (said to 'believe' or 'know') as 'the truth-holder' (e.g. John in our example). The something that he holds as true I shall refer to as 'the proposition' – it is the object of the truth-holder's knowing or believing. The statement about the truth-holder and the proposition – the belief-statement or knowledge-statement – may be referred to briefly as 'the statement' or 'the assertion', or more fully as 'the statement (or assertion) of truth-holding'. He who asserts the statement will be termed 'the author'.

The author of a belief-statement or a knowledge-statement necessarily commits himself to two judgements on matters of fact: first, that the truth-holder does hold the proposition as true, and second that the proposition either is or is not certainly true.

Now when a belief-statement is made in the grammatical third person (with such grammatical subjects as 'John', 'he', 'they'), the author and the truth-holder are two different persons, and their judgements on the truth of the proposition, both of which are conveyed by the statement, are typically independent. But this cannot be the case when the belief-statement is made in the first person singular, with grammatical subject 'I': here author and truth-holder are one and the same person, and their conveyed judgements on the truth of the proposition cannot be independent. These are two significantly different kinds of situation, and the difference is so great as to cause the sense of 'believe' to alter between the two cases. It can therefore be seriously misleading to apply the term 'belief-statement' to cases of both kinds, as if there were no relevant distinction. We must therefore specialise further terms. A 'belief attribution' shall be a belief-statement in the third person, attributing believing to one or more persons other than the author. A 'belief avowal' shall be a belief-statement in the first person singular, which asserts the believing of the author himself.[73]*

A similar distinction may be made formally between knowledge-attributions and knowledge-avowals, but here there is not a parallel substantial distinction of meaning. To assert a knowledge-attribution is to assert that a third person holds a proposition as true; but it is also to assert that, in the judgement of the author, the proposition is indeed true. It is a contradiction to assert 'this proposition is true but I do not hold it as true'; hence every author who asserts that someone else knows something implies that he, the author, knows it also. Hence knowledge-attributions are also implicitly knowledge-avowals.[74] We need examine knowledge-statements no further. We should, however, bear in mind that normally a belief-statement is made because the author is unwilling to make a knowledge-statement.

A belief-attribution, then, is made when someone holds a proposition as true, but the author is not prepared to assert it as true. This may be because (a) the author judges it to be false, or (b) he is not sure it is true, or (c) he suspects that asserting it as true might annoy other people. Cases (a) and (b) can be covered by saying that the author doubts the truth of the proposition; all three cases by saying that the author recognises doubt concerning its truth. Very often the case is (a), so that to use 'believe' in the third person is frequently understood as conveying that the author reckons the proposition is false, and hence that its believer is mistaken. This was plainly intended by Leach when he wrote, 'But Professor Spiro (and all the neo-Tylorians who think like him) desperately wants to believe that the evidence can tell us much more than that . . .'.[75] In other cases one cannot be sure whether the depreciatory connotation was intended or not; but, intended or not, it is likely to be felt by many readers. I feel rather sure that it was a wish to avoid this that led Evans-Pritchard to try so hard not to use belief-terms in his account of Nuer religion; and it may affect other sensitive authors in the same way. This would help to account for the apparent fact that in the ethnography of other religions the use of belief-terms is inversely correlated with the quality of the study.

The situation is necessarily different with belief-avowals. It would be a contradiction for the same person to assert, as believer, 'I hold this proposition as true,' and, as author, 'I judge it to be false'; hence there are no cases of type (a), only of types (b) and (c). That is, the author of a belief-avowal implies either that he doubts the truth of what he holds to be true (type (b)), or that he recognises the doubts of others (type (c)).

In everyday, non-religious contexts belief-avowals are commonly of type (b). One may say, 'I believe it will rain this afternoon,' meaning thereby 'I think but am not sure that it will': the intention of this idiom is to highlight the doubt, to warn the hearer not to regard the proposition as certainly true. Sometimes in religious contexts belief-avowals are intended to convey the doubt of the believer; more often, perhaps, this is unwarrantably supposed by the hearer – especially if he is himself an unbeliever.

Often, and I think most often, religious belief-avowals are not intended to convey the doubt of the believer – rather, in fact, to deny or conceal it, if indeed there is any. Belief-terms are selected, rather than knowledge-terms, in order to recognise the doubt of others. There may be various reasons for such recognition. One may be simple courtesy: if a speaker is aware that his hearer does not share his views and says, 'I know that such-and-such,' he implies that his hearer is defective in not knowing it too. 'I believe that such-and-such' allows that it is not unreasonable to be of a different opinion. This would be one reason why informants speaking to an anthropologist might use belief-terms regarding tenets the truth of which they do not doubt in the least. On the other hand, when a Christian says, 'I believe that . . .' (if he ever does in a religious context) his purpose may be to recognise not the legitimacy of doubt but its sinfulness, and to vaunt his own state of grace in being free of it. Very often, however, the purpose of acknowledging that others do not share one's own beliefs is social: beliefs are treated as emblems of social groups and membership thereof. 'I believe (and you do not)' then signifies primarily that you and I are members of different social groups. This might be another reason for informants to use belief-terms in speaking to an anthropologist.

It also explains why politicians say 'I believe' so often – indeed, with tiresome frequency, once one is alert to it. In a political speech 'I believe that such-and-such' is both an invitation to those of like mind to join the politician's support group, and an implication that there are others of unlike mind, unbelievers, opponents, against whom we must unite. It is these functions of partitioning the field and mobilising support that account for the fact that the 'such-and-such', the content of the pretended belief, is often vacuous, vapid, or even nonsensical.

Now the author of a belief-attribution does assert that the truth-holder (termed 'believer') holds the proposition as true. What could be his evidence for this judgement? It might be that the truth-holder has said 'I believe that . . .', or that he has said 'I know that . . .'. More often it is that he has simply asserted the proposition, or consented to it, or implied it. From the bare belief-attribution we cannot infer which of these lies behind it. The use of belief-terms is triggered by the *author's* recognition of doubt: it therefore cannot tell us whether or not the truth-holder has recognised doubt. But this is often, perhaps very often, overlooked. Often we take it for granted that a belief-attribution is a report of a belief-avowal. We assume that a report 'they believe that such and such' tells us that each of them has said, or would say, 'I (or we) believe that such-and-such.' This is a fallacy. It derives from our failure to see the important differences between belief-attributions and belief-avowals. It is reinforced by our expectation, derived from our Christian culture, that in matters of religion truth-holding will be expressed by belief-avowals: if indeed they believe that such-and-such, surely they will want, like Christians, to avow, 'We believe . . .'. It may be further reinforced by the fact that, for reasons of courtesy or social discrimination, informants speaking to an anthropologist may make belief-avowals as they never would in speaking among themselves. It is further reinforced by the fact that the anthropologist thinks they are speaking of believing-that when they are really speaking of believing-in.

Needham fails to see the distinction between belief-attributions and belief-avowals, and regularly assumes that the former must be reports of the latter. This is the basis of his curious argument that because in some languages it is uncertain how, or even whether, a speaker could make an unambiguous belief-avowal, ethnographic belief-attributions concerning peoples who speak such languages must be defective.[76] Together with his failure to distinguish between 'faith' (believing in) and 'belief' (believing-that) it accounts for his failure to understand the words of Evans-Pritchard's that he criticises. Quite plainly, when Evans-Pritchard wrote, 'There is in any case, I think, no word in the Nuer language which could stand for "I believe",' he meant that Nuer has no idiom for making belief-avowals. To demonstrate, as Needham does at length, that there are idioms for *attributing* 'belief', or for attributing or avowing *'faith'*, is beside the point.

I have little doubt that failure to distinguish between belief-attributions and belief-avowals is largely responsible for the delusion that belief-attributions are descriptions of inner mental states. If both are instances of one indistinguishable category of belief-statements, it is legitimate and easiest to analyse these on the basis of those one makes oneself. When I say 'I believe that . . .', I am normally referring to an inner mental state with which I am acquainted. It is, sometimes, a fascinating because puzzling one: sometimes it combines the ill-assorted elements of some conviction (holding as true) and some doubt (not quite holding as true). Hence it is natural that one's own believing should be seen very much as a matter of one's inner mental state. Since holding as true is, often at least, a mental operation or condition, in principle anyone else's believing is also an inner mental state. But to suppose that an *attribution* of belief is so largely a description of an inner mental state that it cannot properly be made without knowledge of that state, always was absurd. I have never met anyone, no matter how unsophisticated, who was not very well aware that one can rarely know much about the inner mental state of another person. The practice of making belief-attributions could never have arisen if they had been understood as descriptions of the unknowable. In fact they are not. A belief-attribution states what a person apparently holds as true on the basis of inference from what he observably says and does. There is a latent reference to the truth-holder's inner mental states: but his mind, as usually in the practical affairs of life, is treated as a 'black box',[77] attention being directed to its inputs and outputs. This is perfectly straightforward, or was, until philosophers confused matters by first confounding belief-attributions with belief-avowals, and then speculating on the basis of introspection instead of studying the actual use of language.

It is entirely understandable why ethnographers writing about religion and magic and the like have often used belief-terms. When their informants asserted or affirmed factual propositions, or seemed to do so, it was inevitable that their ethnographers, not having been reared in the same cultural tradition, did not regard these propositions as certainly true: hence it was natural to report that the informants 'believed' them. Moreover in most cases the ethnographers, whether they were Christian missionaries or positivist anthropologists, felt sure that the tenets of the informants were false: so the connotation of error carried by belief-terms made them seem the more apt. We have already remarked some other factors which reinforced these.

Now it is quite possible to use belief-terms properly in contexts where any misunderstanding to which they might give rise is harmless. It is also possible to use them properly in more critical contexts if one takes care, by stipulation and qualification, to rule out deleterious misinterpretations. But it is difficult if one is aware of all the misunderstandings that can arise, and virtually impossible if one is not. The latter seems to have been the normal condition of ethnographers. Consequently their belief-attributions cannot be taken as yielding a great deal of reliable information, except where (as is often the case) we are given further information which helps us to interpret them more closely. The prevalence, such as it is, of belief-attributions in the ethnographic literature cannot be taken as reflecting the prevalence of 'belief' (believing that . . .) in other cultures.

In fact there is a simple knock-down argument which shows that there cannot be religious 'belief' of a kind which would support a view contrary to Robertson Smith's. As I shall explain more fully later (Chapter 13), it is believing-that, factually, that might reasonably be taken as a basis for practice. Affirming a proposition symbolically will not do; believing-in does not always have specific implications for practice and, to the extent that it does, is rather a product than a precursor of practice. But, in matters of religion, the tenets, 'beliefs', propositions that a person is said to believe always embody 'mystical notions' which, by definition, 'transcend sensory experience'.[78] For this reason, a person can never get sufficient objective evidence for their factual truth. If he does hold them as true, it is either as a result of his practice ('If one must act as though one believed . . .'), or as a result of their cultural factuality. But cultural factuality implies that practice is already established; moreover, as is readily observable, as an individual grows up in such a culture he becomes accustomed to participating in the practices before he can form his own judgement on the truth of the 'beliefs'. Further, because mystical notions transcend sensory experience, propositions embodying them cannot yield unambiguous prescriptions for practical conduct in the empirical world. In short, religious propositions cannot be believed apart from practice, and even if they were so believed could not really found practice.

All this would be obvious if we did not wallow in the confusions carried by notions of belief. These confusions are not unmotivated: our terminology of belief both expresses the bias of our own religious culture and obstructs its refutation. It is with 'belief' rather as it is with incest:[79] in both cases anthropologists have found it difficult to think about, or even perceive, the facts clearly because socialisation into the values of our own culture prevents us from doing so.

Notes to Chapter 11

1 A good example is Lewis (1980) – see particularly his statements on pp. 11 and 19, where he too refers to many ethnographic reports which are at least consistent with the conclusion.

2   Smith (1927), p. 16.
3   *Ibid.*, p. 20.
4   *Ibid.*, p. 21.
5   *Ibid.*, p. 17.
6   *Ibid.*, p. 18.
7   Durkheim (1915), p. 36; (1912), p. 50.
8   Langer (1951), pp. 97–8 and *passim*.
9   Barth (1975), p. 225; cf. Langer (1951), p. 233 f.
10 See Ornstein (1973, 1975) and the literature cited therein.
11 Langer (1951), p. 81 f.
12 Cf. Barth (1975), pp. 224–8.
13 This assimilation seems to underlie Leach's statement 'In sum then, my view here is that ritual action and belief are alike to be understood as forms of symbolic statement about the social order' (1954, p. 14). I would not agree that they are only about the social order, nor that they as easily interpreted as Leach's analyses often imply.
14 Needham (1972), p. 6.
15 See Wittgenstein (1966), pp. 59–60, and Pears (1971), p. 174 (quoted below).
16 Southwold (1979), p. 635 f; Sperber (1975), pp. 102–6; Langer (1951), p. 260.
17 E.g. Evans-Pritchard (1937), p. 478; (1976), p. 204.
18 Pears (1971), p. 174, quoted in Gudmunsen (1977), p. 102.
19 Needham (1972), p. 2.
20 *Ibid.*, p. 5.
21 *Ibid.*, pp. 6–7.
22 *Ibid.*, p. 32.
23 *Ibid.*, p. 3. That there is a unitary concept of belief, that it implies some particular mental state, and that this implies a common human psychological capacity, are the initial assumptions from which he begins; much of his argument is directed to demonstrating that all three are false.
24 *Ibid.*, p. 108 and chapter 7.
25 *Ibid.*, chapters 7–10.
26 *Ibid.*, pp. 192–3.
27 *Shorter Oxford English Dictionary.*
28 Leach (1969), especially pp. 99, 102.
29 *Ibid.*, p. 88.
30 I give reasons for this interpretation in Southwold (1979), pp. 628–9.
31 Leach (1968b), p. 655.
32 Needham (1972), p. 6.
33 For trenchant criticism of Durkheim's position, see Lukes (1973), pp. 6–8, 11–12, 16–22; Hallpike (1979), pp. 41–57.
34 Cf. Hallpike (1979), pp. 42–8.
35 Geertz (1966), pp. 24–5.
36 Leach (1968c), p. 103.
37 Leach (1969), p. 103.
38 *Ibid.*, pp. 107–8.
39 *Ibid.*, pp. 86–7.
40 Dixon (1968), p. 653.
41 Spiro (1968).

42 Roth (1903), p. 22. As I point out, this does not impute ignorance of any causal connection between copulation and pregnancy; neither does any other of the few sentences Roth wrote. Roth comes nearest to imputing that in words which neither Leach nor Spiro quotes. Thus the heading to this section of his report is: 'Sexual History. Conception not necessarily due to copulation' (p. 22). And on p. 23, after having discussed some other aboriginal groups, he wrote, 'When it is remembered that as a rule in all these Northern tribes, a little girl may be given to and will live with her spouse as wife long before she reaches the stage of puberty – the relationship of which to fecundity is not recognised – the idea of conception not being necessarily due to sexual connection becomes partly intelligible.' Even this does not impute ignorance of *any* causal connection.

43 Leach (1969), p. 89.

44 Spiro (1968), p. 246.

45 *Ibid.*, p. 256.

46 Needham (1972), p. 4.

47 *Ibid.*, p. 21.

48 Evans-Pritchard (1956).

49 Needham (1972), p. 3.

50 *Ibid.*, chapter 2.

51 Needham (1972), p. 23, quoting Evans-Pritchard (1956), p. 9.

52 Needham (1972), p. 23.

53 *Ibid.*, pp. 24, 37.

54 It is not always easy to decide whether by use of a belief-term an author is imputing belief. For example, this conclusion could not be drawn if the belief-term occurs in a passage the author is quoting from another writer: can it be when he seems to be paraphrasing rather than directly quoting? I would point out also that counting rare occurrences of a word in a book is a task, like proof-reading, in which some errors are almost inevitable. However my count, though corrigible, clearly shows that belief-terms are rare in this book.

55 Because it seemed to me that Needham misrepresented Evans-Pritchard in discussing the one passage he did cite, I thought to look for some other instances of Evans-Pritchard's use of belief-terms. The unexpected difficulty I had in finding any convinced me that the most significant fact was not his use but his abstention from use.

56 Lewis (1980), p. 113. See also other passages listed in his index under 'belief'.

57 Needham (1972), p. 23.

58 Gombrich (1971), pp. 4–6.

59 *Ibid.*, p. 6.

60 This is shown very clearly in Evans-Pritchard, e.g. (1937), pp. 120, 475; (1976), pp. 57, 202.

61 There is also the kind of truth which philosophers call 'logical' or 'analytic', which applies to such tautologies as '$2 \times 2 = 4$'. I put this aside since we rarely use belief-terms in connection with such propositions (cf. Braithwaite, 1967, pp. 30, 38).

62 Lewis (1980), p. 186.

63 *Ibid.*, p. 187.

64 Cf. Langer (1951), p. 202.

65 Buddhism provides an interesting illustration. Buddhists very commonly say they believe in (*visvāsa karanavā*) Lord Buddha, who they are quite emphatic does not exist. One would not suspect a logical paradox in this case, since we would understand believing in Lord Buddha to mean having confidence in the wisdom of his teaching. But Buddhist ritual attitudes to Lord Buddha are largely similar, though not identical, to Christian ritual attitudes to God. If it seems to us paradoxical to believe in God without believing that he exists, this may be largely because our view of religious attitudes has been confused by the intrusion of an inappropriate, and confused, notion of existence.

66 Leach (1969), p. 99.

67 Gerard Manley Hopkins, 'The Wreck of the Deutschland', stanza 24.

68 Evans-Pritchard (1956), p. 9, quoted in Needham (1972), p. 23.

69 1972, chapter 3.

70 Gombrich (1971), pp. 58–60.

71 For example, in works included or cited in Griffiths (1967), e.g. pp. 29, 89, 144.

72 Philosophers usually add a further criterion, that the knower is justified in, has sufficient warrant for, holding the proposition to be true. But in practical usage, I think, we rarely attend to this criterion: we assume that if a person judges truth correctly he has good reason for his judgement. – I have used the term 'certainly' because Needham takes it up from Kant's distinction between knowing and believing (Needham, 1972, p. 54 and *passim*). I do not mean it in some strong sense such as 'absolutely incorrigible'. I mean simply that the more uncertain we feel that a proposition is true, the less ready are we to say that someone 'knows' it: 'certain' here implies that we are not recognising substantial doubt.

73 Belief-statements in the first person plural ('we') are mixed, combining an avowal on behalf of the author with attributions to others. In many cases, however, their reference is rather collective than plural, and their force more normative than descriptive: i.e. they assert a dogma adherence to which is emblematic of membership of our collectivity as contrasted with yours. They are thus especially difficult to parse.

74 Hintikka (1962), pp. 61–2, suggests a similar point.

75 Leach (1969), pp. 88.

76 Needham (1972), chapter 3, especially p. 38.

77 See, e.g., Ashby (1964), p. 86 ff.

78 Evans-Pritchard (1937), pp. 12, 81; (1976), pp. 229, 31.

79 Lévi-Strauss (1949), chapter 2.

12

Buddhist practice and belief: ritual, ethics, and Dharma

The one sentence in which Robertson Smith came closest to summarising his position was the last one of the last passage I quoted:

The conclusion is, that in the study of ancient religions we must begin, not with myth, but with ritual and traditional usage.

It is quite evident that he meant us to understand the same conclusion of belief in place of myth. One of the major reasons for his conclusion as stated was that 'the ritual was fixed and the myth was variable, the ritual was obligatory and faith in the myth was at the discretion of the worshipper'. As we saw (Chapter 11), he had already made just the same remarks about belief as he here makes about myth. It is clearly implicit that he would say of belief what he next says of myth: 'the myth is merely the explanation of a religious usage; and ordinarily it is such an explanation as could not have arisen till the original sense of the usage had more or less fallen into oblivion'. But his final point against taking a myth as an explanation for the origin of a ritual, that we cannot take the myth to be a narrative of real occurrences, cannot quite so obviously be transferred to apply to beliefs. Some beliefs or dogmas are quite credible even when interpreted in a literal sense: we can imagine people engaging in ritual practices because they have judged the belief to be true. The argument therefore requires to be modified, as we have already done. Some beliefs or dogmas are not obviously incredible as myths tend to be; but they are not sufficiently credible to motivate action, except in circumstances where such action is already antecedently established. Their weakness is not that they are fantastic, it is simply that, apart from practice, there are no available grounds to convince anyone of their truth.

In doing my fieldwork in Sri Lanka I was more or less aware that I ought to follow Robertson Smith's methodological prescription, as it is the foundation for sound anthropological enquiry into other religions. I suspected, too, that some other research on Buddhism had been inadequate because it had ignored Robertson Smith's advice and had given undue, and indeed central, analytical primacy to matters of belief.[1]* But it seemed to me nearly impossible to carry through the programme I thus judged to be appropriate: in two fundamental respects Buddhism seemed to be refractory to Robertson Smith's approach.

Naturally enough, in a study of the rite of sacrifice, when Robertson Smith was arguing for the primacy of practice over belief, it was mainly ritual practice that he was referring to. It is in this sense that his position has most evidently been taken up into the methodology of anthropological research on religion: to the extent that we are loyal to his position we focus our enquiries on rituals rather than on beliefs. But to seek to make sense of Buddhism through study of its ritual appears decidedly eccentric, since Buddhists say, what their practice broadly supports, that ritual is of minor importance in Buddhism.

To make this clear, we need to distinguish between various categories of what might be taken to be Buddhist rituals.

In the first place, there is a distinction between rituals in which Buddhists engage while specifically stating that they are non-Buddhist, no part of Buddhism, and those which they do classify as Buddhist. This is an emic distinction, that is one made by the actors themselves, and we know very well that emic categories are not necessarily the most appropriate for use in a social-scientific analysis of the phenomena. But there are good reasons why we too should adopt this distinction.

In the first place, religion is very much a matter of attitudes, states of mind, interpretations of experience: what the actors think is thus constitutive of a large part of the phenomena, more so than when we are considering institutions in which empirical, pragmatic considerations are relatively more determinative. With institutions of the latter kind, for example the economic, the political, or those concerned with the procreation and rearing of children, we often find a structure of behaviour determined by pragmatic considerations which is inadequately represented, or more or less purposively misrepresented, in the explicit emic categories of the actors; in such cases adequate analysis of reality may well require that we go beyond the categories of the actors. Just because religion is less closely linked to hard empirical facts, this consideration may be less applicable to it: in a certain sense the religious facts are created by the actors, so the way they create them is the way they are. The difference is no more than relative, but I think significant.

Secondly, the emic distinction of the Buddhist is not arbitrary, but is based on distinctions more fundamental. It is evident – and actual Buddhists say this fairly clearly – that the distinction between Buddhist and non-Buddhist rituals is based on a distinction between supposed means of efficacy. A Buddhist ritual is always constructed as a means of

earning Merit (*pin*), and the supposed benefits it brings are seen as
deriving from the Merit earned. Non-Buddhist rituals are always overtly
concerned with influencing or controlling spiritual beings: with
propitiating gods, or with appeasing, binding, or driving away the more
harmful spirits, that is, demons and ghosts. My informants regularly
referred to such non-Buddhist rituals as '*sāntikarma*'. This is a noun
formed from the verb '*sāntikaranavā*', which the Sinhalese–English
dictionary renders as 'to calm, etc.; appease, pacify'. '*karma(ya)*' in the
relevant sense means an act or deed; it is formed directly from the verb
'*karanavā*', which means 'to do *or* to work' in a very wide sense (like
French '*faire*'). '*Sānti*' is a form of the adjective '*sānta*', which means
'calm, quiet, tranquil; content; mild'.[2] Thus the meaning of '*sāntikarma*'
can be summarised as 'an act (*or* work) of appeasement', and this fits well
with my impression of what people seemed to think they were about in
performing such rites. I should add that those people I asked did not seem
to be conscious of '*sāntikarma*' as designating a distinct and unitary
category of rites: rather, they applied the term to each of a number of rites
considered particularly but not as a class. Also, to judge from the
literature, their use of the term does not appear to be standard Sinhalese
usage.[3]

This, partly implicit, categorisation of rites further relates to a more
basic distinction. As we saw earlier (Chapter 7), my informants regularly
said that cultic practices directed to gods and other spirits were no part of
Buddhism, *Buddhāgama*, and did not constitute any other *āgama* (very
roughly, 'religion') because they were oriented to *laukika*, worldly,
concerns; whereas, by contrast, *Buddhāgama*, and any other *āgama*, is
concerned with *lōkōttara* (roughly, supra-mundane, sacred) matters. To
us, who tend to define religion in terms of orientation to gods and similar
spiritual beings,[4] it seems very strange to hear people saying that cults of
gods and the like are *ipso facto not* religious. Most of the explanation lies
in the fact that the concept of *āgama* is different from our usual concept of
religion, so that although the two terms have a largely common domain of
reference they are not synonymous. I shall suggest shortly that the
Sinhalese Buddhist concept of *āgama* may be superior for analytical
purposes to our own concept of religion. The other part of the explanation
is that the usual translation of the Sinhala words '*deviyō*' and '*devata*' as
'god' is distinctly misleading. These concepts refer to imagined beings
which do not have important attributes of the Christian, and more
generally Semitic, concept of God. In *our* terms these beings are creatures
not Creator, they are more like than unlike human beings. With regard to
their powers they might be termed superhuman beings: though in
relation to 'spiritual', *lōkōttara*, matters they are actually inferior to
human beings. Only a human being can attain Nirvana, and a 'god' who
wishes to do so – as most of them are supposed to wish – must first be

reborn as a human. Thus the apparent paradox is merely the result of mistranslation. At the level at which it could be said that both Christianity and Buddhism are concerned with *lōkōttara* matters, the difference is that in Christianity theistic concepts are employed to express and symbolise such matters, whereas Buddhism employs a non-theistic idiom.

Sometimes in answer to our questions, and very commonly in more normal contexts, the villagers we knew would say that '*laukika*' refers to one's concerns in this life, '*lōkōttara*' to one's concerns for the next life (rebirth). This is plainly a long-established formulation, for Knox wrote, referring more narrowly to the 'religious' festivals of the Sinhalese:

Now of these there are two sorts, some belonging to their gods that govern the Earth, and all things referring to this life; and some belonging to the Buddou, whose province is to take care of the soul and future well-being of Men.[5]

At first sight this reduction of the fundamental polarity of *laukika* and *lōkōttara* to a simple distinction between the present life and the life to come, in the context of the notion of Rebirth, looks like a cheapening, if not betrayal, of what Buddhism is really about. I shall explain later that this verdict is incorrect, and derives from much too crude and literalistic an interpretation of the Rebirth idiom (Chapter 14).

I accept that the distinction the Sinhalese themselves make between Buddhist rites and non-Buddhist rites (*sāntikarma*) is analytically valid; most other writers on Sinhalese and other Theravāda Buddhist countries who deal with 'religious' phenomena do likewise. Tambiah, however, treats Buddhism and the spirit cults in north-east Thailand as components of one religious field;[6] and still more definitely Obeyesekere maintains that among the Sinhalese the unit to be studied is Sinhalese religion (he calls it 'Sinhalese Buddhism') as a whole, with what the actors themselves distinguish as Buddhism and non-Buddhism being integrally connected elements of one system.[7] To a large extent the difference between their standpoint and mine is one of theoretical orientation, and I do not consider that Tambiah's position is either wrong or fruitless. But I do consider that Obeyesekere's position goes too far, and has been made to appear plausible by selection of the evidence.

On the one hand, Obeyesekere understresses, indeed virtually neglects, the fact that Sinhalese regularly say, and indeed insist, that there is a fundamental distinction between Buddhist and non-Buddhist cultic practices, in both of which most of them participate. On the other hand he overstresses the significance of the fact that those who engage in non-Buddhist cultic practices regularly include some reference, even address, to the Buddha. This is not, as Obeyesekere supposes, because the people see *sāntikarma* and Buddhism as linked variants within one field of 'religion': as we have seen, non-English-speaking Sinhalese Buddhists do not have such a concept of 'religion'. It is rather because almost any significant public activity, and a great range of other activities, are given a kind of legitimacy by thus formally relating them to Buddhism – much as we do by bestowing the title 'Royal' on associations and other institutions as a mark of acceptability and honour. It is not just non-Buddhist rites which begin with some formal homage to Buddhism: so, for example, do the school day and most political meetings. Rather similarly, most buses carry on the front, inside or out, a Buddhist flag and/or a picture of the Buddha. We need not agree with the cynical villagers that this is because the style of driving makes heavy demands on every kind of protection one can get. I would, however, accept, and indeed endorse, the inference that education, politics, and public transport, as well as *sāntikarma*, are viewed as under the rule or protection of Buddhism, *Buddha Sāsana*, Buddhendom, which is pre-eminent in the world. But this is to take us right away from the foreign concept of 'religion' which underpins Obeyesekere's analysis.

Having made this distinction, we can point out that the more elaborately ceremonial and symbolic – i.e. typically 'ritual' – rites in which Sinhalese engage are in fact non-Buddhist. This applies both to the large-scale ceremonies, such as the Äsala Perahära in Kandy,[8] and to the elaborate exorcist rites most characteristic of the southern Low Country.[9] By contrast, the dominant characteristic of what Sinhalese and I would categorise as genuinely Buddhist rites is that they are spare, in both senses of the word. The form of the rites is extraordinarily simple and so devoid of symbolic elaboration that they only just resemble ritual at all. And the Buddhists say, and in the main show by their actions that they think, that such rites are inessential to Buddhism and dispensable for Buddhists.

There are two basic forms of Buddhist rite. One is *pūjā*, an offering, which is Buddhist in as much as the offering is directed to the Buddha, and laid before some emblem of him, whether an image or picture, or some other object symbolically associated with him, such as a Bo-tree or a *dāgäba*.[10] What is offered is most characteristically flowers and/or lamps, but it may be food and/or (non-alcoholic) drink, and occasionally other items, e.g. a toothbrush 'to clean his teeth after eating'. Both the word '*pūjā*' and the practice are clearly continuous with similar ritual forms in Indian religion generally; and indeed among the Sinhalese there are also *pūjās* to gods.

On the face of it, the *Buddha pūjā* is clearly an instance of a ritual form found in nearly all human cultures, that of the offering; and when the offering is of food or drink it would satisfy Robertson Smith's definition of a sacrifice.[11] But there is an apparent difficulty. In most cultures the offering is made to please the god or similar recipient, and in the hope of receiving from him some reciprocal favour. But Sinhalese Buddhists never offer this explanation of the *Buddha pūjā*, and in fact repudiate it if one suggests it to them. They insist that when he died the Buddha ceased to exist, and consequently cannot receive offerings nor do anything in response. If one asks why then do they give *Buddha pūjā*, a few refer it vaguely to custom, but most offer the standard reply that they do it for the sake of the good effect on the giver's mind.[12] Some explicate as follows. Giving is an expression of gratitude; by giving to the Buddha we enhance our sense of gratitude to him for the Dhamma he taught to us; by enhancing our sense of gratitude we strengthen our feeling of the value of the Dhamma; and this in turn motivates a stronger commitment to the Dhamma and to actually realising it in one's conduct of life.

This is an extremely sophisticated explanation; and when one hears it from an apparently unsophisticated peasant one is strongly tempted to think that he could not possibly believe it, but is merely parroting a sophisticated doctrine he has been taught. Gombrich, in particular, does state such a conclusion, though without explicitly underestimating the peasants. He declares that while at one level, the cognitive, the peasants may sincerely believe what they say, at another, the affective, which is that of what they 'really believe', their behaviour shows that they believe that the Buddha does exist, as a supernatural godlike being, who receives their gift, and responds.[13]

This contention is rather persuasive: when one observes *Buddha pūjā* one does strongly feel that of course the Buddhists feel they are making an offering to a real being. I was once permitted to watch a woman making an unusually elaborate offering to Lord Buddha in her home – it was she who included the toothbrush – and in the course of what she was doing she remarked, 'If I did not imagine [or 'think' – *hitanavā*] that Lord Buddha receives my offerings I could not do these things,' though when I took her up on this she stated firmly that of course she knew that Lord Buddha does not exist. I ought to add that she was an unusual person, regarded, rightly I think, by most of the villagers as eccentric.

Nevertheless I think that Gombrich's argument must be accounted unsound. While it is true that we say a person does not really believe what he says if his conduct is radically inconsistent with his holding it true, the converse is not valid. We cannot conclude that a person really believes the truth of what is consistent with his conduct even though he does not say it, or denies it. This is because in general, and certainly in this particular instance, any given course of conduct is consistent with the truth of at least two different propositions: hence we need further evidence to determine which of them it is that he actually holds as true.[14] If we agree with Gombrich that we cannot rely on what people say they believe, however sincerely, the conclusion must be that there is no way we can be certain what anyone really believes: neither his conduct nor his avowal, separately or together, puts the matter beyond reasonable doubt. For most practical purposes I think we can often be fairly confident what a person believes; but once one pursues the critical analysis on which Gombrich embarks one has to conclude, not as he does that we can explain ritual conduct by a different kind of belief, 'affective belief', but that belief is too unknowable to serve as a thoroughly satisfactory explanation for observable conduct.

There is a further weakness. Our conviction that when they are performing *Buddha pūjā* Buddhists feel, affectively believe, that the Buddha is real, is largely a projection of our own feelings in the situation: and our feelings are conditioned by the fact that we have been reared in a theistic religious culture, as Sinhalese Buddhists have not. It is exceedingly difficult, practically impossible, for us to know what they feel. I think it more probable than not that some of them sometimes do feel that they are making a gift to real person: that is surely true at least of the eccentric lady I have cited above. I would certainly agree that feelings, emotions, are an important element of religious behaviour; but it confuses analysis to identify them with belief.

In fact the *Buddha pūjā* seems to me to lend significant support to Robertson Smith's thesis. Among Sinhalese Buddhists and most other peoples we find the same ritual form of offering, but the Buddhists account for it by beliefs radically different from those provided in most other cultures. If we have to decide between the two kinds of explanation, the Buddhist and the theistical, as the common explanation for the common ritual form, there is much to be said for preferring that of the Buddhists. As a result of his own analysis, and revealing no awareness that he had been anticipated by the Buddhists, Durkheim wrote of rites generally that their 'true justification . . . does not lie in the apparent ends which they pursue [e.g. influencing the gods], but rather in the invisible influence which they exercise over the mind and in the way in which they affect our level of consciousness'.[15] I am confident that anyone who has himself sincerely participated in religious ritual will acknowledge that this is true, if not perhaps the whole truth.

I would in fact go further and suggest that all explanations of offering-ritual are *ex post facto* rationalisations, and not the real bases of participation in the rituals. Obviously most people participate in a ritual because it is established and one is expected to participate. But some people are more strongly motivated to perform the ritual than this would account for;[16*] and we have to posit some further source of motivation to account for the fact that people must have started to perform the ritual before it became established. Just as it is natural when one is happy to sing and to dance, and even for an atheist to thank or to praise God, so too it seems to me that many basic ritual forms are spontaneous modes of human expression which bypass rational analysis. I was puzzling about

Buddha pūjā when I got an invaluable clue from Appuhamy's son, a toddler. I had called at the house and had been talking to his parents for some minutes when the boy took from his mouth a sweet he had been sucking and offered it to me. I suspect that, whether it be innate or learned at a very early age, the act of offering, especially food, is a very basic item in the repertoire of human expression and communication; and that it is gratifying to employ it irrespective of any calculation of how it may alter the world beyond oneself. I think that this is the basic source of offering rituals, which are thus, as to their core, generated independently of whatever hypotheses and theories may come to be offered to rationalise them.

Buddha pūjā may be performed in the home, before a Buddha shrine, when it is normally a very simple ceremony indeed, or more publicly at a Buddhist temple, usually in the image-house;[17] sometimes at other public shrines. In village temples a *Buddha pūjā* is held every Poya day, the Buddhist 'sabbath', which is the full-moon day of each month; sometimes more frequently. Apart from the basic rite of conveying offerings to and laying them before the Buddha image, there is some chanting of standard Buddhist texts, and a sermon is given by the priest. Apart from the sermon, the procedure lasts about twenty minutes, and is very simple. In Polgama, on normal Poya days, no more than about fifty people (from a village of 730) attended, and they were mainly women and children.

On three Poya days, those of Vesak, Poson, and the *Kathina pinkama*,[18]* the ceremonies are somewhat more extended, though still very simple by comparison, say, with Hindu ritual. They are also better attended, though many people stressed to me that attendance was as much for fun – for the sake of the attendant festivities – as for devotion. I was fairly often told by villagers that rituals are good for those who find them beneficial, but there is no kind of religious obligation to participate and one can be a perfectly good Buddhist without ever doing so; and I never heard a contrary view expressed. Some people, especially those inclined to the middle-class variety of Buddhism, say that a really good Buddhist ought *not* to participate in public ritual.

The other principal form of Buddhist ritual consists of presenting alms (*dānē*) to Buddhist clergy, for which they reciprocate by giving teaching (or preaching – *bana*). Often the *dānē* consists of giving a meal to a set of clergy who have been invited. The *bana* may consist of giving a sermon in Sinhala, or chanting scriptural texts in Pali, a language which few laymen know, though they often have a general idea of what the scripture is about. Such ceremonies are usually referred to as *dānē* or as *bana*, sometimes by other terms: people seemed largely indifferent to the terminology. There is so little symbolic behaviour involved that these are rituals in little more than the wide sense that could be applied to almost any conventionalised pattern of behaviour.

These ceremonies are commonly held at people's homes – most usually, in fact, if we exclude from the category the routine presentation of meals (*dānē*) to clergy at their temples.[19]* The most important are the *mataka dānēs* held at certain fixed intervals after a person's death; in Polgama most people held only the one which has to take place on the seventh day. People said that the purpose was to earn Merit and transfer it to the deceased in the hope that it might ensure him a better rebirth; it seemed rather clear to me that the principal, if unacknowledged, motivation was to lessen the chance that the deceased might persist as a ghost (*prēta*) likely to cause trouble to his surviving relatives. Mortuary ceremonies in many cultures seem to be largely concerned with laying the ghost; here too we seem to have a basic ritual form for which Buddhists provide a rationalisation of a relatively unusual kind.[20]*

An interesting variant of the basic *dānē/bana* is the ceremony known as *pirit*, the ostensible purpose of which is to gain protection against various potential dangers, mainly of supernatural origin; it may also be used to counteract actual dangers, notably sickness, especially when these are thought to be supernaturally caused, as by sorcery. The *dānē* is often dispensed with, and the *bana* consists of the chanting of certain scriptural texts held to be especially appropriate. The *modus operandi*, which most of the informants whom I asked explained to me, shows this rite to be an ingenious compound of Buddhist and non-Buddhist elements. Gods are always summoned to the ceremony by token offerings in specially constructed simple shrines, and by offerings of sound, i.e. music. Thus the gods are given the opportunity to earn Merit by hearing the *bana*, and this is augmented by the Merit the people earn in the same way and transfer to the gods. In return, the gods bestow the protection which is sought, which is mainly within their, *laukika*, domain. In short, this is an offering (*pūjā*) to gods of Merit earned by a typically Buddhist rite. Although *pirit* ceremonies incorporate rather more symbolic items than do other ceremonies of the *dānē/bana* type, they are still comparatively simple. In fact it is not even necessary to have Buddhist clergy for a *pirit* ceremony: it can be, and often is, conducted by laymen who know the chants.[21]

Clergy regularly insist that it is most important for laymen to give them *dānē*, and that this is among the most effective ways of earning Merit; laymen, on whom the economic motivation of this is not lost, tend to be somewhat sceptical. I got no suggestion that it is essential for a Buddhist to participate in ceremonies of the *dānē/bana* kind; but it was clear that nearly everyone would be most reluctant not to hold a *mataka dānē* after a death, or not to have clergy present at a funeral ceremony, to which their active contribution is in fact exiguous.[22]* Apart from occasions of death, however, it was rare for Polgama households to have ceremonies of the *dānē/bana* kind, *pirit* included.

Thus it would seem implausible, not to say obstinate, to maintain that Buddhism should be approached through study of its ritual; and it would be rather fruitless too, since the rites are so spare and simple that there is little to be said about them. At the same time it looks equally obstinate to maintain that belief, doctrine, is only of secondary importance in Buddhism. Buddhists constantly lay stress on the importance of the Dhamma, the doctrine, in their religion.

Entirely correctly, Gombrich writes: 'The most frequent religious act of Buddhists is the recitation of a few lines in Pali. Many Buddhists recite them daily in private; their recitation begins, and often punctuates, every public religious occasion.' He then quotes them, with approximate English translation, and summarises them thus: 'The first line is a salutation to the Buddha. The next nine lines are the Three Refuges (*tisarana*) thrice repeated. The last five lines are the Five Precepts (*pan sil*).' He comments, most aptly:

A person who takes the Three Refuges and Five Precepts is thereby a Buddhist layman. There is no ceremony for conversion to Buddhism beyond the recital of these lines, so anyone who says these words and means them can rightly call himself a Buddhist. To go so far and then to keep the precepts is considered sufficient for great religious progress.[23]*

Gombrich further remarks:

The objects of the Three Refuges are the Three Jewels (*triratna, teruvan*): most people asked to explain Buddhism (*Buddhāgama*) would begin here. The Buddha is the founder of the religion, the Dharma is the truth he discovered, the Sangha is the vehicle for preserving and propagating that truth.[24]

It is not difficult to see that in the structure of this triune sacred, it is the Dhamma (Dharma) which is central and most salient. Village Buddhists regularly say that the Buddha does not exist, and that they venerate him as the discoverer and first teacher of the Dhamma. Similarly, as Gombrich says, the Sangha too is respected, by most clergy and laymen, principally as preserver and teacher of the Dhamma. It therefore appears that Buddhists themselves define Buddhism primarily as a matter of doctrine, formulated belief.

Certainly when I was doing my fieldwork it seemed to me that Buddhism could not reasonably be accommodated to Robertson Smith's view of religion; and, as on other matters, I doubt if I should ever have been sufficiently impelled to challenge this judgement but for my emotional protest at the kind of conclusions to which it conduces. I shall now show that its plausibility depends in part on an unduly restricted view of what Robertson Smith was arguing, and more on a misunderstanding of Buddhism which results from too hasty and uncritical a rendering of the facts and concepts into our own categories.

Although Robertson Smith, when he argued for the primacy in religion of practice over belief, was referring mostly to ritual practice, he was not doing so exclusively. This emphasis in his presentation arose from the fact that he had made his argument in the context of a study of the rite of sacrifice. In fact he was well aware that in the societies he was studying religion was not a specialised institution, separated from other aspects of life, as it tends to be with us. In particular he saw that what we distinguish as religious and as political institutions were in other societies integrally linked and continuous – a point which has been confirmed by much subsequent anthropological research. Thus in the third of the passages which I quoted above (Chapter 11) he wrote: '. . . the oldest religious and political institutions . . . were parts of one whole of social custom. Religion was a part of the organised social life into which a man was born . . . to the ancients it was a part of the citizen's public life . . .'[25]

It is in fact an oddity that we, in our own culture, tend to think of religion and political affairs as two separate, independent, and even incompatible provinces of life.[26] It results in part from the highly differentiated and specialised character of our social system, which leads us to treat almost any major aspect of life as the distinct province of a special and specialised institution; this in fact makes it harder for us to understand how society actually works, and often has detrimental effects on the practical conduct of these various aspects of life. Thus we both misunderstand and mismanage our economic affairs by treating them, in practice and in theory, as the special province of Economics. Politics is debased by being treated as exempt from the moral considerations which are typically handled by religions; as by the compensatory tendency to inflate political ideologies, such as Socialism, into quasi-religions. Education tends to become ineffective and irrelevant by being regarded as the specialised province of academics and teachers, rather than as an integral aspect of the conduct of real life.

Religion is made more or less irrelevant by being treated as a peculiar activity of special days, special buildings, and special people of peculiar costume and diction. This no doubt is not unmotivated: in a normal society religion is pre-eminent in the world, but there are always those who would prefer to escape from this. It was a crucial factor in our cultural history that Church and State came to be seen as somewhat independent and opposed institutions, with the eventual upshot that it was the State, and the politicians who work it, who became in fact pre-eminent in the world, with the Church largely confined to unworldly, that is irrelevant, concerns. Such a development is potential in any, or at least any universalistic, religious culture, because of the real difficulty of maintaining the proper balance between Transcendence and Immanence, between the facts that religion must not be of the world but must be in the world. It is made more probable when religion is infected by Manichaean views.

The worst of this did not occur in Buddhist civilisation, in part because the technological base did not encourage excessive specialisation, in part because the constitution of the Sangha made the separation of Church and State practically impossible. Although Western scholars once presented Buddhism as an asocial, apolitical religion, and this is still the popular view in the West, there is now a substantial body of scholarly literature which puts it beyond doubt that throughout its known history Buddhism has been integrally involved and concerned with the political order.[27] I cannot agree with Ling[28] that the scriptures show that the Buddha himself took a large interest in political matters, simply because I cannot agree that the scriptures tell us anything much about the historical Buddha; but the scriptural evidence which Ling has assembled does show that even among the clerical authors of the scriptures the view was widespread that Buddhists should concern themselves with political affairs. Weber, who relied on the work of the earlier scholars, was quite wrong when he wrote, 'Ancient Buddhism represents in almost all, practically decisive points the characteristic polar opposite of Confucianism as well as of Islam. It is a specifically unpolitical and anti-political status religion . . .,'[29] as he was when he wrote, 'Finally, ancient Buddhism had been simply apolitical. An inner relation to political power was hardly discoverable for it'[30]; and followed this with a lengthy exposition of how King Asoka radically transformed Buddhism to make it what we know from history. Possibly events may have followed that course, and the readiness of scriptural authors to endorse a political orientation may have been a consequence of the changes, if that is what they were, instituted by Asoka. But once we bring scripture under that kind of suspicion, as we should, we have no sound evidence for claiming that before Asoka Buddhism was thoroughly apolitical. 'Ancient Buddhism' is either unknowable or not as Weber described it.

There is indeed an apolitical strain in the Buddhist scriptures, most evident in the rhinoceros verses, which are far from unique in their tendency. But we cannot definitely say from the evidence that this was earlier than the contrary tendency, still less that it was characteristic of the Buddha himself; on the contrary, all the evidence we have suggests that the two tendencies have run as parallel streams throughout Buddhist history.[31*] As we have already remarked (Chapter 9) the rhinoceros tendency is to some degree linked with the more enclosed, if not secluded, clergy; I associate it with the more Manichaean forms of Buddhism which, as in our own tradition, are linked with excessive emphasis on celibacy. Weber's view is inescapably speculative; for what speculation is worth, there is more to be said for an alternative guess. The Buddha himself, I suggest, taught a kind of religion which was substantially different from that of the Indian ascetic tradition, but because the greater part of his disciples were drawn from those committed to that tradition, after his death they rejected his innovations (which perhaps they did not understand) and taught a doctrine more orthodox in terms of the more familiar Indian tradition. This has undoubtedly happened to other notable innovators in human history, and clues that it did happen with regard to the Buddha are not lacking. I draw attention only to one set of clues.

It is so clear from the scriptures as to be generally accepted without challenge that the Buddha's own favourite among his disciples was Ānanda, and it was to him that the Buddha left charge of the Sangha after his death. Ānanda, however, was not an *arhat*, i.e. he had not attained Nirvana, as most of the other disciples had. How very odd that a Buddha who supposedly considered the attainment of Nirvana to be the essential goal of a *bhikkhu* should actually have preferred as his chief associate and chosen successor[32]* one who had conspicuously failed to attain! It is clear, of course, that the other *bhikkhus* found it intolerably odd, for at the First Council held immediately after the Buddha's death Ānanda was declared sinful, required to do penance, and deposed from the leadership, which passed to *bhikkhus* of the more traditional mould.[33] However, scholars are generally agreed that the First Council never occurred but is an historical fiction:[34] the yarn should thus be interpreted as reflecting a tradition that Buddhism did revert to a more traditional, non-Buddhist, mould soon after the Buddha himself was out of the way, and was also an attempt to legitimate this reaction. Further, according to Frauwallner, the yarn about the First Council, and the supplementary yarns about Ānanda's deficiencies, derive from the *Skandhaka*, and were either selected from tradition, or simply invented, by the author of that work.[35] I find that several of the less attractive features of Buddhism stem from the *Skandhaka*, as Frauwallner has described it. I cannot say how much historical basis there may be for any of the stories about Ānanda, and in the end it does not much matter: even if they are sheer legend, they do indicate an established tradition that the Buddhism of the Buddha was rejected or altered by those who made themselves his leading disciples after his death. I suspect that yarns in which Ānanda appears in a favourable light will positively correlate with the less Manichaean strand in Buddhendom.

If this speculation is sound – and it has at least as much right to be considered so as the alternative speculation favoured by Weber – then Asoka did not radically alter Buddhism, but rather restored or sustained an original Buddhism. It seems to me quite possible that although original Buddhism was transformed by an élite among the Sangha, the authentic religion was carried on by laymen and their more immediate clerical pastors, and realised without essential change by Asoka, who on the evidence of his Edicts appears to have been little concerned with the Buddhism of the monastic tradition. But again, it seems to me of little importance to guess what the facts may have been: by the crucial test of the *Kālāma Sutta* I should prefer to trust Asoka's understanding of Buddhism to that of a monkish élite.

Now Asoka does have something very interesting to say about ritual in Buddhism. In his Rock Edict IX he remarks that people perform various ceremonies, and refers to what we would term curative rites and several kinds of rites of passage. He continues:

It is right that ceremonies be performed. But this kind bears little fruit. The ceremony of Dharma (*Dharma-mangala*), on the contrary, is very fruitful. It consists in proper treatment of slaves and servants, reverence to teachers, restraint of violence towards living creatures, and liberality to priests and ascetics. These and like actions are called the ceremonies of Dharma.[36]

This suggestion, that ethical action is analogous to ritual, echoes what I had sometimes thought when I was doing fieldwork. Then, as I puzzled over the fact that ritual, which according to anthropological theory should be crucial in any religious system, was nearly lacking in Buddhism, it crossed my mind that ethical conduct was in some ways functionally analogous to ritual in other systems. When I asked them what as Buddhists they should do, my informants regularly replied by speaking of ethical conduct; and it seemed rather evident that much of this conduct, notably not killing animals, and liberality to clergy, was plainly emblematic if not symbolic.

Now I am not suggesting that the meaning of the term 'ritual', already too various, should be extended further to cover ethical conduct *per se*; it is surely more expedient to restrict the meaning of the term to conventional stylised symbolic action, especially of a ceremonial kind. But I am suggesting that there is a significant analogy of function. Geertz has written:

... it is in ritual – i.e. consecrated behaviour – that this conviction that religious conceptions are veridical and that religious directives are sound is somehow generated ... In these plastic dramas men attain their faith as they portray it.[37]

And

The main context, though not the only one, in which religious symbols work to create and sustain belief is, of course, ritual ... For the overwhelming majority of the religious in any population ... engagement in some form of ritualized traffic with sacred symbols is the major mechanism by means of which they come not only to encounter a world view but actually to adopt it, to internalize it as part of their personality.[38]

I am suggesting, that is, that ethical conduct is an alternative means by which people can come to adopt and internalise a world view, that it too can create and sustain belief. Buddhism is indeed remarkable, in a comparative view of religions, for the large extent to which it relies on this means, and the notably small extent to which it makes use of 'ritualized traffic with sacred symbols'.

If what I have suggested is sound, it shows how right Robertson Smith was to include under religious practice both 'ritual and traditional usage'. That political action should also be regarded as part of religious – that is, ethical – practice is entirely consistent with the way that many of my informants spoke,[39]* as it is of a very large part of Buddhist historical usage, and not least the deeds and the words of Asoka.

In one of the passages most often quoted, Asoka, referring to himself as he usually did by his title Priyadarsi ('one who sees to the good of others'),[40] had inscribed in his Pillar Edict VII:

King Priyadarsi says:

I have ordered banyan trees to be planted along the roads to give shade to men and animals. I have ordered mango groves to be planted. I have ordered wells to be dug every half-kos [about a half-mile], and I have ordered rest houses built. I have had many watering stations built for the convenience of men and animals.

These are trifling comforts. For the people have received various facilities from previous kings as well as from me. But I have done what I have primarily in order that the people may follow the path of Dharma with faith and devotion.[41]

The last sentence has usually been interpreted as meaning that Asoka sought to create circumstances in which people would have sufficient leisure and freedom from affliction to be free to devote their minds to religious pursuits.[42] It may well have that meaning too, but the principal meaning is more profound. Asoka saw his provision of measures of welfare as a means of teaching Dharma, on the principle that an example is worth a thousand words. The passage quoted is part of a long Edict which is all concerned with the various means he has adopted for the promulgation of Dharma. A later section in it reads:

King Priyadarsi says:

Whatever good deeds I have done the people have imitated, and they have followed them as a model. In doing so, they have progressed and will progress in obedience to parents and teachers, in respect for elders, in courtesy to priests and ascetics, to the poor and distressed, and even to slaves and servants.[43]

But this notion of teaching by example does not fully represent Asoka's thought. To be quite clear about what he was saying we need to examine the concept of Dharma, and its Pali equivalent, Dhamma.

Gombrich remarks, '*Dharma* can be and has been translated in a thousand ways: "righteousness", "truth", "the Way", etc. It is best not translated at all.'[44] In a way this is true, and one can go on without end registering and discussing the innumerable shades of meaning that it has borne in its usage by various persons. But if one is primarily concerned to understand the concept, matters are very much simpler. In his *Buddhist Dictionary* Nyanatiloka gives for 'Dhamma':[45] 'literally the "Bearer", Constitution (or Nature of a thing), Norm, Law (*jus*), Doctrine; Justice, Righteousness; Quality; Thing, Object of Mind; "Phenomenon"', and a little later refers to 'The Dhamma, as the liberating law discovered and proclaimed by the Buddha ...'. This does indeed cover the major meanings of the term, and is much simpler than Gombrich's thousand translations. Nevertheless, perceived from our standpoint, Nyanatiloka does seem to have presented us with a ragbag of senses. But the basic concept is very simple; it is only because it is unfamiliar to us that we find it hard to follow the logic of its more particular application to what, in our conceptual schema, seem very different things.

A *dharma* is simply the true nature of a thing, its basic and inherent characteristics. The *Dharma* is simply the true nature of the cosmos. It comprises the whole system of natural laws which define and constitute the cosmos, and, with reference to man as part of the cosmos, the moral law. In Buddhism, of course, there is no notion of these laws as having been decreed by a law-giver, a God: they are simply the inherent structure of reality. The Dhamma of the Buddha, therefore, is not primarily a theory or doctrine that he taught; it is simply the way things are, which he discovered and saw, and explained to others. It is liberating simply because suffering and inadequacy (*dukkha*) are the product of error, of not understanding how things are; to bring to completion one's inherent potential (one's *dharma*) it is necessary to understand how things are, oneself and the cosmos of which one is an integral part – and sufficient to do so through and through without residue. That is all.

From this basic concept it is evident how the more specific senses arise as particular applications. In some contexts Dhamma is the explication of reality, the teaching of how things really are: thus 'doctrine' is a bit like one sense of '*Dhamma*', though neither so like, nor so central to the meaning as we from our peculiar Western standpoint imagine. Asoka's own definition, though still partial, represents a much greater part of what the concept means in practical terms for Buddhists:

King Priyadarsi says:

Dharma is good. But what does Dharma consist of?

It consists of few sins and many good deeds, of kindness, liberality, truthfulness, and purity.[46]

It may have been noticed that I have not gone into the issue of whether and how far the Buddhist concept of Dhamma is the same as the wider Indian concept, or concepts, of Dharma. Nor have I considered the question, which has been much discussed, whether Asoka's concept of Dharma was specifically Buddhist at all.[47] These are good academic questions, but relatively trivial. My villagers regularly told me that a good man was a good Buddhist whether he called himself a Christian or a Muslim, or anything or nothing. This is not only sound common sense, but an inescapable consequence of the concept of Dhamma when it is properly grasped. By this excellent criterion, Asoka was a good Buddhist, wherever he may have got his ideas from.

So too was Sīlaratana, who almost certainly did not get his ideas direct from Asoka. When he told me that he had devoted himself to social service because the Buddha enjoined his disciples to go out and proclaim Dhamma to the people, I had found his logic incomprehensible (Chapter 3); now that we have understood what Dhamma is, the logic is obvious. More remarkably, Sīlaratana's reading of his calling was justified by its fruits. He sowed Dhamma, and what he reaped was Dhamma: 'It consists of few sins and many good deeds, of kindness, liberality, truthfulness and purity.' These were indeed the characteristics of the people of Polgama: not perfectly, in fact very far from it, but by properly human standards, if my observation is to be trusted, genuinely.

Once again, therefore, the view of Robertson Smith stands firm. The supposition that Buddhism is basically a matter of doctrine, of belief, derives largely from distorting the concepts into our own conceptual frame. Dhamma is not doctrine, except derivatively, and even then not exactly: in the religious life Dhamma is primarily what Asoka defined it to be, practice.

Notes to Chapter 12

1   In particular, the work of Spiro and Gombrich, as remarked above in Chapter 1.
2   Carter (1924), p. 622.
3   I have encountered it only once in the literature, in Obeyesekere (1981), p. 65.
4   Cf. Southwold (1978), p. 362.
5   Knox [1681] (1966), p. 148.
6   Tambiah (1970).
7   Obeyesekere (1963).
8   See especially Seneviratne (1978).
9   See Kapferer (1977, 1979a, 1979b, 1979c), Obeyesekere (1969), Wirz (1954), Yalman (1964).

10 Gombrich (1971), p. 76–7.

11 Smith (1927), pp. 214, 218.

12 Cf. Gombrich (1971), pp. 117–18.

13 *Ibid.*, chapter 3, notably pp. 139–40, 142.

14 Cf. Southwold (1978), p. 366.

15 Durkheim (1915), p. 360; (1912), p. 514. I have followed Lukes's translation (1973, pp. 473–4).

16 For example, the eccentric lady referred to above. In her unusually elaborate and frequent offerings she was not conforming to established custom: she went far beyond it, evoking rather amusement than approval. It is my impression that in any society there will be found a minority of people whose ritualism is regarded as excessive, so that it cannot plausibly be attributed to a wish to satisfy the expectations of neighbours.

17 *Vihāra-gē*.

18 Fixed by a lunar calendar, the dates for these vary somewhat from year to year; but they commonly occur towards the end of May, June, and November respectively.

19 These presentations are often made with some formality, and should be accounted as rituals. Partly because they are routine, partly because they involve only the recipient clergy and members of the family making the presentation, I perceive them as minor in comparison to the *dānes* I go on to discuss.

20 Gombrich analyses *mataka dānes* in detail, and sees these rites as basically Hindu rites which have been given elaborate Buddhist rationalisation (1971, pp. 229–43).

21 It is then called *gihi pirit*, 'layman pirit'.

22 It is described by Gombrich (1971, pp. 241–2). The acts of receiving a cloth and chanting while water is poured are so brief and inconspicuous that one can easily not notice them. Far more conspicuous are the eulogies to the deceased, in which clergy may speak on the same terms as laymen, and the disposal of the corpse by cremation or burial, before which the clergy leave.

23 Gombrich (1971), pp. 64–5. The Three Refuges amount to affirmations of confidence in the Buddha, the Dhamma, and the Sangha. Taking the Five Precepts is affirming intention to abide by this ethical code – for its content, see Chapter 6, n. 18.

24 Gombrich (1971), pp. 67–8.

25 Smith (1927), p. 21.

26 Cf. Ling (1973), p. 26.

27 The arguments are developed and the evidence reviewed most usefully in Ling (1973) and Tambiah (1976).

28 Ling (1973), p. 140 f.

29 Weber (1967), p. 206.

30 *Ibid.*, p. 237.

31 The point is clearly made by Sarkisyanz (1965, p. 36). I have the impression that the two tendencies are significantly associated with basic social or political orientations, the rhinoceros tendency with those of a conservative kind, the more politically active with those of a radical kind. This is what should be expected in any complex society composed of human beings like

ourselves.

32   According to scripture, the Buddha declined to constitute himself as in any
     sense authoritative ruler of the Sangha, or to authorise anyone to succeed to
     such a position: he merely asked Ānanda to take care of the Sangha in his
     place. See, e.g. Ling (1973), p. 128.

33   Thus Weber (1967, p. 224).

34   Thus Bareau (1955, pp. 27–30) and Frauwallner (1956, p. 64), both quoted by
     Gombrich (1971, p. 41 n. 4).

35   Frauwallner (1956), pp. 64–5, 162.

36   Nikam and McKeon (1959), p. 46. Tambiah (1976, p. 67) also notes the
     significance of this text.

37   Geertz (1966), pp. 28–9.

38   Geertz (1968), p. 100.

39   Many people, however, maintain that a cleric ought not to be actively
     involved in party politics.

40   Nikam and McKeon (1959), p. 26n.

41   *Ibid.*, pp. 64–5.

42   E.g. Sarkisyanz (1965), p. 28.

43   Nikam and McKeon (1959), p. 35.

44   Gombrich (1971), p. 60.

45   Nyanatiloka (1972), p. 47.

46   Nikam and McKeon (1959), p. 41.

47   Tambiah (1976, chapter 5) argues cogently and at length that it was.

13

Instrumentalism and sapientalism

Robertson Smith maintained, as we saw (Chapter 11), that we get our peculiar notion, that in religion belief is primary and practice derivative, from our Christian tradition. But where did our Christian tradition get it from? It is unusual in other religious traditions; from my demonstration that we perceive it in Buddhism when it is not really there at all (except to the extent that some modern Buddhists have been misled by us), I should be sceptical of any apparent evidence that it is found elsewhere, and incline to regard it as unique. We Christians certainly did not get it from the Hebrew foundations of our tradition, which in this respect at least were robustly sound.[1] Probably we got it from our foundations in the thought of the Greeks.

But it is not of first importance to know where we got it from, nor to count how many partners, if any, we have in our error: it is more useful to show, as I shall now do, the basic reason why it is and must be an error. In what follows I shall make some observations on what I choose to term the basic nature of religion. Though I suspect that it is, what I have to say may not be true of all religions. The term 'religion' is so loosely applied that it refers to a range of phenomena which are very various superficially, and may be so profoundly. It is absurd to assume *a priori* that the set of all things that have been called religions is a well formed homogeneous (monothetic[2]) class, so that what is true of any must be true of each. If there is some religion, or collection of religions, of which what I say is not true, so be it: I am not talking about them. I claim only that my remarks are true of those religions of which they are true, and that this is not an empty set. It certainly contains Buddhism, and to the best of my understanding Christianity also, at least as it used to be; and to me at least it seems a probable hypothesis that it has many other members. Just how many I leave to future enquiry to determine.

Much of Gombrich's analysis of Sinhalese village Buddhism is built on a distinction between two kinds of belief. 'Cognitive' beliefs are what people sincerely say they believe; 'affective' beliefs are what people really believe, in their hearts, as evidenced by their behaviour. 'What people really believe I am aware to be ultimately unknowable; but this does not mean that it is nonsense to talk about it. Only a pure behaviourist refrains from making inferences from what people really do to what they are thinking or feeling.'[3]

What has happened here is that by taking such care to avoid the Scylla of pure behaviourism Gombrich has let himself fall into the Charybdis of attributing belief in ways which are unwarranted and which actually preclude satisfactory analysis. We have already seen how he thinks that the offering of *Buddha pūjā* shows that Sinhalese really believe that the Buddha exists; and how this is both logically unsound and an obstacle to perceiving the real analytical problem (Chapter 12). Similarly, when he confronts the issue raised by the fact that he categorises Sinhalese Buddhism as a religion, but religion is usually defined in terms of theism, 'belief in deity or deities', he dismisses it by remarking, 'Whether a definition which equates religion with theism holds on the cognitive level is therefore controversial; the only level on which I think it certainly holds is the affective: Sinhalese Buddhists behave, at least with regard to the Buddha, as if they believe in a supernatural being.'[4] The evidence for this claim is mostly the same as that on which he founds the other claim, and thus the conclusion is logically unsound for similar reasons. Here too the analysis is theoretically stultifying: for we ought to see that Buddhism really does challenge our conventional definition, or conception of religion, and by facing the challenge go on to produce a more satisfactory concept.[5]

The last chapter of Gombrich's book, 'Conclusion', is an admirably sensitive and insightful discussion of two main tendencies in contemporary and historical Buddhism, framed largely in terms of his contrast between cognitive and affective religion. It may be that his reliance on this too easy and superficial distinction cocooned Gombrich from facing up to the real challenge that the evidence, his evidence, presents, so that he states the conclusion it points to, that the voice of the people is the voice of the Buddha,[6] not definitely, but as an extremely tentative query. Whether or not this is a case in point, the real objection to giving primacy to belief in the analysis of religion is not so much that it is ill-warranted by fact and by logic, as that it diverts us from the kind of analysis which produces better understanding.

It is one of the marks of an excellent book that its author makes it plain where he has gone wrong. I do not mean this as a backhanded compliment; we learn from mistakes, not least those of our colleagues, and hence we learn most easily from those whose argument is as clear when they are wrong as when they are right.[7] Gombrich qualifies for this sincere accolade (as for many others).

Not only is he very plain that his analysis hinges on concepts of belief: also he explains, as many do not, why:

> A religious action is based on a belief about facts and directed to certain aims. Either the belief or the aims may change. What does not change is the relation between these two: that the action based on the beliefs and directed to the aims follows the rationality principle. If it does not it is not amenable to systematic study.[8]

Now we know, in view of our discussion of Robertson Smith's position and related matters, that the assumption that 'a religious action is based on a belief about facts' is highly questionable. Gombrich has done us the service of explaining that, for him at least, the assumption is a consequence of 'the rationality principle'.

He also explains what the rationality principle is, and how it leads to emphasis on belief to account for religious behaviour. His words are so revealing that I quote them at some length:

> It may seem paradoxical that the social study of religion should concentrate on the rational, but Popper, the begetter of what he calls the 'rationality principle', has shown that there is no other way. The rationality principle is the zero principle, the basic assumption of the social sciences; it is the principle that in so far as behaviour is amenable to social study, it is the behaviour of people acting in what they conceive to be their best interests. Its application to the sociology of religion has been expounded by I. Jarvie in his interesting and provocative book *The Revolution in Anthropology*. If we see a man in an agricultural community oppressed by a drought enter a special building (called, maybe, a church), get on his knees, fold his hands and start muttering, we may assume that he is insane, in which case we can offer no further testable explanations of his conduct, or that he thinks his actions may bring rain. And if that is what he thinks, we must assume that he thinks some entity is capable of giving him rain, and that that entity, which begins to look rather human in its emotions, will be placated by his suppliant posture and humble gesture, and listen to his words ... Conduct is rational if it consists in using what seem appropriate means to attain given ends: the man praying for rain is acting rationally. What are given to him are the beliefs that make those means seem appropriate and the ends he wishes to attain; in this case that rain should fall.[9]

Of course I am not suggesting that everyone who over-uses the concept of belief to account for religious behaviour has been misled by Popper. Rather, I argue that Popper's 'rationality principle' is simply a rigorous formulation, and to that extent an exaggeration, of a set of assumptions that are deeply embedded in our culture and which are the real source of the trouble. It is revealing to note the inadequacy of analysis which results when one embraces Popper's extreme formulation of more general assumptions. Jarvie's interpretation of ritual behaviour associated with rain and drought is crude; if this is not immediately evident to the reader, he may compare it with Lienhardt's sensitive and insightful remarks about rain ritual among the Dinka.[10]* It is a measure of how far a man's insight can be blocked by his theoretical preconceptions that Gombrich, normally so sensitive, could approve such a travesty of ritual behaviour.

No doubt there really are people in other societies as naive as Jarvie's imagined mutterer: naivety is as common, and as uncommon, in other societies as in our own. But my conclusion from my own experience as a fieldworker, as from that of others, is that when the behaviour of most people, typical people, in another society appears to us unintelligible and more or less silly, the fault lies with us, not with them; and the remedy is to search ourselves to discover why we cannot fathom their good sense and rationality. To assume that they are either insane or naive, as Jarvie in effect does, is impertinent, in both senses: it is insulting, and it is irrelevant to, and a diversion from, an analysis which would fit the facts and teach us something worth learning. It is all too easy to compound our arrogance by selecting as typical those relatively few members of the other society who actually are as naive as our biased misinterpretation implies.

When Jarvie and Gombrich attempt to account for religious behaviour by the application of Popper's extreme formulation of assumptions common in our culture, the result is a *reductio ad absurdum*. That is a valuable, if unintended, contribution. It remains to diagnose the looser and usually tacit, and hence less obviously wrong, assumptions which more generally lead to our common overestimate of the place of belief in religious behaviour and religious systems.

Some human behaviour is more or less automatic or physically determined: we do not normally need to appeal to psychological or sociological theory to explain why a man breathes, or trips over an unseen obstacle. Social scientists normally distinguish as 'action' behaviour which is voluntary, purposive, and more or less rational; where we can, and often do, go wrong is in mistaking its purpose and its rationale. I suggest that we can properly say of all human action that its object is to ameliorate experience. This may not be the most proximate goal, and it may not be easy to understand how the actor supposes his action will achieve such a goal. Further I assume that the goal is the amelioration of the actor's own subjective experience. While this seems plain of most kinds of action, it is questionable with regard to altruistic action. But this can be accommodated by arguing either (or both) that the actor's goal is the satisfaction of perceiving himself as altruistic, or that he has enlarged his sense of subjectivity, his identification of self, to include those we would normally regard as others.

Much, and probably most, human action is predicated on the assumption that our states of subjective experience are determined by the states of our environment, the world about us. Since the 'I', that which has states of experience and chooses actions, is a psychic or mental entity, its environment, for purposes of this analysis, includes the body, the physical organism. Given the assumption, in order to change our state of subjective experience (for the better) we have to change the state of the world which determines it. Action which is oriented to changing the state of the world as a means to the end of changing one's state of subjective experience is often termed 'instrumental';[11] I shall specialise the term in just this sense.

For instrumental action to be effective we require information and more or less rational analysis based upon it. We need information on how different possible states of the world correlate with different states of subjective experience; and we need information on how different possible states of the world are causally connected with one another, so that we can reckon what actions of ours will deflect the course of events to produce the states we seek. Holding constant the adequacy of our rational analysis, the better the quality of the information we have the more effective our instrumental action will be. Ideally we seek perfect information, that which is certainly correct, which we term 'knowledge'. We may indeed attain it on matters of particular fact, but definitive and incorrigible general information about the world is rarely attained, and very probably, as Popper maintains,[12] unattainable. In the strict sense, then, we do not require certain and incorrigible 'knowledge' in order to act effectively. What logically we do need are beliefs, in the sense of propositions held to be factually true: our action will be the more effective the more nearly our beliefs are indeed factually true, the more nearly they approach asymptotically the ideal of 'knowledge'. The pursuit of 'knowledge', or perhaps more exactly, more and more warranted beliefs, together with the improvement of rational analysis, is what we call 'science'. That science is such a dominant element of our culture is a measure of our commitment to the instrumental strategy of action.

I have been using the term 'belief' in the more basic inclusive sense, in which knowledge is a sub-class of belief. I have done so in order to make clear that what is held to be factually true is a necessary basis for any rational instrumental action: necessarily, instrumental 'action is based on a belief about facts', since without it there can be no coherent link between the action proposed and goal sought. If religious action is instrumental action, then it too must be 'based on a belief about facts', as Gombrich asserts. In practice, we more often use the term 'belief' in the exclusive sense, according to which belief is always less than knowledge. And we tend to apply the terms according to the bias that what we hold to be true is knowledge, but what you hold to be true, and we do not, is merely belief. Hence we tend to suppose that science, and action rooted in science, is based on knowledge, whereas religion is based on belief; and we feel the more confident of this because Christians have always said that their religion is based on belief, without our noticing that either this is belief in a different sense, or else the Christians are as confused as the rest of us. This tends to obscure the fact that our view of religion as based on belief, in the ordinary sense, derives from a tacit analogy between it and science and technology, and instrumental action generally.

I have defined instrumental action as action directed to altering the state of the world, one's environment, as a means to altering one's subjective state of experience, which it is taken to determine. The strategy of ameliorating experience by such means I shall call 'the instrumental strategy'. The system of assumptions, thought and action – including the necessary basis of action in beliefs about facts – of which this strategy is part, I shall term 'instrumentalism'. To the extent that a person has adopted this system as a model for action, or a model of action, or both, I shall term him an 'instrumentalist'.

I have not the least doubt that much, probably most, human action is, in large part at least, instrumental and has an instrumentalist rationale. Wherever it is so, the instrumentalist model is a proper basis for interpreting and analysing it. To this extent, Popper's 'rationality principle' is sound. It becomes unsound when we recognise the fact that some human action, wholly or largely, is not instrumentalist, and is radically misunderstood if we treat it as if it were. Such action has its own, different, kind(s) of rationale and hence rationality. To appropriate the term 'rationality' for instrumentalism alone is tendentious and misleading, since it implies, contrary to fact, that non-instrumental action is necessarily non-rational, and suggests that it is irrational and hence more or less unintelligible. This leads Jarvie and Gombrich, and many others, to assume that religious action, much of which in fact is non-instrumental, must be analysed on instrumentalist assumptions, which in fact are inept for the purpose; and thus to assume, as we have seen, that 'a religious action is based on a belief about facts' or else 'is not amenable to systematic study'.

There is nothing at all wrong with instrumental action, or with instrumentalist analysis of it. The error comes in when it is assumed that all action, or at any rate all rational and intelligible action, is instrumental, and consequently it must be analysed on the instrumentalist model, for 'there is no other way'. This error can properly be termed 'positivism', in a sense close to that of Gellner when he writes, 'Pure positivism, in the traditional sense, consists *au fond* of recommending that all thinking should emulate the ways of science, whatever they be, or pack up.'[13] I enlarge the term a little to include the bias that all action should emulate the ways of instrumentalism or else be dismissed as non-rational. In this somewhat extended sense, positivism is the real root of the delusion that belief is basic to religious practice. It has plainly distorted Gombrich's analysis. I think that it is the basis of the conventional Western misunderstanding of Buddhism, as also of our usual misunderstandings of religions generally, our own included.

I would not suggest that all rational action which is not instrumental follows the same pattern, has the same kind of rationale: without having gone into the matter much, I think it is not so. I wish merely to describe and define one system of rational non-instrumental action which seems to be important in, indeed crucial to, much religious practice.

The instrumentalist is wrong if he assumes that subjective experience is wholly determined by the state of the environing world, for its quality is largely shaped by what we make of what is given. Proverbially, the difference between an optimist and a pessimist is revealed in their reactions to a bottle of whisky half consumed: the optimist rejoices that the bottle is still half full, the pessimist complains that it is already half empty. Naturally not all givens are as neutral as this one, and it is harder to rejoice in kicks than halfpence; but over a wide range, at least, the quality of experience is shaped by what we make of it, by the way we construe and construct what is given to us by the world. Thus an alternative strategy for ameliorating experience is directed to changing the way we interpret and evaluate the givens of experience, and behind them the giver, the world. Where instrumentalism is directed to ameliorating given experience by altering the giver, the world, this strategy is directed to ameliorating experience by altering the maker, who construes it this way or that, the self. Since the experiencing self is a mental or psychic entity, and construals are mental or psychic products, the relevant alterations are always changes of mind and of states of consciousness. But because the psyche is not a free-floating entity, alterable at will as easily as we 'change our minds' in the sense of the everyday idiom, but is rooted in our whole active being, emotive, dispositional, conative, and rational – and is shaped by our actions as much as it shapes them – the effective changes of mind are much more than this: they amount rather to change of being, of self, to conversion, that is turning round of the whole persona.

This was once clearly understood by Christians, whose term for the inner change, of mind and of self, was rendered in English as 'repentance'. Thus Richardson explains: '. . . though the Greek word *metanoein* is often used for "repent", in its New Testament usage it implies much more than a mere "change of mind"; it involves a whole reorientation of the personality, a "conversion" '.[14] This is from Richardson's article on the biblical terms 'repent, repentance, convert, conversion'. It will be evident that the concept is central to the teaching of the New Testament, as the call to 'Repent' is basic to the reported mission of Christ. It is still encountered in modern Christianity, though often in impoverished, not to say debased, form.

In fact there is now no word in English which clearly designates this crucial Christian concept: conversion means largely joining a Church or sect, and 'to repent' means especially 'To feel regret, sorrow or contrition for (some fault, misconduct, sin, or other offence)'.[15] This was certainly an important aspect of the biblical concept, since the change of mind and being that was called for was always seen as a return to submission to the sovereignty of God (otherwise, kingdom of Heaven), renouncing the rebellion that was termed 'sin'; but it does not adequately represent the aspects that are brought out by Richardson's explication of the meaning of '*metanoein*'. Perhaps there never has been an English term that adequately designates the concept, since the dictionary does not register Richardson's sense in its entries for 'repent' and 'repentance'.[15]

There certainly is a rational strategy for ameliorating experience by altering the mind and the self, rather than the environing world; it is parallel to, and alternative to, the instrumental strategy – though the two are not mutually exclusive, and no one survives who is not often an instrumentalist. This strategy too is part of a system of assumptions, thought and action which parallels instrumentalism, though as we shall see it differs significantly from it not only in content but also in structure. It is this system, I am arguing, which provides the rationale for at least a large part of religious practice, and to recognise this is to see why religion is misunderstood when it is analysed on the instrumentalist model. This system is very plainly basic to Buddhism, as I think it is to New Testament Christianity. In Buddhism, however, the concept of changing the mind, of reorienting the personality, carries no connotations of regret or contrition, of sin or offence. There is no concept of a sovereign God to whose allegiance one should return after rebellion; rather the notion is that of acquiring understanding, right view, or Dharma, the way things truly are, replacing ignorance and delusion by wisdom (*pañña*).

In analysing this system, and contrasting it with instrumentalism, it would be convenient to have a clear and definite term by which to label and refer to it; but it is difficult to find a satisfactory one. In an earlier essay,[16] taking a hint from Richardson, I coined the terms 'repental' and 'repentalism'. But they have met with objection, for it seems that no one finds it easy to think of repentance in terms not of regret and contrition but of the concept which Richardson explicates for '*metanoein*'; and I suppose it is true that the Christian formulation of the concept is incurably slanted by Semitic notions of a sovereign God. Various other possible terms have seemed to have more drawbacks than advantages.

I have therefore settled on the term 'sapientalism', from 'sapience', wisdom. It is indeed tendentious to imply that wisdom is the peculiar prerogative of this system, but no more so than the common presumption that rationality is that of instrumentalism; and perhaps the devil has had the best words long enough. There is, moreover, an established practice of contrasting wisdom with rationality in the narrow sense which associates the latter term peculiarly with science and scientific technology.[17] Thus, with contrition for any implication that sapientalism alone is wise, I shall adopt this term as a not altogether inadequate label.

Henceforth, then, the strategy for ameliorating experience by changing the mind and the self will be termed 'sapiental'. The system of assumptions, thought and action of which it is part will be 'sapientalism'. To the extent that a person has adopted this system as a model for action, or a model of action, or both, I shall term him a 'sapientalist'.

In principle, it is possible for there to be sapiental strategies directed to different goals and employing different tactics, and there need be no conflict between sapientalism and instrumentalism. But, as we shall see, there are good reasons why a sapiental system should take a form we categorise as 'religious'; and, so far as I know, all sapiental systems that have become firmly established in a culture are, in large part at least, 'religious'. Most often, but not invariably, a society has one, or one dominant, religion. Such a society therefore has one established sapiental, religious system, counterposed to the instrumentalism of everyday, secular life. Often the sapiental system is more or less critical of the instrumentalism of the same society. This might be accounted for by the fact that if instrumentalism is regarded as satisfactory, the sapiental system and its professionals or priests tend to appear superfluous.

There is, I think, a more fundamental reason for the typical duality of sapientalism and instrumentalism, and the tendency of one or both to criticise and oppose the other. Actual sapiental systems manifest features – holism, and expression in music, dance, and pictorial imagery – which are typical of the operations of the right hemisphere of the cerebral cortex, as instrumentalism manifests features of the thinking of the left hemisphere.[18] The duality of sapientalism and instrumentalism in cultures may thus be rooted in the fact that our minds employ two notably different modes of thought, which are largely specialised in the two divisions of the cerebral cortex. This would help to account for the fact that sapientalist thought is often critical of instrumentalist thought: because the left hemisphere and its thought tend to be dominant, the right hemisphere has to fight for due recognition.

There is, however, a more basic reason for opposition between the products of thinking of the two hemispheres. Left-hemisphere, instrumentalist, thinking is fundamentally egoistic[19] – though not necessarily egotistic – and analytic, concerned with making and marking distinctions. Right-hemisphere thinking tends to be holistic and synthetic, overriding distinctions in its perception of patterns and gestalts. This is carried over into the sapiental systems it produces: it is highly characteristic, for example, of religions to present a picture of the cosmos as an ordered, harmonious society, or, less often, as an integrated system of another kind. There is, at best, some difficulty in harmonising analytic and synthetic thought, and in striking a balance between the centrality of the ego postulated in instrumentalist thought, and its subordination to a larger whole as postulated in sapientalist thought; and since in action egoism tends to become egotism, disruptive of the unity proclaimed by sapientalism, the roots of conflict are evident.

This may be part of the reason why religion is not only important in most societies, but is also 'eminently social', as Durkheim put it with unwary zeal.[20] Rational, instrumentalistic thought and action are not necessarily egotistical; on the contrary, most people understand that unalloyed egotism is evil. But reason, it seems, is hard pressed to provide sufficient motivation for altruistic conduct without which society, and hence the welfare of all and each, are the worse. Religion seems to be more apt for this purpose, in which undoubtedly it has some success.[21]*

The implication in what I have written, that what we call the 'soul' or 'spirit' is basically the right hemisphere of the cerebral cortex in operation, may appear shocking. But this is not a reductionism which reduces the spiritual to the physiological – on the contrary, it enhances the body as spiritual, as the doctrine of Creation requires. – I should, for clarity, point out that the terms *ātma(ya), ātman, atta*, which in other religious systems refer to the soul, in Buddhism refer rather to the ego, and that terms like *hita*, 'mind', are used for the sapiental mind (see below, Chapter 14). This may usefully remind us that the two hemispheres are not independent, so that any simple identification of cultural systems as exclusive products of one hemisphere or the other is inexact.

The problem for sapiental systems is to show man, ordinary worldly man, that their alternative construal is truer and better than his, and to convert him to it, at all the expense of effort and deprivation that is required fully to realise it. It is not easy: on the face of it it is impossible.

Since a sapiental system presents to man an alternative construal of experience, another, deeper truth, and requires him to accept and realise it, one might suppose that here too, as in an instrumental system, belief is basic. If it is so, the similarity is purely nominal, for 'belief' in the one is of a very different kind from 'belief' in the other. As Wittgenstein observed, referring to religion, 'Also, there is this extraordinary use of the word "believe". One talks of believing and at the same time one doesn't use "believe" as one does ordinarily.'[22]

Instrumentalism requires belief, many beliefs about facts, because without them its strategy is inapplicable; at the same time, since these are beliefs about matters of empirical fact, their truth can, at least in principle, be established. But sapientalism, because it is not directly concerned with action on the world, does not require such beliefs about facts. A sapiental system may be presented as a set of assertions, about, say, God and salvation, or *anatta* and Nirvana: and as these are claimed to be true, it may appear, or be made to appear, that they are to be believed. But these are not beliefs about empirical facts of the same kind, and cognitive attitudes to them are not of the same kind. This is sometimes noted by ethnographers – see the passages on the Dinka and the Azande quoted below. More generally, it is the distinction we have noted between 'faith' and 'belief', 'believing in' and 'believing that'. The difference in cognitive attitudes is a response to a difference in their objects. When sapiental assertions are projected as 'truths' about the objective world, their 'truth' is of a symbolic or mystical kind, which 'transcends sensory experience' and hence cannot be established by the same means by which truth is established in instrumentalism. In these cases often, and still more often in Buddhism, which more regularly presents its assertions as 'truths' about inner subjective reality rather than about outer objective reality, it is often said that one comes to know them by experience. Thus a priest told me, referring to a quite well known simile, that Nirvana cannot be described, as one cannot describe the flavour of a mango to one who has not tasted mangoes. The 'truths' of instrumentalism one gets to 'know' analytically – French *savoir* – but the 'truths' of sapientalism one gets to 'know' by acquaintance – French *connaître*. Parallel to this distinction between two kinds of 'knowing' is a distinction between two kinds of 'believing' – naturally, since as we have seen, the concepts of 'knowing' and 'believing' are closely related (above, Chapter 11). Belief in the sense of believing-that resembles the knowing termed *savoir*, faith or believing-in resembles the knowing termed *connaître*.

Thus what is loosely and ambiguously called 'belief' differs as between instrumental and sapiental systems both in the cognitive attitudes referred to and in their foundations, the ways in which they are acquired. So-called 'belief' functions in different ways in the two kinds of system: in instrumentalism it is the necessary foundation for practice, whereas in sapientalism practice is a necessary foundation for it. This results from the fact that the two kinds of system result from different approaches to life, hence different strategies for ameliorating experience, which involve different attitudes to matters of fact. The basic difference is well brought out in the passage I quoted earlier in which Pears summarises the views of Wittgenstein on religious belief:

A religious tenet is not a factual hypothesis, but something which affects our thoughts and actions in a different way . . . the meaning of a religious proposition is not a function of what would have to be the case if it were true, but a function of the difference it makes to the lives of those who maintain it. Religious beliefs, unlike scientific beliefs, are not hypotheses, are not based on evidence, and cannot be regarded as more or less probable.[23]

In the Pali lines, so often recited, the adherence to which is sufficient to make one a Buddhist (see Chapter 12), it is very striking that there is no profession of belief, no credal formulation. The Three Refuges include a profession of cleaving to the Dhamma, but as we have seen, 'Dhamma' does not essentially mean doctrine or belief. At most, it might be said that by reciting the Three Refuges one implies belief that the Buddha did exist, and the Dhamma does, and that each is properly so termed. But then, among village Buddhists at least, in referring to this conventional formulation of adherence, the Three Refuges are mentioned very much less frequently than the Five Precepts. Village Buddhists very often say that the Five Precepts are the core of Buddhism, and sometimes that they are virtually all that is essential. In this they recognise that it is practice, ethical conduct, which is basic, and belief need not even be mentioned, since it arises, of its own, and only, out of practice.

We might put the difference in another way. Instrumentalism accepts the world as given, and seeks to ameliorate experience within its constraints, so that its guiding ideas must be responsive to, as far as possible correspondent with, the given reality. But sapientalism is differently oriented, it is not responsive to the given, but creative, making new. And since it claims that its construal of reality is truer than that of natural, secular man, more in harmony with the ways things really are, it must, implicitly or explicitly, deny that the world of secular man is really *given*. In Buddhist philosophy, which is only an explication and development of what is implicit and latent in Buddhist thought generally, it is quite clearly said that the world we take as given is not in fact given as we perceive it. There is reality, the objective existent, but its structure is not as we perceive it: the world that secular man perceives is, as to its form, itself a human construction, a construal of reality. Thus Buddhist sapientalism either denies the supposedly given veridical character of the world that secular man constructs, in relation to the existent, and says that he perceives; or, which comes to the same thing, defines a world as a product of construal, and says that therefore there are two worlds, the world of the secular construal and the other world of the sapientalist's construal. This idiom is also used in Christianity, though usually without the same clear recognition of its epistemological basis. It is potentially confusing, since the term 'world' gets to be used in two different senses, one to refer to the common substrate of the existent, the other to refer to two different construals of it. But the ambiguity is inherent, for it derives from the necessary apparent paradox that we have seen to be manifested in a variety of puzzling claims: for example that humanity is both divine and counter-divine, that the holy is both transcendent and immanent, that Nirvana is *samsāra*, that the *lōkōttara* is both the opposite of the worldly and pre-eminent in the world, that religion is not of this world yet in the world.

Small wonder that claims so counter-intuitive and nearly un-intelligible cannot readily be believed by secular, commonsense man. But these are inner mysteries, and the basic difficulty of converting man to a sapientalist system is far more exoteric. An advocate of a particular sapientalist system – let us say a Buddhist – tells secular man that he has a different, better construal of reality, and urges him to adopt it in place of what he already has, to convert himself to it through and through, which confessedly will be no easy task. What can motivate the secular man to agree with him? His own construal, his own 'world', is familiar to him – he knows it by acquaintance and lives by it; why should he change, and extinguish the 'world' he lives in? He may be told of this other construal, other 'world', and told that it is better: but why should he believe (credit) this? How can he credit it, when he is told that this other world is radically contrasted with what is familiar to him, and can be realised only at the end of a long and strenuous process of 'conversion', so that his actual experience tells him nothing of it? If he is to believe what he is told, this belief cannot be warranted by evidence or experience. If belief there can be, it must be, as both village Buddhists and Christians make clear, unwarranted belief, Faith (Sinhala *visvāsa*), which is certainly very different from the kind of belief basic for instrumental strategies. 'Faith is the assurance of things hoped for, the proving of things not seen.'[24] But how, as the Kālāmas asked, is one to know in what to have Faith; and how is such Faith to be motivated?

It may be pointed out that this world, experience as we encounter it, is unsatisfactory. No one would dispute that. But is it so unsatisfactory that it must, at great pains, be extinguished and replaced by another, not seen, not known, and to appearance not unequivocally more satisfactory? The disease (dis-ease) is real enough: but is the medicine effective, and is it not, as it appears to be, worse than the disease itself?[25]* There is no answer to these questions capable of convincing the unconvinced. The basic fact is that both worlds, both construals, are closed systems, logically disconnected, so that there is no bridge of reasoning by which one can cross from one to the other. The advantage of speaking of Faith is that it makes clear that if one is to cross at once a leap is required. But most of us are poor leapers, and besides we want to be sure where to leap.

The basic fact, that there is no bridge of reasoning, is obscured in the Western and modernist presentation of Buddhism, which insists not only that Buddhism is a rational and scientific philosophy (which, internally, in large part it is), but also that it makes a universal rational appeal (which it cannot). This mistaken impression is sustained by the account which is given of the Buddha preaching in a style of logical, scientific analysis.[26] But the account derives from a misreading of the sources. The 'discourses of the Buddha' were composed not by him but by other men, the authors of the scriptures, centuries later. Many of them were evident pedants. More importantly, they were composing at a time when Buddhism was already established, so they were preaching to the converted, which is a very different matter. Even so, if their accounts are read less selectively and more carefully, it is far from evident that their Buddha, in whom there may or may not be historical as well as mythical elements, was a teacher who sought to convert by rational analysis. He is more often portrayed as impatient with philosophical argument, replacing it with an urgent appeal to act. This is most vividly expressed in his ironic parable of the man wounded with a poison arrow, who declares that he cannot let the surgeon remove the arrow until he knows every last detail about the archer, his bow, the arrow.[27] When he does himself engage in logical argumentation, it sometimes appears that his purpose is ironic, intended to show its ultimate futility: a point which becomes explicit in Mahāyānist writings, and perhaps unduly exaggerated in Zen Buddhism.

The alleged rational approach of the teaching of the Buddha and of Buddhism is often attributed to its summary in the form of the Four Noble Truths. The first of these, and the foundation for the rest, is the proposition that all life is *dukkha*, which means suffering but much more than that, unsatisfactoriness, dis-ease. But it is quite mistaken to take this as a proposition capable of winning the assent of natural, secular man. When the alleged Buddha first propounded the Four Noble Truths, in his first sermon,[28] he was preaching not to secular men but to ascetics, that is, to those who were already converted to at least the first, unworldly, truth.

One does not often encounter the Four Noble Truths, the complete formula as such, in village Buddhism;[29] but the first of them is very familiar. Regularly when I asked people why they wanted Nirvana, they would reply that all life is *duka* (suffering). When I asked them to enlarge on this, they would regularly mention death, disease, poverty, oppression, which are indeed comprehended under the concept of *dukkha*. When I tried to probe further by expressing puzzlement or scepticism, most of them would only repeat stubbornly, 'All life is *duka*.' This made me feel they did not really believe what they were saying: an impression one gets too from the evident enjoyment they take in life, and their zest for more both in the present life and in future rebirths.

In this they show their good sense. As Gudmunsen writes, 'If duhkha is interpreted solely as "pain-sensation", however broad in scope this is meant to be, the statement [all life is duhkha] appears simply false.'[30]* It is only as privative of Nirvana that life can be recognised as through and through *dukkha*: 'The point of the first Holy Truth is to describe not empirical fact but the way in which the ordinary world is evaluated from the standpoint of Nirvana.'[31] There is thus an *impasse*. Men cannot directly be drawn to the other world, of Nirvana, because they do not know it in experience. Rather they must be turned from this world, which they do know, by condemning it. But the condemnation depends for its plausibility on knowledge of that which is not known. The *impasse* has its parallel in Christianity: 'For whosoever would save his life shall lose it: and whosoever shall lose his life for my sake shall find it.'[32]

I suggest, on the basis less of extensive enquiry than of logical considerations, that all sapiental systems face such an *impasse*, because of the lack of any logical bridge between the two 'worlds'. This is nicely illustrated in Nyanatiloka's article on the Eightfold Path in his *Buddhist Dictionary*. He says, in effect, that the Path should not be regarded as a vectored sequence, for its structure is circular. He identifies step 1, termed 'Right View', with Wisdom (*pañña*), and says that if the Path were truly linear:

one should have realized, first of all, Right View and penetration of the truth, even before one could hope to proceed to the next steps . . . ; and each preceding stage would be the indispensable foundation and condition for each succeeding stage. In reality, however, the links 3–5 constituting moral training (*sīla*), are the first three links to be cultivated, then the links 6–8 constituting mental training (*samādhi*), and at last Right View, etc., constituting wisdom (*pañña*). It is, however, true that a really unshakable and safe foundation to the path is provided only by Right View . . .[33]

It is this basic circularity, and hence closedness of sapiental systems, that creates the characteristic difficulty for those who would advocate one of them – as also for those who would analyse them not in abstraction but in the world of men. Where can the system best be entered, and how can those who are without be led to enter? There are devices which can be used to diminish the difficulty, and it is the employment of such devices by sapiental systems which gives them the character of religions. The difficulty, it should be noted, is very much reduced in societies in which the religion has become established: then the circularity of the system becomes a source of strength rather than of weakness. But a universalistic religion, at least, does not become established before it has converted some who were not born into it, and the features it must have to achieve this persist. Indeed, they are always needed if the system is to flourish, since mere adherence falls far short of thorough conversion, and men are largely secular men for all they have been reared in a particular religious tradition. '. . . long after Peter's confession, the Lord says to him, "when thou art converted . . ."'[34]

The devices I have in mind, by which people can be led to recognise, accept, or suppose the truth and validity of a sapiental system, enough for them to cleave to it and in time realise more, are of four kinds. Typically all, or most, of them are employed by the same system, and there may be others I have overlooked.

First, as we have seen, there is Faith, unwarranted belief. This is not the same thing as credulity, though doubtless it comes more easily to the credulous. It also comes more easily in a society where a religion is established, so that its doctrines or tenets have the aura of cultural factuality. It is not credulity, since Faith is usually not much a matter of believing-that; indeed, without cultural factuality, and even with it, the more important tenets of a religion are often incredible, because they are either unintelligible (mysteries) or practically meaningless. It is very much more a matter of believing-in, which is having trust or confidence.

The second device, no doubt not consciously contrived, is to present sapientalism in the more familiar, commonsensical, instrumentalist idiom. In systems which do this, what Buddhism accurately treats as inner states of mind are projected on to outer reality and figured as the work of gods and godlike beings. I owe this perception to Lienhardt's *Divinity and Experience: the Religion of the Dinka*.[35] In fact I might have learned it from Buddhists, who quite often say that the various spirits in which people believe are essentially projections of their own states of mind.[36] Where this idiom, this transformation is employed, it is made very easy for us to analyse the system on the instrumentalist model, for the people themselves to a large extent approach it in the same way. It then requires very careful discrimination to see that people believe in their gods rather than believing propositions about them, and that their belief is of a somewhat different kind than that which they have towards matters of empirical fact. Lienhardt writes:

Thus even for the Dinka themselves, a Power [godlike being] is not an immediate *datum* of experience of the same order as the physical facts or events with which it is associated. To refer to the activity of a Power is to offer an interpretation, and not merely a description, of experience . . .[37]

More simply, Evans-Pritchard had noted, of a basic magico-religious notion of the Azande:

. . . that even to the Azande there is something peculiar about the action of witchcraft . . . It is not an evident notion but transcends sensory experience. They do not profess to understand witchcraft entirely . . . Indeed, I have frequently been struck when discussing witchcraft with Azande by the doubt they express about the subject, not only in what they say, but even more in their manner of saying it, both of which contrast with their ready knowledge, fluently imparted, about social events and economic techniques.[38]

It further requires careful discrimination to see that their belief, whatever it amounts to, is not basic to practice as it is in pure instrumental systems.

This device, as we have remarked, enables people to handle a sapiental system as if it were a system of the more familiar instrumental kind. It also facilitates Faith, since it is easier to trust and have confidence in a figure conceived after a human model than in a subtler abstraction. For the same reason it is better able to arouse and channel emotion. And also, I think, it provides greater scope for elaboration in presentational symbolism. It is small wonder, therefore, that almost all sapiental systems do resort to theism. What is more remarkable is that two, Jainism and Theravāda Buddhism, have survived without it. I can see only one inherent advantage that a non-theistic sapiental system has: it can flourish in a situation where the existence of gods is dubitable by many, as is likely to have been true of that which gave birth to both these systems.[39] Why they survived in less plural cultural situations is harder to understand; I guess Theravāda Buddhism survived in competition with more typical religions largely because it was different, and this was an asset to societies on the fringe of pan-Indian civilisation, concerned to differentiate themselves from the centre.

It is because nearly all religions do resort to the theistic device that we normally define religion, more or less plainly, in terms of theism. If we take such definitions seriously we have to say that Buddhism is not a religion. But no one who is acquainted with actual Buddhism doubts for a moment that it is a religion: in this he registers the fact that in a variety of ways it strikingly resembles what we are sure are religions, and notably Christianity. To categorise phenomena in a way that obliges us to say that Christianity and Buddhism are members of two basically distinct classes, religion and non-religion, seems perverse, and is. Hence theism cannot be the essential definitive characteristic of religion.[40] I am suggesting that sapientalism is, at least of the greater and more interesting part of that class. I have not, to be sure, done much to show that theistic religions are essentially sapiental systems. I have relied for that on Lienhardt's analysis, which is that of a tribal theistic religion, conducted by a man who himself is a Catholic. We may both be mistaken. But if we are not, then it must appear that Buddhism, so far from being doubtfully a religion at all, is actually the clearest case of what a religion really is, because almost uniquely, in it sapientalism is not obscured by being presented in instrumentalist idiom.

The third device is to resort to presentational symbolism of various kinds. This is especially apt for dealing with what is basically an *impasse* of reason, for presentational symbolism is well suited to expressing and conveying what more 'rational' – better, 'logical' – forms of discourse cannot. This is why, for example, ritual is usually so important in maintaining and indeed promoting faith in sapiental systems, as Geertz puts it so well in a section which merits close study.[41] 'For it is in ritual – i.e. consecrated behaviour – that this conviction that religious conceptions are veridical and that religious directives are sound is somehow generated.'

It is for the same reason that so much of religious thought – if that is not too constrictive a term – is organised by those master-symbols for orientation which I have called 'Marks', and which Geertz aptly refers to as 'templates for producing reality'.[42] These too, as vehicles for meaning, for interpretation and control of experience, can reach out beyond the confines of the closed sapiental system. When we see how a basic problem is that of establishing a link, a bridge, a way that can be travelled, between two separate construals of reality, two 'worlds', we see once again how very apt is the Ndembu metaphor for a religious symbol, a *chijikijilu*, a landmark or hunter's blaze. In its literal sense:

> as a *hunter's blaze* it represents an element of connection between known and unknown territory, for it is by a chain of such elements that a hunter finds his way back from the unfamiliar bush to the familiar village . . . Its ritual use is already metaphorical: it connects the known world of sensorily perceptible phenomena with the unknown and invisible realm of the shades.[43]

I have already remarked that ritual appears to be relatively spare in Buddhism; and I think it is more widely true that Buddhism makes less use of presentational symbolism than most religions do. This is connected with the fact that Buddhism treats as inner states of mind what in other religions are projected as the work of deities and the like: for one of the functions of such projection is, as Lienhardt makes clear, to facilitate the collective control of experience by symbolic means, especially in ritual.[44] Nevertheless, I think that we commonly underestimate the place of symbolism in Buddhist thought. Western scholars, in seeking to present their view of Buddhism as a rational, not to say positivist, system, tended to dismiss those features which would not easily fit that mould as mere superstitious accretions. But there is more to them than that: as so often, what superficially appears mere superstition can be better understood as sound symbolic thought. I shall, for example, suggest that the view of village Buddhists, that Nirvana can hardly be attained except in the lifetime of a Buddha, can be taken as a symbolic recognition of the ambiguous relation of the *lōkōttara* to the world.

Because Buddhism makes comparatively little use of the other devices for conversion or the awakening of faith, it relies very heavily on a fourth device, which is that of practice generating 'belief'. As Evans-Pritchard remarked, 'If one must act as though one believed, one ends in believing, or half-believing as one acts'; and if this is true for strangers, including such more or less reluctant strangers as anthropologists, it must surely be all the more true for people indigenous to the system, to the culture. Practice, here, may be ritual practice, or it may be straightforward ethical practice, and we have seen how, in Asoka's view, these are by no means radically different. Buddhists themselves are very well aware of this effect, and they frequently stress that just as it is true that having a right or good state of mind tends to lead to right or good conduct, so too good conduct tends to produce good states of mind. We have seen how they draw upon this principle to explain *Buddha pūjā*: necessarily since, given that they hold that Lord Buddha does not exist, they are precluded from rationalising their offerings in instrumentalist idiom, as is normal in other cultures. Indeed, it is very characteristic of Buddhists to see ethical matters primarily, though not exclusively, from the sapientalist point of view, and to say that one does good for the sake of gaining a good state of mind, and avoids evil because it produces bad states of mind. This is formalised in the concepts of Merit (*pin*), which one gets by doing good, and Demerit (*pau*), which one gets by doing ill. Karma, the process[45*] by which good deeds are rewarded and evil deeds 'punished', is seen as operating through mind: thus people regularly say that one's next life, in the sequence of Rebirth, is generated by one's state of mind at death, which is itself the product of one's conduct throughout life. To a foreigner it actually seems somewhat selfish and priggish to hear people explaining that they do good to benefit themselves: as, for example, they will say they they give to a beggar more in order to gain Merit than to benefit the beggar. I did, however, find that most people did not so much dismiss the latter kind of effect as treat it as secondary in importance.

I conclude, therefore, that it is in the nature of sapiental systems, as contrasted with instrumental, that practice, whether it be more of the ritual or of the ethical kind, must precede belief: for belief cannot surely be attained by any other route, and even if some degree of belief is produced by socialisation, in cultures where the religion is already established, it is relatively ineffective, largely a matter of lip service and convention, until it is filled out by the products of practice.

Notes to Chapter 13

1 See, e.g., Parkes (1960).
2 A monothetic class is one in which every member possesses each of a set of common properties: every member resembles every other with respect to these properties. See Needham (1975). In Southwold (1978) I argued that what we call 'religion' should be seen not as a monothetic but as a polythetic class.
3 Gombrich (1971), pp. 4–5.
4 *Ibid.*, p. 9.

5   I argued this in Southwold (1978).
6   Gombrich (1971), p. 327; I commented on this above, Chapter 1.
7   'Truth will sooner come out of error than from confusion' – attributed to Francis Bacon in Peter (1980), p. 170.
8   Gombrich (1971), p. 15.
9   *Ibid.*, pp. 12–13, referring to Jarvie (1964), pp. 111–14.
10 Lienhardt (1961), pp. 280–1. A parallel comparison is furnished by Winch's insightful interpretation of Zande magic, developed in opposition to that of MacIntyre (Winch, 1970, pp. 101–6, especially p. 106).
11 E.g. Beattie (1966), p. 63.
12 In many places, e.g. Popper (1968), pp. 278–81.
13 Gellner (1968), p. 259.
14 Richardson (1950), p. 192.
15 *Shorter Oxford English Dictionary.*
16 Southwold (in press).
17 E.g. Hallpike (1979), pp. 490–5.
18 See, e.g., Ornstein (1975).
19 *Ibid.*, pp. 55, 61, 156; cf. Bohm (1980), p. xi.
20 Durkheim (1915), p. 10; (1912), p. 13.
21 I am not arguing that religion always, or even usually, leads people to be more altruistic than they otherwise would be.
22 Wittgenstein (1966), p. 59.
23 Pears (1971), p. 174.
24 Hebrews 11, v. 1.
25 'It is interesting that the way the Four Noble Truths are expressed corresponds to traditional Indian medical practice . . . The medical flavour of the Buddha's teaching seems to indicate an attempt to apply protoscience to religious problems' (Smart 1964, p. 33). Ling similarly notes that 'the Buddhist way is essentially a therapy' (1973, p. 112). It is of course common for religious teachings, including that of Christ, to be presented as therapies.
26 E.g. Weber (1967), p. 225.
27 *Majjhima Nikāya, Cūla-Mālunkya-sutta* (No. 63), quoted in Rahula (1967), p. 14.
28 See, e.g., Rahula (1967), p. 16.
29 Cf. Gombrich (1971), p. 70.
30 Gudmunsen (1977), p. 13 ('*duhkha*' is the Sanskrit form of the word which is *dukkha* in Pali). It is of course a familiar point that *dukkha* means much more than 'suffering' in any ordinary sense – see, e.g., Gombrich (1971), p. 69, Rahula (1967), p. 16f.
31 Gudmunsen (1977), p. 13.
32 Matthew 16, v. 25.
33 Nyanatiloka (1972), p. 93 (on *magga*).
34 Richardson (1950), p. 192, citing Luke 22, v. 32.
35 Lienhardt (1961), especially pp. 149–59.
36 Cf. Ortner (1978), p. 99.
37 Lienhardt (1961), p. 148.
38 Evans-Pritchard (1937), p. 81; (1976), p. 31.
39 Ling (1973), chapter 5.

40 As I argued in Southwold (1978).
41 Geertz (1966), pp. 28–35.
42 *Ibid.*, p. 9.
43 Turner (1969), p. 15.
44 Lienhardt (1961), chapters VI and VII.
45 Strictly, '*karma*' means volitional action, not its effects nor the process by which these are produced (Rahula, 1967, p. 32). The inexact extension of the term which I have used is common among Sinhalese Buddhists.

14

Conclusion: Rebirth and Nirvana

We can now solve the problem with which we began, the problem rooted in the apparent fact that villagers do not want Nirvana but seek a happier rebirth instead, and consequently are not really Buddhists.

We have already remarked (Chapter 6) that the evident reluctance of village Buddhists to talk about Nirvana can be explained by the mystery and ineffability of a concept of an undesirable *summum bonum*. Gombrich perhaps puts the point better when he heads his concluding chapter with a quotation from Davy (1821):

What this Niwane is, is a religious mystery: priests are rather averse from answering questions on the subject; they say, it is forbidden to discuss its nature, and on the principle that if men understood it they would not like it but prefer worldly things, as flies do bad smells.[1]

When I tried to probe village Buddhists on the reasons they gave for wanting Nirvana, their replies suggested that they had not thought about the matter and found it uncomfortable to be pressed to do so. This too can be partly explained on the same basis. There is also a more obvious reason. They are told, and accept, that no one can attain Nirvana for thousands, if not millions, of years to come. No one in his right mind gives much thought to considerations which can have no practical relevance except in such a remote future. I went too far in attributing this lack of practical interest to rejection of Nirvana as a goal; and my conviction that I could, if it had been decent, have pressed them to admit that they did not want Nirvana, was not well founded.

I made a false inference from the fact that the one man, Banda, whom I did feel able to press hard enough, did admit it: Banda was far from a typical village Buddhist, but was strikingly inclined towards the characteristic positions of middle-class Buddhism. Since I knew him well, this should have given me pause; I guess I was incautious because his confession so nicely confirmed what I felt sure was true of village

Buddhists generally. I did not see the significance of his anomalous attitudes until I noticed a parallel in Spiro's report. He tells us that one of the villagers of Yeigyi, actually the headman, said that he preferred Nirvana to a wealthy rebirth, but on further probing admitted privately to the reverse preference.[2] More strikingly, he cites two men who unhesitatingly told him that they did not want Nirvana; one is a Government engineer and the other a businessman, both residents of Rangoon.[3] Since there is evidence that in Burma as in Sri Lanka interpretations of Buddhism broadly correlate with social class, this admittedly meagre data suggests that it is some of those who are inclined to middle-class Buddhism, in which Nirvana is regarded as actually attainable, who in fact do not want it. This directly inverts our usual prejudice that it is village Buddhists who do not want Nirvana and are thereby shown to be deficient. Though the evidence is too meagre to be more than suggestive, the tentative conclusion is predictable if the priests cited by Davy read human psychology rightly. We might perhaps say that village Buddhists are protected from not wanting Nirvana by being taught that they are in no danger of getting it.

The question of whether Nirvana is to be taken as a proximate goal, readily attainable, or only as an ultimate goal, a beacon or lodestar, is crucial to our assessment. When Gombrich argued that in village Buddhism the aim has shifted 'from *nirvana* to heaven or even to earth', he maintained 'But most Sinhalese villagers do not want *nirvana* – yet. They are like St. Augustine who prayed "Make me chaste and continent, O Lord – but not yet".'[4] Spiro develops a parallel analysis, at much greater length, and he too uses the same analogy: 'They have not rejected nirvana, they merely – like St. Augustine in the matter of celibacy – wish to defer it'.[5] The parallel is the more striking since Gombrich and Spiro were writing virtually simultaneously, and neither refers to the work of the other.

Yet the analogy which impressed them both is rather obviously fallacious. We know that St. Augustine's prayer for chastity was insincere because we know that anyone who genuinely wants chastity can have it now – hence deferment implies lack of wholehearted desire. But the situation is quite different regarding village Buddhists: they know that no one can attain Nirvana now, so it would be senseless to seek it now. Hence from their not seeking it now there can be no inference about the quality of their wanting it. That both Gombrich and Spiro were convinced there was such an inference indicates a further but tacit assumption, that villagers say Nirvana is not attainable now *because* they do not want it. Gombrich states it on another page where he writes, 'In fact most people, even monks . . . display very little liking for *nirvana*. Accordingly, *nirvana* has been postponed in the popular mind to the coming of Maitrī, in some remote future era; it is so difficult to attain, and we are not sure we want it anyway.'[6] The assumption depends on a further tacit assumption: that Nirvana *can* be attained now, by those who want it enough to make sufficient effort. This is what is uncritically assumed in the Western interpretation of Buddhism, and in middle-class Buddhism.

But these assumptions are arbitrary and biased at best; and I shall argue that they are unreasonable and misconceived. I frequently asked village Buddhists why they thought no one could attain Nirvana until the coming of Maitrī. They regularly replied by citing the Buddha's prediction that after his death the spiritual capacities of his followers would steadily decline, so that Buddhism would die out altogether after 5,000 years. The half-way point, the 2,500th anniversary of Buddhism, was celebrated in 1956. Since Nirvana is so difficult to attain, we of this age in which spiritual capacity is already more than half-way to extinction can hardly hope to attain. Indeed, this has been the situation for many centuries past, for the last person to attain in Sri Lanka was Maliyadeva, who lived a very long time ago. Villagers do not say how long ago, for in practice Maliyadeva is more a figure of legend than of history. They do say he lived in the reign of King Dutugämunu, who is also in practice a largely legendary figure; the historical Dutugämunu reigned from 101 to 77 B.C.[7] In effect, villagers are saying that no one has attained for millennia past or can for millennia to come.

The villagers have excellent authority for their view. Gombrich shows that the view that the *Buddha Sāsana* would last only 5,000 years, and would steadily decline over that period, derives from Buddhaghosa[8] (fifth century A.D.), the great scriptural commentator, of whom he writes, 'To this day Buddhaghosa's Buddhism is in effect the unitary standard of doctrinal orthodoxy for all Theravāda Buddhists ...'.[9] If one appeals beyond Buddhaghosa to the canonical scriptures, one finds that according to them the Buddha predicted that his *Sāsana* would last only five *hundred* years.[8] Since Buddhaghosa lived about nine hundred years after the Buddha's death, he knew there was something wrong with that. (It may be worthy of remark that the scripture alleges the Buddha made his absurdly gloomy prediction after he had been prevailed upon, against his better judgement, to admit women to the Sangha.)[10]*

Thus the notion that it is *villagers* who have changed the aims or goals of Buddhism by not wanting Nirvana now is hard to sustain; and Spiro's statement, with which he introduces his lengthy argument that in the Buddhism of villagers we have a shift of goal from that of canonical Buddhism, is at least misleading: '... early Buddhism ... could hardly have perdured as the religion of an unsophisticated peasantry without undergoing important changes'.[11]

If we allow that villagers have sound authority for their view that Nirvana is not now attainable, we must also allow that their usual attitude towards meditation, one of indifference tending to scorn, so contrasted with that of middle-class Buddhists, is quite reasonable. The eight steps of the Eightfold Path leading to Nirvana are commonly grouped under three heads: the first two are grouped as wisdom, the next three as morality, the remaining three as meditation.[12] It is a matter of debate among learned Buddhists whether and how far the steps of the path are to be viewed as sequential, but Spiro cites Buddhaghosa as maintaining that they are.[13] On this well authorised interpretation, morality has to be mastered before tackling meditation. If one also accepts that the end of the path, the attainment of Nirvana, is many thousands of rebirths in the future, then it is reasonable to consider that major application to meditation is a concern for the future, and virtually to equate, as village Buddhists usually do, Buddhism in the here and now with moral understanding and practice. Conversely, the great concern of middle-class Buddhists with meditation implies their supposition that the attainment of Nirvana is within reach.

The view of village Buddhists on the attainability of Nirvana does not deserve to be as easily depreciated as it has been; on the other hand, the contrasted view of middle-class and Western Buddhists against which it is disparaged ought not so readily to be taken for granted. Occasionally when middle-class Buddhists assured me that Nirvana can be attained, with application, by some in the present lifetime, and by most within the next few rebirths, I asked them if they knew anyone who had attained. Their responses were curiously uncomfortable and evasive. Usually they said that if anyone attained he would be a meditating monk remote in the jungles, so they would be unlikely to meet him. One man, whom I met in southern Sri Lanka, said he knew one monk who he thought had attained, though of course he could not be sure. When I asked why not, he replied that the monk could not tell anyone he had attained, since to boast of spiritual attainments is one of the four gravest, *pārājika*, offences against the Vinaya Rule. In fact, this is a convenient mistake: what the Rule forbids is *falsely* claiming spiritual attainments. If it actually forbade true claims to spiritual attainments, the Buddha himself and a great many of his immediate disciples would be convicted as grave sinners, on the evidence of the scriptures. Similarly, the more usual claim that there doubtless are attainers, only somewhere else, is an example of a familiar dodge for evading the confrontation of dogma with empirical evidence: thus Azande, who are aware that every witch-doctor they know is a fraud, evade the conclusion that all are by claiming that there must be genuine witch-doctors somewhere in Zandeland.[14]

The need for evasive responses is rather obvious. If it were indeed true that Nirvana can be attained at worst within four rebirths – or even eight, as those of less confidence maintain – and if in every generation a cohort of even one hundred people apply themselves diligently to the quest as meditating monks, then within a few centuries one hundred would be attaining in each generation. The fact could hardly be concealed even if, contrary to the Buddha's own example, the attainers lay low in the jungles. Since it is quite evident that the real state of affairs is entirely unlike this, the dogma must be wrong.

I never asked middle-class Buddhists where they got their dogma from, partly because I did not wish to be offensive, partly because the answer seemed quite obvious to me. The scriptures make it plain not only that the Buddha urged his followers diligently to seek Nirvana, but also that many thousands of them did attain in the same lifetime – some, indeed, instantaneously. Now if one makes the assumption that the scriptures are historical accounts about the historical Buddha and his contemporaries, basically ordinary human beings like ourselves, then it is shown that human beings, such as we are, can attain. But of course it is this assumption, and those who swallow it, that truly merit the description 'unsophisticated'. A little learning about historical method is indeed a dangerous thing; with a more adequate grasp it is quite plain, as we have remarked, that scriptures cannot be taken as historical accounts of their purported subjects. Indeed, if those who wanted, and want, to read the scriptures as history were less arbitrarily selective they would have to allow for the facts that, according to the scriptures, the Buddha was eighty-eight cubits tall, flew through the air, could have lived for ever if only Ānanda had not been too obtuse to see that he was being asked to request Him to do so, and so on and so on. To dismiss all this as superstitious legend is to be blind to the religious purpose it served. The function of such legends, as with comparable material on the life of Christ, is to convey that we are not dealing with scientific accounts of a normal human being in ordinary history, but with myth and symbolism about a superhuman being (*mahāpurisa*) in a supernormal period. To confuse myth with history, and to take the behaviour of mythical beings uncritically as a charter for ourselves is a grave delusion: as it would be to argue, in many religious traditions, that since the founding ancestors were incestuous, so too should we be. The stories that thousands attained Nirvana in the lifetime of Gotama Buddha do not warrant the naive interpretation that the same must be possible for us, living in normal time. On the contrary, since at the time the scriptures were written it must have been as evident as it is today that no one does attain, their purpose must have been to demonstrate the contrast between a Buddha's lifetime and normal time, with a view to conveying symbolically that Nirvana appertains not to time but to eternity (in our terminology), and thus that it is to be understood as an ultimate ideal, not a proximate goal. The message is completed by saying that once again many will attain in the lifetime of Maitrī, the next Buddha and another plainly superhuman personage.[15]

The teaching that the attainment of Nirvana is not an event of ordinary time, but of periods of supernormal, sacred time in which a Buddha is manifested, is itself symbolic. The difference between two kinds of time, ordinary and supernormal – otherwise figured as the difference between time and eternity – stands for the difference between two worlds, the *laukika* and the *lōkōttara*. To say that Nirvana is not attainable in ordinary time is to say that the *lōkōttara* is not of this world. Though it is pre-eminent in the world, and may be made more so, we are not close to its perfect realisation in the world.[16*] The teaching, or imagery, that Nirvana was discovered by Gotama Buddha, that the products of that discovery are, diminished, with us now, and that Nirvana will not again be completely realised until Maitrī Buddha dwells among us, is evidently similar to Christian teaching about the onetime incarnation, and future second coming, of Christ. Both, as we saw above, seek to recognise both the transcendence of the holy and its actual, imperfect, immanence. It is the remoteness of perfection from the way things now are that is expressed in the doctrine that Nirvana cannot be attained until the next Buddha comes; that this is a matter more of symbolic than temporal futurity may be suggested by the fact that Buddhists are very vague about the chronology.

I have to conclude that the view of village Buddhists on the attainability of Nirvana is consistent with a proper reading of the scriptures, whereas the other view seems to derive from an indefensible misreading of them. It is supported too by the plain fact that no one does attain. Still more importantly, in my view, it is validated by the test of fruits. As we saw, the recognition that one can be in no hurry to attain Nirvana fits with the understanding that one should be of service to others; unmistakably often, though I would not say invariably, the impetuous pursuit of a solitary Nirvana is associated with a deficiency of human sympathy, and a degree of selfishness which is sometimes gross (see above, Chapter 6).

In the light of this, the fact that most village Buddhists seem to be more interested in attaining a better rebirth than they are in attaining Nirvana does not indicate a change of aims, but rather a rational ordering of proximate and ultimate goals. Since Nirvana is the ultimate goal, and since our first and best opportunity of attaining it will be during the lifetime – 80,000 years[15] – of Maitrī, our best strategy is to bring ourselves to the point of readiness to attain at that time. That must be done through a long process of spiritual improvement through many births, in each of which one has the capacity to progress further because of the karmic fruits of one's achievement in the previous birth. This is just the strategy that village Buddhists say they are following. If it is mainly the next birth, the next lifetime after the present, that they talk about, this limitation may be regarded as pragmatic good sense. Many villagers say that *lōkōttara* matters are those concerned with the (next) life to come, *laukika* matters those concerned with the present lifetime. This need not be seen as vulgarisation of the concepts: given the framework I have outlined and justified, it is a prudent focusing on matters of more immediate practical concern.

Thus Rebirth theory, though it may appear to conflict with the rather naive concept of Nirvana that one finds among Buddhist modernists, is in harmony with the concept when it is properly interpreted. Indeed, the harmony may go deeper than I have so far shown. It has often been argued that Rebirth doctrine is inconsistent with the true Buddhist doctrine, since it implies that there is a soul to transmigrate, whereas Buddhism denies the reality of the soul (*ātma, atta*). I do not wish to enter into all the theological subtleties of this, but rather to remark that Gombrich perceives a comparable inconsistency and regards it as important. He argues 'that people affectively believe that *they* will survive death and be reborn' and 'I think that this affective belief in personal survival . . . is the basis for a whole system of affective religion which diverges from official doctrine'.[17] I am sure he is right that people do assume a continuity of personal identity between one lifetime and the next; but I query his interpretation.

Some of the most interesting conversations I had during my fieldwork were with a man I call Appuhamy. He was a skilled motor mechanic with a job in a garage in Kurunegala town. Occupationally, therefore, he was not a typical villager, but might rather be categorised as lower middle-class; as a member of the Radala families, however, he was knowledgeable about and interested in the affairs of the village. He had more than a smattering of English, was well read and highly intelligent, with a forceful, original mind. He meditated every night before going to bed, and assured me that an intelligent fellow, if he had not the defilements Appuhamy was striving to remove in himself, could certainly attain Nirvana in his present lifetime. Both the meditation and the view about Nirvana are characteristics, usually diagnostic symptoms, of the kind of Buddhism I associate with middle-class Sinhalese. Unlike other adherents of that kind of Buddhism, he was exceedingly scornful of forest-dwelling meditating monks. In one of our conversations, when we were not even talking about religion at all, he suddenly exclaimed:

Appuhamy. I think the monks in *arañña* [secluded monasteries] are off their heads [*pissu*]! Maybe I'm crazy myself just for having visited to take a look. Cutting themselves off from people in the jungles, indeed!

Anthropologist. But isn't meditating and training the mind good?

Appuhamy. How do I know what they really get up to in the night? I reckon those monks are just inventing methods to get their meals provided. It is we people who sweat and look after children who should really get Nirvana.

I heard from several other people a similarly caustic judgement on forest-dwelling monks, though not so vividly expressed.

It was in another conversation that Appuhamy made some statements that throw considerable light on the place of ideas about Rebirth in village Buddhism. Between the fact that it took place towards the end of my fieldwork, and the fact that I did not fully understand what he was saying, I did not follow up its implications with other people. But it does suggest a revised interpretation of what they said. Appuhamy had been telling me that he meditates every night, and went on:

Appuhamy. When I am meditating I am fighting with the *ātmaya. Ātmaya* and mind [*hita*] are competitors, and mind must win.

M.S. (anthropologist). What is *ātmaya*?

A. By *ātmaya* I mean the next birth. If you are doing wrong, troubles come to the body [*sarira*] and after death these go to the *ātmaya.*

M.S. What happens after death?

A. The body is destroyed and what is left of the person is the *ātmaya.* If a person does good, his life now is good and his *ātmaya* is also good. This is my own idea.

M.S. What is *ātmaya* like?

A. In English a noun is the name of a person, place, thing, etc., and Pali *atta* is the same.

M.S. Why did Lord Buddha teach *anatta* [doctrine of no soul/self]?

A. He meant that people must finish this *ātmaya.* The end of *anātmaya* is Nirvana.

M.S. I can't understand that.

A. I'm sorry, I can't explain it. Before a person gets Nirvana he must find *anātmaya. Anātmaya* means there is no more *ātmaya.*

Now Appuhamy was an exceptionally intelligent man. I doubt if any other layman I knew could have explained his concepts so well, still less have related them to a correct understanding of the Pali terms of the scriptures. But I do think that Appuhamy's understanding was implicit in the usage of more ordinary people. When I asked people what Nirvana is, the most usual, standard response was (translated to me as) 'No suffering, no Rebirth'. This is orthodox enough as it stands. But what they actually said was '*Duka nää, ātma(ya) nää*'. In Sinhala (at least among Buddhists) *ātma(ya)* does not mean a soul, but typically has the meaning of a 'life-span', i.e. of any life in a succession of lives linked by Rebirth[18] – hence the translation I was given. But in terms of Appuhamy's explication '*ātma(ya) nää*' is equivalent to '*anātmaya*', i.e. *anatta*, the fundamental and most distinctive doctrine of 'the Buddha', and this makes the standard Sinhalese statement still more orthodox. In talking of Rebirth Sinhalese do assume a continuity of personal identity (*ātmaya*) from birth to birth, but this would appear not to be an 'affective belief' divergent from and clashing with official doctrine and 'cognitive belief', as Gombrich supposes. As Appuhamy says, the continuity of personal identity is real; but it has the reality of all worldly constructions – that is to say, it is ultimately delusory and has to be overcome sapientally, to be overcome by the realisation of *anatta*, which is Nirvana.[19] The doctrine of Sinhalese villagers differs from that which has been commonly attributed to the Buddha only in this: he is supposed (mistakenly, I have argued) to have taught that *atta*, the delusion of separate permanent selfhood, can be eliminated, and replaced by the perfect realisation of the truth of *anatta*, which is Nirvana, in the present lifetime: but Sinhalese villagers see it as a vastly more long-drawn-out process. Until it is completed, the delusory, imperfect sense of personal identity will persist and be manifested in the continuity of Rebirth. Once again, they are not posing Rebirth as an alternative goal to Nirvana, but rather as a condition through which, and eventually from which, the attainment of Nirvana is to be reached.

There is, moreover, another, more symbolic way in which emphasis on Rebirth harmonises with more philosophical Buddhism. In the latter, the doctrine of *anatta* teaches that the sense of separate selfhood which both generates and is sustained by ego-centred desires is delusory, and all living creatures are as one. In Rebirth doctrine, this teaching of the synchronic indistinction of all living beings is transformed into a statement of their diachronic potential identity. The ethical effect is similar, and probably more readily apprehensible. People will say, and appear to mean, that they hesitate to kill an animal because they can well imagine themselves as an animal in another birth. They say, too, that a husband hesitates to beat his wife because the karmic consequence of that is to be reborn as a wife with a cruel husband. These are fancies, no doubt, but they are fancies which greatly assist one to see oneself in the place of another, which is the foundation of ethical objectivity, and of dissolving the sense that one's own ego is of any special importance.

To see one's dharma, one's true position in the cosmos and hence one's ethical duty, in terms of the philosophy of *anatta*, is to see things from the standpoint of Nirvana, which is not attained in completeness until the future. To see it in terms of Rebirth is to see it in terms of present conditions, in which the sense of self is still strong.[20*] To take this view is appropriate for village Buddhism, in which, as we have seen, right action, conduct, practice, is of critical importance. Action is in the present, for action tomorrow is half-way to inaction: the more seriously one takes the importance of action the more one attends to the present, and in attending to the present one must see it as one presently does. Rebirth theory provides a rationale and a motivation for ethical action now: it appeals to man as he actually is, very far from perfect, and provides a bridge by which a man in whom the sense of self is still powerful can be led through right action to loosen that sense of self. Appuhamy, at least, did not regard Rebirth theory as true, except provisionally: on the contrary, he spoke of the construal of reality which it expresses – *ātmaya* – as that which he was fighting to displace. I have no direct evidence that other villagers saw it in that way explicitly. It may not be unduly generous to suggest that they may do so implicitly.

Just as accepting the present, though provisional, reality of the self in Rebirth theory provides a way, through right action, of beginning to realise *anatta* in experience, so too Rebirth theory can serve intellectually to point to a recognition of the philosophical case for *anatta*. By heightening the natural man's assumption of the separate and lasting nature of himself it brings it more sharply into focus, and lays it more open to questioning: as the priest I met took occasion of my doubting Rebirth to question my confidence in the continuity and solidity of the I who had seemingly taken part in the events which had led to our encounter in a Sinhalese village (see above, Chapter 4). I have no evidence that such philosophising is explicit in the minds of ordinary villagers; but as they are Buddhists too, it may be implicit.

This is not to say that Rebirth theory is a necessary foundation for Buddhism. Though most people with whom the matter came up told me that it was, there were some even among villagers who said it was not; and in this they reflected those scriptural passages which present the Buddha as saying Dhamma is wise if there is no rebirth, and still more wise if there is. We might say that the supposed reality of rebirth is a cultural datum in this part of the world: it clearly is in Sinhalese culture, and on the evidence of the scriptures it was in that of the Buddha, or, to be more cautious, in that of the scriptural authors. It is not inconsistent with the philosophy of *Buddha Dharma*, but on the contrary, as we have seen, can serve as a foundation for grasping it.

There is more to it, however, than a cultural idiosyncrasy, a notion which has cultural factuality in some parts of the world but not in others. It is a remarkably rich metaphysical concept, and there are two senses in which I find it true, though I do not believe rebirth occurs, and am not now a participant in Sinhalese culture. I remarked one of these earlier, when I wrote of its figurative value as a metaphor for representing the hidden complexities of our inward being: we are many persons stacked within us, who may be unfolded as we imaginatively project ourselves over many lifetimes (Chapter 4).

The other follows from my observation that if we are to be logical about it the Rebirth doctrine is practically meaningless: since I cannot know now, and he cannot know then, whether some future person who bears the results of my present deeds is or is not *me*, it makes no practical difference which it is. This cuts both ways. If holding Rebirth to be true adds nothing to our understanding of our life, holding it to be false subtracts nothing. Hence the Sinhalese view of reality is our view, though we deny rebirth. Two important things are left of their theory of Rebirth even when the physical factuality of rebirth is discounted. The first is the law of Karma: that evil deeds produce suffering, and good deeds happiness. The second is that there is life after death. If I deny rebirth, whether through not having been brought up with the theory, or like Appuhamy through fighting with the *ātmaya*, I recognise that it will not be my life. To a Buddhist, however, this is the best of it, since the disease (*dukkha*) of this present life is just my misapprehension of it as mine.[21]

Thus we seriously underestimate the Buddhism of villagers when we suppose that in it an interest in Rebirth has been substituted for concern with Nirvana. The two conceptions are deeper than they appear when they are interpreted too literally, and they are harmonious: 'For now we see through a glass, darkly; but then face to face: now I know in part, but then shall I know even as also I am known' (I Cor. 13, v. 12, A.V.). Gombrich's conclusion, that the voice of the people is the voice of the Buddha, stands, not as a query but as a truism: there is no other voice of the Buddha to be heard.

Notes to Chapter 14

1   Gombrich (1971), p. 318, quoting Davy (1821), p. 216.
2   Spiro (1971), pp. 78–9.
3   *Ibid.*, p. 79.
4   Gombrich (1971), pp. 16–17.
5   Spiro (1971), p. 79.
6   Gombrich (1971), p. 322.
7   *Ibid.*, pp. 284–6, 29.
8   *Ibid.*, p. 284 n. 28.
9   *Ibid.*, p. 43.
10 Cf. Thomas (1975), p. 109. At the (fictional) First Council, Ānanda was required to do penance for having persuaded the Buddha to admit women. These yarns come from the *Mahā-parinibbāna-Suttanta*, which Frauwallner attributes to the author of the *Skandhaka* (1956, p. 162).
11 Spiro (1971), p. 66.
12 E.g. Gombrich (1971), p. 70.
13 Spiro (1971), p. 44 n. 13.
14 Evans-Pritchard (1937), pp. 185, 193, 475; 1976, pp. 107, 202.
15 E.g. Gombrich (1971), p. 289.
16 It cannot be perfectly realised in one person alone, because it is the antithesis of separate individuality. But if each must wait for all, and travel in convoy, progress will plainly be slow.
17 Gombrich (1971), p. 73.
18 *Ibid.*, p. 71.
19 Rahula (1967), p. 65.
20 It is clear in philosophical Buddhism that there are two kinds of truths, conventional truths and ultimate truths: the former are not wholly false in their contexts. The reality of the self is a conventional truth. See, e.g., Rahula

(1967), p. 55. I think some villagers, at least, have some sense of this distinction, though I find no explicit exposition of it in my field-notes.

21 E.g. Rahula (1976), p.51.

Appendix

Terminology

'monk', 'priest', clergy; *Saśana*; 'temple'
and its components; 'Buddhism' and 'religion'

The term 'monk' is standard in the literature on Buddhism to refer to members of the clergy. It may seem petty and pedantic of me to refuse to conform, and to prefer the term 'priest', which is itself unsatisfactory. Words, however, are not neutral labels, but carry connotations which colour the picture one presents, to the point where the reader's image of the reality can be seriously distorted.

The word 'monk', in ordinary contexts, normally means, and is likely to connote, a person who has secluded himself from the everyday life of the world in order to devote himself to a contemplative religious life. My own reading about Buddhist 'monks' had led me to expect that they would be much like that, and I was surprised, even shocked, to find that most Buddhist clergy are quite different. I found it absurd to think of such clergy as 'monks', and perverse to describe them as such. It seems strange that a term so evidently inappropriate has become standard.

This is not the result of mere linguistic insensitivity; as with so many other errors, it results from our Western misinterpretation of Buddhism, which also it subtly serves to sustain. We term Buddhist clergy 'monks' because we imagine that this is what they are expected by others, and themselves intend, to be. As I show in Chapter 9, this is largely untrue: their actual vocation is of a kind that has little of the monkish to it. The standard terminology suggests that the clergy conform, more or less, to a role-model or pattern of life which in fact, mostly, they do not hold, and hence neither conform to, nor intend or are expected to conform to. Further, the word 'monk' naturally suggests the pattern of Christian monachism, which is alien to the Buddhist tradition – although I think it has influenced many of those today whom I refer to as the Buddhist 'forest-dwelling monks'. As Dutt points out, 'Between Buddhist monk-communities and monasteries and their counterparts in the Christian world, there was an ideological and hence functional difference. Isolation from society was never the cue of Buddhist monachism' (1962, p. 25).

Because the term 'monk' is descriptively inept and theoretically pernicious I will not use it for the village clergy I write about. It is not easy to decide on what term should be used. One of our research assistants used regularly to refer to Silaratana as 'the Rev.'. This seemed to me an admirable rendering of colloquial Sinhalese usage into colloquial English; but I fear it is too vivid, and vulgar, for me to adopt in writing. I often thought that the word 'parson' is quite close in meaning to the word used in Sinhala – but it is too distinctively Anglican. 'Minister' describes rather well how village clergy see their function – but in its religious usage I find its connotations too dour.

Faced with such difficulties, it might seem an obvious recourse to use the indigenous term untranslated. I dislike this practice, since I find that any but the most sparing use of foreign words is apt to confuse the reader: who in any case normally substitutes his own translation. The standard and by far the commonest term by which Sinhalese refer to and address Buddhist clergy – and also refer to the Buddha – is 'hāmuduruvō', pronounced more nearly as 'hāmdrū'. This used to be a standard term for lay members of the highest caste, the Goyigama, and especially the Radala aristocracy (as evidenced by Knox, 1681), and is still occasionally used as an honorific term of address to laymen. It translates quite closely as 'lord'. It is entirely apt to translate 'Buddha Hāmuduruvō' as 'Lord Buddha' and I have done so; but to refer to ordinary members of the clergy as 'lords' would be more misleading than helpful.

Another indigenous term, sometimes used in the literature on Buddhism, is 'bhikkhu'. This was the term applied to the original members of the Sangha, the community of those who left lay life to follow the Buddha as religious virtuosos. It is still sometimes used by Sinhalese to refer to members of the Sangha, which is now an order of clergy. But it is used mainly in writing, sometimes in speech by clergy: it is rare, and invariably pretentious, for a layman to use it in speech. Its use of modern clergy, who are radically unlike the original *bhikkhus*, is romantic when it is not canting. As a standard term for actual clergy it is quite as unsuitable as 'monk'.

English-speaking Sinhalese use the words 'priest' and 'monk' indifferently for the men termed *hāmdrū* in Sinhala. 'Priest', too, has drawbacks. As Spiro points out, the Buddhist cleric is not primarily a ritual officiant, as the word 'priest' connotes (1971, p. 280). This is rather more true of ideology than of actuality, particularly if we widen the scope of what might be considered ritual in Buddhism (see Chapter 12). On the other hand, the actual functions and status in society of village clergy do seem to be notably similar to those of rural Catholic priests, in, say, Spain or Ireland. This comparison will, I think, give the reader a helpful image of the reality, provided he bears in mind Spiro's reservation – and allows for the unavoidable fact that terms drawn from one culture never describe exactly the realities of another.

By specialising the term 'priest' to refer to most Buddhist clergy, those who follow the vocation of ministry or teaching (see Chapter 9), I release the term 'monk' to refer to those others to whom it is reasonably applicable: namely those who do withdraw from the society of laymen to pursue the contemplative life. It is hard to restrict its usage to such clerics only, especially when quoting or referring to the work of other writers: sometimes I have had to follow their usage of the word where I thought 'priest' or 'cleric' would have been more suitable. Hence when I have wanted to emphasise my own narrower range of reference, I have sometimes qualified 'monks' as 'meditating' or 'forest-dwelling'.

I use the terms 'priest' and 'monk' for men who are fully qualified members of the Sangha, having received their (higher) ordination (*upasampadā*), normally taken at about the age of twenty. As is conventional, I use the term 'novice' for those who have not yet received *upasampadā*, but have entered the Sangha as junior members by the ceremony technically called 'Robing' (*mahanakala*), and by various other terms including 'lower ordination'. In Sinhala a novice is addressed and referred to as *'punchi* (or *poḍi*) *hāmuduruvō'*, literally 'lordling'; but priests often like to use the Pali term *sāmanera*, which they say means 'son of a *sāmana* (i.e. cleric)'.

As a collective term to refer to priests, monks and novices without distinction I use the term 'clergy'; it is in standard use in Sri Lanka, and describes their actual social position quite accurately. It suggests the useful singular term 'cleric'. Its connotation of literacy and some learning is also appropriate, for these are important features of the status.

With much misgiving, I have used the standard term 'temple' to translate what Sinhalese call a *pansala* or *vihāra*. What is referred to is a set of buildings and a tree set in and around a yard which is kept swept and sometimes sanded. The buildings are normally the *pansala* or *āvasa*, the house in which the priest(s) and novice(s) reside, which I call the 'presbytery'; the image-house (*vihāra-gē*), which is used mainly for offering rituals (*pūjā*) and for private devotions; the preaching hall (*banasala* or *dharmasala*), which, more commodious than the image-house, is used for larger ceremonies, for Sunday school, and for meetings oriented to Buddhist interests; and the *dāgäba*, or *vehera*, a solid, dome-shaped construction which is supposed to contain a relic, and is therefore a suitable focus for devotions directed to the Buddha (or, more exactly, his memory). The tree is a Bo-tree (*ficus religiosus*), which gives welcome shade and does, by its beauty alone, evoke religious sentiments; it is regarded as a relic of the Buddha and hence as an appropriate focus of devotions. Often one or more of these five elements is absent. The buildings are sometimes quite beautiful, and sometimes rather scruffy; but rarely is a village 'temple' much like the grandiose ritual edifice that the word might suggest.

Indeed, the connotation of ritual function that the word 'temple' has is itself misleading. As Gombrich rightly says, 'The essential of a Buddhist temple, the fact by virtue of which it is in use, is that one or more monks live there' (1971, p. 75). This focus, and understanding, is indicated by the fact that, in my area at least, the word *pansala*, which more specifically refers to the presbytery, is used by extension to refer the whole complex, the 'temple'. The more familiar, and probably more common, term, *vihāra*, originally meant 'a place where clerics reside', so the import is the same. Where the religious centre of a Christian community is the church, the house of God, and the presbytery (vicarage, etc.) is attached and subordinate, it is the other way about in Buddhendom: the image-house in which the Buddha is represented and chiefly worshipped is called the *vihāra-gē*, literally 'monastery-house'. This is logical: unlike our God, the Buddha is held not to exist, and hence the sacred is most really manifested in the members of the Sangha.

Largely through my aversion to plaguing the reader with foreign terms, I have drawn more freely on the terminology of Christianity than is usual in writing about Buddhism. I recognise the perils of this, but also the perils of seeming unidiomatic, quaint, or opaque. In the main I think understanding is better furthered by suggesting resemblances between Christendom and Buddhendom than by hiding them behind a peculiar terminology – so long as the imperfectness of the analogies is kept in mind. I have used the terms 'ecclesiastic' and 'ecclesiastical', but have held back from speaking of the 'Buddhist Church' for there is no such concept. In contexts comparable to those in which Christians would naturally speak of the Church, Buddhists refer either to the Sangha – which is less inclusive – or to the *Buddha Sāsana*, Buddhendom, which is more inclusive, since it is the whole nation, indeed civilisation, seen with religious reference. There is no comprehensive specifically religious organisation which includes both the clergy and laity. Indeed, there is not much organisation to the body of clergy, the Sangha itself: its senior members have little effective authority over anyone other than novices seeking higher ordination. The Sinhalese Sangha is divided into three autonomous Nikāyas or fraternities, of which the two larger are further subdivided; these are not sects, since they differ hardly at all on points of doctrine.

The danger of distortion through inappropriate terminology, which makes factual description problematic, extends also to the more comprehensive and hence basic terms. As I remark in Chapters 1 and 10, it is misleading to speak of 'Buddhism', as the word is usually understood, since the prime reality is not an -ism but a civilisation; and on the same grounds it can be misleading to term it a 'religion'. The issues are admirably discussed in Ling (1973), chapter 1, and I have made some further remarks on the matter in Southwold (1978). As the word 'religion' has various senses, 'The answer to the question whether Buddhism is a religion is thus both Yes and No' (Ling, 1973, p. 18). In this book I have normally categorised it as a religion because I am arguing that the study of Buddhism – or, preferably, Buddhendom – is illuminated by the anthropological study of religions, and vice versa.

Bibliography

Ames, M. M. (1962), *Religious syncretism in Buddhist Ceylon* Ph.D. Thesis, Harvard University.
— (1964a), 'Magical animism and Buddhism: a structual analysis of the Sinhalese religious system'. In E. B. Harper (ed.), 1964, pp. 21–52.
— (1964b), 'Religion, politics and economic development in Ceylon. An interpretation of the Weber thesis'. In M. E. Spiro (ed.), 1964, *Symposium on new approaches to the study of religion*, Seattle, University of Washington Press, pp. 61–76.
— (1966), 'Ritual prestations and the structure of the Sinhalese pantheon'. In M. Nash (ed.), 1966, *Anthropological studies in Theravada Buddhism*, New Haven, Yale University Press, pp. 27–50.
Ashby, W. Ross (1964), *An introduction to cybernetics*. London, Methuen.
Bareau, André (1955), *Les premiers conciles Bouddhiques*. Paris, Presses Universitaires de France.
Barth, Fredrik (1975), *Ritual and knowledge among the Baktaman of New Guinea*. Oslo, Universitetsforlaget; New Haven, Yale University Press.
Beattie, John (1966), 'Ritual and social change'. *Man* (N.S.), 1, pp. 60–74.
Bechert, Heinz (1966), *Buddhism, Staat und Gesellschaft in den Ländern des Theravada Buddhismus*, vol. I, *Allgemeines und Ceylon*. (Institut fur Asienkunde in Hamburg.) Frankfurt am Main, Metzner.
Bechert, Heinz (1978a), 'Contradictions in Sinhalese Buddhism'. In B. L. Smith (ed.), 1978, pp. 188–98.
— (1978b), 'S. W. R. D. Bandaranaike and the legitimation of power through Buddhist ideals'. In B. L. Smith (ed.), 1978, pp. 199–211.
Bohm, David (1980), *Wholeness and the implicate order*. London, Routledge.
Bowen, Elinore S. (1954), *Return to laughter*. London, Gollancz.
Braithwaite, R. B. (1967), 'The nature of believing'. In A. P. Griffiths (ed.), 1967, pp. 28–40.
Brandon, S. G. F. (1971), *The trial of Jesus of Nazareth*. London, Paladin.
Bruner, Jerome (1962), *On knowing: essays for the left hand*. Cambridge, Mass., Harvard University Press.
Bunnag, Jane (1973), *Buddhist monk, Buddhist layman* (Cambridge Studies in Social Anthropology, 6). Cambridge, Cambridge University Press.
Burghart, R. and Cantlie, A. (eds.) (in press) *Indian Religion*. London, Curzon Press.
Burlingame, E. W. (1921), *Buddhist legends translated from the original Pali text*

of the Dhammapada Commentary (Harvard Oriental Series, vol. xxx) Cambridge, Mass., Harvard University Press.

Carrithers, Michael (1977), *The forest-dwelling monks of Lanka.* D.Phil. thesis, University of Oxford.

— (1979), 'The modern ascetics of Lanka and the pattern of change in Buddhism'. *Man* (N.S.), 14, pp. 294–310.

— (1980), 'Radical asceticism and the Sinhalese case.' Letter in *Man* (N.S.), 15, pp. 195–6.

Carter, Charles (1924), *A Sinhalese–English dictionary.* Colombo, Wesleyan Mission Press (reprinted 1965, Colombo, M. D. Gunasena).

Collingwood, R. G. (1946), *The idea of history.* London, Oxford University Press.

Davies, Paul (1982), *Other Worlds.* London, Abacus.

Davy, J. (1821), *An account of the interior of Ceylon.* London, Longman.

Department of Census and Statistics (Sri Lanka) (1973), *Statistical pocket book of the Republic of Sri Lanka 1973.* Colombo.

De Silva, K. M. (ed.) (1977), *Sri Lanka: a survey.* (Institute of Asian Affairs, Hamburg). London, C. Hurst.

Dixon, R. M. W. (1968), 'Virgin birth'. Letter in *Man* (N.S.), 3, pp. 653–4.

Durkheim, E. (1895), *Les règles de la méthode sociologique.* Paris, Alcan.

— (1912), *Les formes élémentaires de la vie religieuse.* Paris, Alcan.

—(1915), *The elementary forms of the religious life* (trans. J. W. Swain). London, Allen & Unwin.

Dutt, Sukumar (1962), *Buddhist monks and monasteries of India.* London, Allen & Unwin.

Evans-Pritchard, E. E. (1937), *Witchcraft, oracles and magic among the Azande.* London, Oxford University Press.

— (1956), *Nuer religion.* London, Oxford University Press.

— (1965), *Theories of primitive religion.* London, Oxford University Press.

— (1976), *Witchcraft, oracles and magic among the Azande* (abridged edition, ed. Eva Gillies). London, Oxford University Press.

Flew, Antony (ed.) (1979), *A dictionary of philosophy.* London, Pan.

Frauwallner, Erich (1956), *The earliest Vinaya and the beginnings of Buddhist literature.* Rome, Is. M.E.O.

Geertz, Clifford (1966), 'Religion as a cultural system'. In Michael Banton (ed.), *Anthropological approaches to the study of religion* (ASA Monograph 1). London, Tavistock, pp. 1–46. (Reprinted in Geertz, C., 1975, *The interpretation of cultures*, London, Hutchinson.)

— (1968), *Islam observed.* Chicago, Chicago University Press.

Gellner, Ernest (1968), *Words and things.* Harmondsworth, Penguin.

— (1973), 'Concepts and society'. In Gellner, E., 1973, *Cause and meaning in the social sciences.* London, Routledge.

Gluckman, Max (1956), *Custom and conflict in Africa.* Oxford, Blackwell.

Gombrich, Richard F. (1971), *Precept and practice: traditional Buddhism in the rural highlands of Ceylon.* London, Oxford University Press.

— (1972), 'Buddhism and society' (review article on Spiro, 1971). *Modern Asian Studies*, 6, pp. 483–96.

Gregory, R. L. (1970), *The intelligent eye.* London, Weidenfeld & Nicolson.

Griffiths, A. P. (ed.) (1967), *Knowledge and belief.* London, Oxford University Press.

Gudmunsen, C. (1977), *Wittgenstein and Buddhism.* London, Macmillan.

Gunasekera, N. D. (1951), 'Some observations on suicide in Ceylon'. *Journal of the Ceylon Branch of the British Medical Association*, 46, pp. 1–11.

Hallpike, C. R. (1979), *The foundations of primitive thought.* Oxford, Oxford University Press.

Hardy, Robert S. (1850), *Eastern Monachism*. London, Partridge & Oakey.

Harper, E. B. (ed.) (1964), *Religion in south Asia*. Seattle, University of Washington Press.

Hintikka, Jaakko (1962), *Knowledge and belief*. Ithaca, Cornell University Press.

Hodge, M. C. (1979), *Buddhist modernism and social change in Sri Lanka, Burma and Thailand*. M.A. (Econ.) thesis, University of Manchester.

Hodge, M. C. (1981), *Buddhism, magic and society in a southern Sri Lankan town*. Ph.D. thesis, University of Manchester.

Horton, Robin (1970), 'African traditional thought and Western science'. In B. Wilson (ed.), 1970, pp. 131–71. (Abridged from *Africa*, xxxvii 1967, pp. 50–71, 155–87.)

Iverson, Jeffrey (1977), *More lives than one?* London, Pan.

Jarvie, I. C. (1964), *The revolution in anthropology*. London, Routledge.

Kapferer, B. (1977), 'First-class to Maradana: secular drama in Sinhalese healing rites'. In S. F. Moore and B. G. Myerhoff (eds.), 1977, *Secular ritual*, Assen, Van Gorcum.

— (1979a), 'Entertaining demons: comedy, interaction and meaning in a Sinhalese healing ritual'. *Social Analysis*, 1, pp. 108–52. (First published in *Modern Ceylon Studies*, 6, 1975, pp. 1–55.)

— (1979b), 'Emotion and feeling in Sinhalese healing rites'. *Social Analysis*, 1, pp. 153–76.

— (1979c), 'Mind, self, and other in demonic illness: the negation and reconstruction of Self'. *American Ethnologist*, 6, pp. 110–33.

Knox, Robert [1681] (1966), *An historical relation of Ceylon*. Dehiwala, Tisara Prakasakayo (2nd edn.). (First published 1681, London.)

Langer, Susanne K. (1951), *Philosophy in a new key* (2nd edn.). London, Oxford University Press.

Lawrence, Peter (1964), *Road belong cargo*. Manchester, Manchester University Press.

Leach, E. R. (1954), *Political systems of highland Burma*. London (London School of Economics), G. Bell.

— (1968a), 'Introduction' to E. R. Leach (ed.), 1968, *Dialectic in practical religion*. (Cambridge Papers in Social Anthropology, 5.) Cambridge, Cambridge University Press, pp. 1–6.

— (1968b), 'Virgin birth'. Letter to *Man* (N.S.), 3, pp. 655–6.

— (1968c), 'Ritual'. In *International encyclopaedia of the social sciences*. New York, Macmillan and Free Press.

— (1969), 'Virgin birth'. In Leach, E. R., 1969, *Genesis as Myth and other essays*, London, Cape, pp. 85–112. (First published in *Proceedings of the Royal Anthropological Institute of Great Britain and Ireland*, 1966.)

Leppard, Raymond (1973), Sleeve note to Mozart's C. Minor Mass; record EMI ASD 2959.

Levi-Strauss, C. (1949), *Les structures élémentaires de la parenté*. Paris, Presses Universitaires de France.

— (1963), 'The sorcerer and his magic'. In Lévi-Strauss, C., 1963, *Structural anthropology* (trans. C. Jacobson and B. G. Schoepf). New York, Basic Books.

Lewis, Gilbert (1980), *Day of shining red: an essay on understanding ritual* (Cambridge Studies in Social Anthropology, 17). Cambridge, Cambridge University Press.

Lienhardt, Godfrey (1961), *Divinity and experience: the religion of the Dinka*. London, Oxford University Press.

Ling, Trevor (1973), *The Buddha: Buddhist civilization in India and Ceylon*. London, Temple Smith.

Ling, Trevor (1980), 'Buddhist values and development problems: a case study of

Sri Lanka'. *World Development*, 8, pp. 577–86.

Lukes, Steven (1973), *Emile Durkheim: his life and work*. London, Allen Lane The Penguin Press.

Malalasekera, G. P. (1928), *The Pali literature of Ceylon*. London, Royal Asiatic Society (reprinted 1958, Colombo, M. D. Gunasena).

Malalgoda, Kitsiri (1972), 'Sinhalese Buddhism: orthodox and syncretistic, traditional and modern' (review article on Gombrich, 1971). *Ceylon Journal of Historical and Social Studies* (N.S.), II/2, pp. 156–69.

— (1976), *Buddhism in Sinhalese society 1750–1900*. Berkeley, University of California Press.

Marga Institute (1974), *Religion and development in Asian societies*. Colombo, Marga Publications.

Medawar, P. B. (1964), 'Is the scientific paper a fraud?' In *Experiment*. ed. David Edge. London. British Broadcasting Corporation, pp. 7–12.

Mus, Paul (1965), 'Preface' to Sarkisyanz, 1965.

Nash, Manning (1965), *The golden road to modernity*. Chicago, Chicago University Press.

Needham, Rodney (1972), *Belief, language, and experience*. Oxford, Blackwell.

— (1975), 'Polythetic classification: convergence and consequences'. *Man* (N.S.), 10, pp. 349–69.

Nikam, N. A., and McKeon, R. (eds. and trans.) (1959), *The edicts of Asoka*. Chicago, Chicago University Press.

Nineham, D. E. (1963), *St. Mark* (Pelican Gospel Commentaries). Harmondsworth, Penguin.

Nyanatiloka (1972), *Buddhist Dictionary* (3rd edn., ed. Nyanaponika). Colombo, Frewin.

Obeyesekere, G. (1963), 'The Great Tradition and the Little in the perspective of Sinhalese Buddhism'. *Journal of Asian Studies*, xxii.

Obeyesekere, G. (1969), 'The ritual drama of the Sanni demons: collective representations of disease in Ceylon'. *Comparative studies in Society and History*, II (2), pp. 175–216.

— (1974), 'Some comments on the social backgrounds of the April 1971 insurgency in Sri Lanka (Ceylon)'. *Journal of Asian Studies*, xxxiii, No. 3.

— (1976), 'Sorcery, premeditated murder, and the canalization of aggression in Sri Lanka'. *Ethnology*, 14.

— (1981), *Medusa's hair: an essay on personal symbols and religious experience*. Chicago, Chicago University Press.

Ornstein, Robert E. (ed.) (1973), *The nature of human consciousness*. San Francisco, W. H. Freeman.

— (1975), *The psychology of consciousness*. Harmondsworth, Penguin.

Ortner, Sherry B. (1978), *Sherpas through their rituals* (Cambridge Studies in Cultural Systems, 2). Cambridge, Cambridge University Press.

Parkes, James (1960), *The foundations of Judaism and Christianity*. London, Vallentine Mitchell.

Pears, David (1971), *Wittgenstein* (Fontana Modern Masters). London, Fontana.

Peiris, William (1973), *The Western contribution to Buddhism*. Delhi, Motilal Banarsidass.

Peter, Lawrence (1980), *Quotations for our time*. London, Magnum.

Pfanner, D. E., and Ingersoll, J. (1962), 'Theravada Buddhism and village economic behaviour: a Burmese and Thai comparison'. *Journal of Asian Studies*, xxi, pp. 341–61.

Phadnis, Urmila (1976), *Religion and politics in Sri Lanka*. London, C. Hurst.

Pieris, Ralph (1956), *Sinhalese social organization: the Kandyan period*. Colombo, Ceylon University Press Board.

Popper, Karl (1968), *The logic of scientific discovery* (revised edition; trans. of *Logik der Forschung*, 1934). London, Hutchinson.

Quine, W. V. O. (1961), *From a logical point of view* (2nd edn.). Cambridge, Mass., Harvard University Press.

Rahula, Walpola (1956), *History of Buddhism in Ceylon: the Anuradhapura period, 3rd century B.C. - 10th century A.D.* Colombo, M. D. Gunasena.

— (1967), *What the Buddha taught* (2nd edn.). Bedford, Gordon Fraser.

— (1974), *The heritage of the bhikkhu* (trans. K. P. G. Wijavasurendra). New York, Grove.

Ratanasara, H. (1974), 'Calling for a positive role for bhikkhus in the national leadership'. In Marga Institute, 1974, pp. 12–34.

Read, K. E. (1966), *The high valley*. London, Allen & Unwin.

Richardson, Alan (ed.) (1950), *A theological word book of the Bible*. London, SCM Press.

Roberts, Michael (1974), 'Problems of social stratification and the demarcation of national and local élites in British Ceylon'. *Journal of Asian Studies*, xxxiii, pp. 549–77.

Robertson, A. F. (1978), *Community of strangers*. London, Scolar Press.

Robinson, James M. (1959), *A new quest of the historical Jesus* (Studies in Biblical Theology, 25). London, SCM Press.

Roth, W. E. (1903), *Superstition, magic and medicine* (North Queensland Ethnography, Bulletin No. 5). Brisbane, Government Printer.

Russell, Bertrand (1905), 'On denoting'. *Mind*, 14, pp. 479–93.

Ryan, Bryce (1953), *Caste in modern Ceylon*. New Brunswick, Rutgers University Press.

Saparamadu, S. D. (1966), 'Introduction' to Knox, 1966.

Sarkisyanz, E. (1965), *Buddhist backgrounds of the Burmese revolution*. The Hague, Nijhoff.

Schmidt, Wilhelm (1931), *The origin and growth of religion* (trans. H. J. Rose). London, Methuen.

Schreiber, Flora R. (1975), *Sybil*. Harmondsworth, Penguin.

Senaveratna, J. M. (1936), *Dictionary of proberbs of the Sinhalese*. Colombo, Times of Ceylon.

Seneviratne, H. L. (1976), 'Aristocrats and rituals in contemporary Ceylon'. In B. L. Smith (ed.), 1976, pp. 97–101.

— (1978), *Rituals of the Kandyan State* (Cambridge Studies in Social Anthropology, 22). Cambridge, Cambridge University Press.

Shorter Oxford English dictionary, 3rd edn.

Sizemore, Chris, and Pittillo, Elen (1978), *Eve*. London, Gollancz.

Smart, Ninian (1964), *Doctrine and argument in Indian philosophy*. London, Allen & Unwin.

Smith, Bardwell L. (ed.) (1976), *Religion and social conflict in south Asia*. Leiden, Brill.

Smith, Bardwell L. (ed.) (1978), *Religion and legitimation of power in Sri Lanka*. Chambersburg, Pa., Anima.

Smith, W. Robertson (1927), *Lectures on the religion of the Semites* (3rd edn.). London, A. & C. Black. (1st edition 1889.)

Southall, Aidan (1956), *A lur Society*. Cambridge, Heffer.

Southwold, M. (1978), 'Buddhism and the definition of religion'. *Man* (N.S.), 13, pp. 362–79.

— (1979), 'Religious belief'. *Man* (N.S.), 14, pp. 628–44.

— (1982), 'True Buddhism and village Buddhism in Sri Lanka'. In J. Davis (ed.), *Religious organization and religious experience* (ASA Monograph 21). London, Academic Press.

— (in press), 'The concept of nirvana in village Buddhism'. In Burghart and
   Cantlie, in press.
Sperber, Dan (1975), *Rethinking symbolism* (Cambridge Studies in Social
   Anthropology, 11). Cambridge, Cambridge University Press.
Spiro, Melford E. (1968), 'Virgin birth, parthenogenesis and physiological
   paternity: an essay in cultural interpretation'. *Man* (N.S.), 3, pp. 242–61.
Spiro, Melford E. (1971), *Buddhism and society: a great tradition and its Burmese
   vicissitudes*. London, Allen & Unwin.
Stcherbatsky, Theodor [1932] (1958), *Buddhist Logic*. The Hague, Mouton. (1st
   edn., Leningrad, 1932, Academy of Sciences of the USSR.)
Stevenson, Ian (1960), 'The evidence for survival from claimed memories of former
   incarnations'. *Journal of the American Society for Psychical Research*, vol. 54,
   pp. 51–71 and 95–117.
Strauss, J. A. and M. A. (1953), 'Suicide, homicide and social structure in Ceylon'.
   American Journal of Sociology, lviii, pp. 461–9.
Tambiah, S. J. (1970), *Buddhism and the spirit-cults in north-east Thailand*
   (Cambridge Studies in Social Anthropology, 2). Cambridge, Cambridge
   University Press.
— (1976), *World conqueror and world renouncer* (Cambridge Studies in Social
   Anthropology, 15). Cambridge, Cambridge University Press.
Thomas, Edward J. (1975), *The life of Buddha as legend and history* (paperback
   edition, from 3rd edn. 1949). London, Routledge. (1st edn. 1927.)
Thompson, E. P. (1978), 'The poverty of theory'. In Thompson, E. P., 1978, *The
   poverty of theory and other essays*. London, Merlin.
Toulmin, Stephen and Goodfield, June (1963), *The fabric of the heavens*.
   Harmondsworth, Penguin.
Turner, V. W. (1969), *The ritual process*. London, Routledge.
Weber, Max (1967), *The religion of India* (trans. H. H. Gerth and D. Martindale)
   (paperback edn.). New York, Free Press.
Whitehead, Alfred N. and Russell, Bertrand (1927), *Principia mathematica* (2nd
   edn.). Cambridge, Cambridge University Press.
Wickremeratne, L. A. (1977), 'Peasant agriculture'. In K. M. de Silva (ed.), 1977,
   pp. 236–56.
Wijekulasuriya, E. (1963), *Some decided cases on our temple laws*. Galle
   (privately published).
Wilson, Bryan R. (ed.) (1970), *Rationality*. Oxford, Blackwell.
Wilson, Ian (1981), *Mind out of time?* London, Gollancz.
Winch, Peter (1970), 'Understanding a primitive society'. In B. R. Wilson (ed.),
   1970, pp. 78–111.
Wirz, Paul (1954), *Exorcism and the art of healing in Ceylon*. Leiden, Brill.
Wittgenstein, L. (1922), *Tractatus logico-philosophicus* (trans. C. K. Ogden and
   F. P. Ramsey). London, Routledge.
— (1966), *Lectures and conversations on aesthetics, psychology and religious
   belief* (ed. Cyril Barrett). Oxford, Blackwell.
Wood, A. L. (1961a), 'Crime and aggression in changing Ceylon. A sociological
   analysis of homicides, suicide and economic crime'. *Transactions of the
   American Philosophical Society* (N.S.), 51.
Wood, A. L. (1961b), 'A socio-structural analysis of murder, suicide and economic
   crime in Ceylon'. *American Sociological Review*, 26, pp. 744–53.
Yalman, N. (1964), 'The structure of Sinhalese healing rituals'. In E. B. Harper
   (ed.), 1964, pp. 115–50.
Ziman, John (1968), *Public knowledge*. Cambridge, Cambridge University Press.

Index

Note. As concepts as well as words are indexed, the word(s) of the entry may not occur in every passage indexed. In each entry, definitions, if any, are listed first, preceded by 'def.'